British political parties today

MANCHESTER
UNIVERSITY PRESS

Politics Today

Series editor: Bill Jones

British political parties today

Second edition

Robert Garner and Richard Kelly

Manchester University Press

Manchester and New York

distributed exclusively in the USA by St. Martin's Press

Published by Manchester University Press
Oxford Road, Manchester M13 9NR, UK
and Room 400, 175 Fifth Avenue, New York, NY 10010, USA

Distributed exclusively in the USA by
St. Martin's Press, Inc., 175 Fifth Avenue, New York,
NY 10010, USA

Distributed exclusively in Canada by
UBC Press, University of British Columbia, 6344 Memorial Road,
Vancouver, BC, Canada V6T 1Z2

British Library Cataloguing-in-Publication Data
A catalogue record for this book is available from the British Library

Library of Congress Cataloging-in-Publication Data applied for

ISBN   0 7190 5104 5 *hardback*
        0 7190 5105 3 *paperback*

First published 1998

02 01 00 99 98   10 9 8 7 6 5 4 3 2 1

Printed by Biddles Ltd, Guildford and King's Lynn

Party is the madness of many for the gain of the few
Jonathan Swift

If the parties fail ... then democracy fails
Houghton report (Cmnd 6601, 1976)

The party's over now.... We've been so bored; Thank the Lord, that the party's over now
Noël Coward

Contents

Figures, tables and boxes

Boxes

Preface and acknowledgements

Since the publication of the first edition of *British Political Parties Today* in 1993, there has been a series of important developments which were crystallised by the result of the 1997 general election: the resurgence of the Labour party under Tony Blair, the deepening crisis within the Conservative party, and the consolidation of support for the Liberal Democrats and the two nationalist parties. In addition, there has been a host of changes and initiatives concerning party policy and party organisation, as well as further questions concerning the role and relevance of political parties in a modern western democracy. In short, events of the last four years merit a revision and update of our original study.

The introductory chapter on the function of political parties has been wholly revised to take account of suggestions we have received from students and teachers. It will now seek to clarify the importance of party activity with reference to recent developments, particularly changes in the position of ordinary party members and the explosion of pressure group activity. In recent years, examination papers have tended to ask questions along the lines of 'Why join a political party?'. This chapter will provide what we think is a comprehensive answer, elucidating the parties' importance in a contemporary context.

Chapter 1 compares the parties' policy programmes and links these to the issue of Britain's political culture, which, again, has come to detain students of British politics more often since the first edition was published. The supposedly consensual tone of modern party politics is examined closely, and areas of convergence and divergence that have arisen in the 1990s are pinpointed. The chapter also highlights the parties' 1997 election manifestos and considers whether voters were offered a choice of ideologies or managerial strategies.

Changes in policy are strongly linked to changes in our party system, and chapter 2 looks at what sort of party system – if any – Britain now has. The 'dominant party system' thesis, popularised after the 1992 election, will naturally be reinspected following Labour's return to power, while chapter 10 provides an update on the parties' electoral performance which includes the 1997 results. The two chapters on party philosophy (3 and 5), meanwhile, will take into account the impact of both 'New Labour' and the state of Conservatism following the end of John Major's leadership.

In the field of party organisation, the many changes since 1993 still bewilder many students and teachers. The assorted articles written by Richard Kelly for *Talking Politics* and *Politics Review* are here encapsulated in two concise chapters which aim to clarify a fiendishly complex area. Labour's 1994 leadership contest, its 'one member one vote' reforms, its dalliance with positive discrimination and its rather brutal centralisation of power are all examined in chapter 6, while chapter 4, on the Tory party, covers the reforms of late 1993, the 1995 and 1997 leadership contests, and the growing demand for greater democracy inside the party – a demand underlined by the accession of William Hague as leader.

In response to comments made by many of our fellow teachers, this edition includes two new chapters. Although the main focus of the book remains party activity in Britain, and principally parliamentary elections, our new chapter 8 considers the UK's 'territorial' parties, namely those of Wales, Scotland and Northern Ireland. It has been written by our old colleague Michael Cunningham, lecturer in politics at the University of Wolverhampton and author of a well received book on the Northern Ireland problem (Manchester University Press, 1991). He analyses not just the aims and doctrines of these parties but also the distribution of power within them – something largely ignored by most textbooks. Such a chapter is justified by the emergence of devolution as a central issue to the new Labour government, but also by the increased likelihood these days of hung parliaments and electoral reform, both of which would give these parties a pivotal role in British politics. The prospect of a hung parliament also justifies a separate and revised chapter on the Liberal Democrats and their centrist forebears (chapter 7).

Chapter 9, the other new chapter, concentrates on party finance, an issue brought to the front of party debate by the 'sleaze' allegations shrouding so much of the last Conservative government. The case for further state aid to the parties will thus be examined, while furnishing students with new data concerning the revenue and expenditure of the main parties. The chapter suggests, though, that the 'problem' of party finance is overstated and easily confused with a more serious malaise afflicting modern political parties.

This connects with our closing chapter, which again considers the impact and potential of governing parties at the close of the century. The question of whether parties 'make a difference' is readdressed, but with more attention being paid to European integration and the constraints of a globalised economy. However, while acknowledging the problems which these phenomena pose, the book closes with a stout defence of political parties in Britain today, reasserting their importance to a society which has become dangerously fragmented and cynical.

Once again, the book has been inspired by the changing demands of A level politics students, with whom the authors have regular professional contact. Yet both authors also have dealings with students in higher education, whose demands too have shifted in recent years. As such, the book has tried to meet the needs of both audiences, combining an array of relevant facts and figures with a large measure of contemporary and historical analysis. The outcome, we hope, is a study germane not just to political parties but to the nature of British politics generally.

In writing this book, we have been fortunate to receive advice and support from our colleagues at the University of Leicester and The Manchester Grammar School, particularly Rod Martin (Head of Politics, MGS) and Steve Foster. For this, we are enormously grateful. We are also indebted to a number of students, in both further and higher education, who took the trouble to read various chapters and make suggestions as to how they could be made more user-friendly. In this respect we should like to thank James Goldstone, Johnny Cohen, Dominic Howorth, Daniel Rosenthal, Leo McBatter, Franklyn Spindle, Dusty Fernandez and Jock Locke. Despite the input of all these colleagues and students, responsibility for the book's contents rests solely with the authors.

This second edition is dedicated to David Kelly, politics teacher and head of sixth form at the Elfed High School, Buckley. His support during the early months of 1997 did much to ensure the book's completion.

RWG, RNK

Abbreviations

AUEW	Amalgamated Union of Engineering Workers
CCO	Conservative Central Office
CLP	constituency Labour party
CSD	Council for Social Democracy
DUP	Democratic Unionist party
EEC	European Economic Community
EU	European Union
FDP	Free Democratic party (Germany)
ILP	Independent Labour party
MEP	member of the European parliament
MP	member of parliament
NEC	National Executive Committee (Labour)
NUM	National Union of Mineworkers
NUPE	National Union of Public Employees
OMOV	one member one vote
OUP	Official Unionist party
PLP	parliamentary Labour party
SDLP	Social Democratic and Labour party
SDP	Social Democratic party
SLD	Social and Liberal Democratic party
SNP	Scottish National party
TGWU	Transport and General Workers' Union
UUP	Ulster Unionist party

Introduction: why do parties exist?

Disraeli once observed that 'the essence of Parliament is party'. If the ensuing century has weakened this view, it is only in the sense that it now appears too narrow: one could reasonably argue, after all, that the essence of modern British *politics* is party activity and debate. It is true that, in recent years, single-issue and special interest groups have challenged the parties' role as the main agent of political participation.[1] Yet this does not alter the centrality of political parties in the British political system. Put simply, any account of British politics which overlooked pressure groups would be defective but still capable of valid observation; any account which overlooked political parties would be nothing short of surreal.

Definitions

When defining political parties, it is vital to consider the political climate in which they operate – something of which the parties are both cause and effect (see chapter 1). Political parties in eastern Europe, for example, have until recently had a very different character to those in western democracies, although it has been argued that parties cannot truly exist in totalitarian systems. As Neumann points out, 'the very definition of party presupposes a democratic climate, since to be "a party to" always means identification with one group and differentiation from another'.[2] Madgwick endorses this idea by claiming that parties are 'organised groups aiming to form or form part of government', and the fact that they can only aspire to this role – rather than being assured it – denotes the sort of rivalry precluded by monolithic regimes, including those (like Nazi Germany) which have a 'party' as their centrepiece.[3]

Hague and Harrop offer another condition, however, which rescues somewhat the status of so-called parties in one-party states (not to be confused with the 'dominant-party systems' discussed in chapter 2). They argue that parties must be mass membership bodies, with membership

1

open to all layers of society and all levels of ability.[4] In this sense, it could be argued that parties in Britain emerged properly only after the 1867 Reform Act, when Tory and Liberal MPs created extra-parliamentary structures in response to the enlarged franchise (see chapters 4 and 7).

In the context of British political history, though, this seems a rather harsh restriction. Research by Martin has confirmed that there was recognised party organisation and competition even during the reign of Queen Anne (1702–14) and probably much earlier.[5] The term 'Conservative party' was common currency in politics after 1833, with the Liberals a recognised force in elections from the 1860s onwards. Indeed, the extension of the franchise was largely the effect rather than the cause of competitive party politics in England.

Aims and functions

In the absence of any fixed definition, caution is naturally required when we consider what parties actually do. In Britain, however, it is possible to cite the following objectives:

Parties seek office

Parties are distinguished from other political alliances by their desire not just to influence those in government (in the manner of pressure groups), but to become, or become part of, the government themselves. The extent to which this is a realistic ambition obviously depends upon the party itself, and for smaller parties the immediate aim is often to act as a quasi-pressure group, securing enough votes to influence the more established parties. During the past thirty years, this has been demonstrated by Plaid Cymru and the Scottish National party (SNP) (affecting Labour's devolution policy in the late 1960s and late 1980s – see chapter 8), by the Green party (affecting the government's environmental policy in the late 1980s), and by the National Front in the late 1970s (affecting Conservative immigration policy). Yet even for these parties, the eventual aim is to get their own hands on the levers of executive authority, albeit in a changed environment. Plaid Cymru, the SNP and the Ulster Unionists, for example, have little interest in holding office at Westminster, yet would be more than willing to do so in a fresh constitutional settlement inside their respective territories.

It must also be noted that hung parliaments, increasingly likely with changes in voting behaviour (see chapter 10), would offer an even greater role to the minor parties – a role which electoral reform would copper-fasten. For parties like the Liberal Democrats, such developments hold out nothing less than the prospect of permanent power at Westminster; with neither of the two main parties able to secure a parliamentary majority, it would be almost impossible for either of them to reach office without the assistance of a sizeable third force. In many other European democracies, hung parliaments have indeed given pivotal power to 'third' parties. The Free Democratic party (FDP) has been a part of the German governments since the 1960s, despite an average vote of only 10 per cent, while in Ireland the Labour party (polling less than a fifth of the popular vote) proved unshakeable in the country's shifting coalitions of 1992 to 1997.

Parties enhance elections

By seeking office, parties give added meaning and clarity to elections. Without parties, voters would be confronted by a bewildering array of independent candidates, each offering a separate vision which had little chance of materialising. Parties clearly make elections more cogent by permitting voters to choose not only a member of parliament (MP) but a government, reinforcing the impression that elections do indeed matter. Through their manifestos, parties enable voters to inspect a number of would-be government programmes and to make a rational choice between the various policy packages.

Parties enhance parliamentary government

By seeking office, parties allow parliamentary government in Britain to function fairly efficiently. Party coherence has allowed British governments to be formed – and changed – quickly after general elections (only once since the war has it taken more than twenty-four hours after polling ended), to endure for reasonable periods (most have lasted at least four years) and to pursue the policies which a plurality of voters supported at the election.

It may be argued that all this is a product of Britain's peculiar two-party system, which has usually given one party an overall majority in parliament. Under Ireland's multi-party regime, party wrangling meant that it took seven weeks to form a government after the country's 1992 general election, while Italy suffered fifty different governments in forty-seven years.[6] But the essential point remains: without *any* party system, such uncertainty and instability would be infinitely worse. Put crudely, parties impose discipline upon, and curtail the independence of, most MPs which, in a parliamentary system like Britain's, is a vital requirement for effective government. It is no coincidence that in France the weak Third and Fourth Republics also contained weakly organised parties, and that the relative stability of the Fifth Republic after 1958 owed much to the instigation of strong party loyalty by supporters of de Gaulle.[7]

Government by party also enhances subsequent elections, in that voters are able to pinpoint blame (or apportion credit) for the way the country has recently been run. In other words, parties help governments to remain democratically accountable. As Kavanagh has written, 'Because parties are disciplined and programmatic, there is a good chance that the majority party can enact its proposals. It can accordingly be judged on its record at the next election'.[8]

Once again, it has to be conceded that these principles work best in a two-party system where one party secures a majority in parliament. Hung parliaments often force a party to dilute its election proposals in the course of post-election deals with other parties, while multi-party governments often obscure accountability in future elections. Furthermore, the rise of third and fourth parties in Britain has already shown that anti-government votes can be split, allowing the governing party to survive a loss of electoral support. Yet even in a multi-party system, the *faute de mieux* factor still holds: a government of party politicians is still more easily held to account at elections than a government of disparate independents, and is still better equipped to follow policies favoured by a large body of voters.

It might be contested that this line of argument actually leads to the suppression of a parliamentary system in that it stresses the primacy of executive action, which, in turn, makes the legislature nothing more than a 'rubber stamp' for government.[9] This idea, fashionable in the 1960s, has since become less tenable, owing to the regular defeat of government policy in parliament.[10] Neither can this be attributed solely to the absence of strong majorities between 1974 and 1979 and 1992 and 1997; even when the government had huge majorities during 1983–92, it still suffered a string of embarrassing reverses at Westminster (the defeat of the 1986 Shops Bill being just one example).

This does not contradict the previous point about the need to limit MPs' independence, nor does it point to a breakdown in party discipline. Instead, it points to a healthy relaxation of party constraint among MPs and perhaps a better balance between executive efficiency and parliamentary scrutiny. Party organisation is still a key aspect of parliamentary life, valued by the vast majority of MPs.

In any case, party unity is not inimical to a potent legislature. It allows, for example, an official opposition to emerge at Westminster, able to articulate public criticism of the government in a systematic fashion. Deals between party managers, notably whips acting 'through the usual channels', enable Commons debates to cover most of the issues of concern to back-bench MPs and to make optimum use of the time reserved for scrutiny and deliberation. Arrangements between the parties can also allow MPs to advance causes which concern either constituents or a section of the public – early-day motions and private members' bills being just two of the options available. All this suggests that party ties are the ally, not adversary, of MPs trying to make their mark. A chamber full of eighteenth-century-style independents would be much less predictable and perhaps more colourful. But it is unlikely that this would make MPs more powerful, either collectively or individually.

Parties are vehicles for change

As Kavanagh indicated in the quote above, parties, through parliamentary government, offer themselves and their voters the prospect of considerable change in society. Edmund Burke stated that the essence of Conservatism was its capacity for change (see chapter 3). Similarly, the survival of a political system relies largely upon its ability to activate radical reform – should such reform be thought necessary by the bulk of electors. The enemy of constitutional stability, and the seedbed of extremism, is often a perception that contemporary needs cannot be catered for by the existing order.

Richard Crossman (Labour cabinet minister 1964–70) once described parties as 'battering rams of change'. By fighting elections in a disciplined way, and by presenting to the electorate a clear agenda for government, they can obtain from voters a mandate to implement certain policies. Once in government, that mandate can then be used to overcome any resistance to those policies from unelected officials, while party discipline can again be used to ensure that those policies get through parliament and become law.

Whether parties in government do make such a difference is examined in the concluding chapter, but suffice to say at this stage that the record of the Attlee and Thatcher governments offers strong support for the thesis outlined above. The capacity for reform that parties may have given our political system may also help explain the lack of progress made by those on the extremes who offer an alternative route to reform – be it through violent revolution, coups or insurrection. The fate of countries which have endured such upheavals is enough to make us grateful for western-style party politics, for all its imperfections.

Parties develop ideas

If parties are to impress voters, and to sustain their reputation as agents of change, there is a clear need to cultivate new themes and update traditional thinking. This point is less applicable to a party in office, when it has bureaucratic expertise and numerous state-sponsored think-tanks to fall back on. But in opposition it remains one of the parties' vital functions, especially as they can no longer expect huge blocks of voters to lend automatic support (see chapter 10).

Recent examples are provided by the Labour party's revised approach to welfare policy, which had its roots first in the internal party inquiry led by Sir Gordon Borrie after 1993 and then in a report overseen by MP Frank Field, and in Labour's fresh thinking on electoral reform, stemming largely from its Plant commission of the early 1990s. The Tories' 'facelift' after 1945, and the nature of Conservatism during the 1950s, also owed much to the pioneering work of the Conservative Research Department.[11]

Yet all this is to take a rather elitist view of the parties' policy-making role, overlooking the influence of ordinary party members. This leads us to the next of the parties' functions.

Parties allow mass participation in politics

The term 'mass participation' is misleading, since an estimated 93 per cent of adults in Britain are not members of political parties.[12] Nevertheless, the 7 per cent who are members do add significantly to the numbers of ordinary citizens involved in political activity. Though each of the main parties have large numbers of 'dormant' members, it has still been estimated that they alone contain over 300,000 people with an active interest in British political life.[13] That political activity does not just consist of full-time politicians and state officials, cocooned perhaps from the lives of ordinary voters, can only be healthy in a modern liberal democracy.

Much has been made (particularly by those who observe the Tories) of the parties' social dimension; it used to be a cliche, for instance, to compare the Young Conservatives with a dating agency. Yet this is to ignore the fact that ordinary party members perform a series of crucial political tasks.

Ordinary members make or break political careers

With the demise of 'independent' MPs, it is almost impossible to get into parliament without the backing of a political party.[14] Although this is often bemoaned, producing (it is said) tribes of identikit MPs, this trend does have virtues from a democratic/meritocratic perspective. Entry into politics as an independent often requires uncommon personal resources and it is frequently the case that, where the party system is weak, the political system has an exclusive or dynastic flavour. The British party network has meant that grocers' daughters and trapeze artists' sons, as well as those from a more privileged background, have reached the height of political power. The parties therefore ensure that political recruitment is not confined to any particular social class and that parliament draws upon a wide catchment area.

The task of choosing parliamentary candidates is almost always done locally (see chapters 4 and 6). With the majority of seats still considered 'safe', and in the absence of American-style 'primaries', the selection of a candidate is often more important than the election itself. Local party members are, in many cases, 'parliamentary gatekeepers', choosing candidates whose election to the Commons is then a formality. It is worth recalling that nearly all members of the Commons, from Tony Blair downwards, owe their positions to the fact that at some stage they impressed a group of local party selectors.

Recent attempts by the party hierarchies to impose candidates upon local activists have not been an unqualified success and even the hint that it is being attempted can prejudice those candidates' chances. The alleged keenness of Tory Central Office to find a winnable seat for black barrister John Taylor caused much friction within the Cheltenham association in 1991 and contributed to the loss of the seat in 1992. Between 1994 and 1996, the often fruitless search for seats by Tory ex-ministers also showed that an established reputation, as well as central party support, are no guarantee of impressing local selectors. Until he was selected for Stratford-upon-Avon in 1995, ex-minister John Maples was turned down by over thirty local Tory associations, despite strong backing from Conservative Central Office.[15]

The fate of Tim Yeo, Tory MP for Suffolk South and a junior minister until 1994, also reminds us that local party members can put a brake on politicians' careers even after they have made it to parliament. Until the Yeo scandal (he had fathered an illegitimate child), it was assumed the Prime Minister's support was the main requirement for ministerial survival. Yeo had this, but was still forced to resign after local Tories expressed disapproval of his conduct (which coincided with the government's 'back to basics' campaign – see chapter 3). If a minister cannot command the support of his local party his position evidently becomes untenable.

At least Yeo was not deselected as a parliamentary candidate, a fate which has befallen nearly two dozen MPs since 1979 after they lost the confidence of their local party – recent examples including David Young (Labour, Bolton South East, 1994), David Ashby (Tory, Leicestershire North West, 1996) and Nicholas Scott (Tory, Kensington and Chelsea, 1996). Again, a high profile at Westminster may not be enough to save an MP if the local party is disgusted with her or his performance. Michael Cocks, a Labour chief whip, was deselected by the Bristol South Labour party in 1986, while former minister David Mellor had to survive a motion of no confidence within the Putney Tory party in 1994. In the case of the Tories, it used to be the case that an MP would suffer such indignities only on account of 'personal' failings, but the reaction of many local Tories to MPs who supported the leadership challenges of 1990 and 1995 indicates otherwise, as did the deselection in Reigate (in 1996) of the 'disloyal' George Gardiner.

Conversely, local parties can save an MP's career even when the party establishments might like to see it ended. As Ranney's study proved, MPs can be grossly rebellious and a constant thorn in their leader's side and survive – providing they have the backing of their local party and electors.[16] It was this factor which encouraged nine 'Euro-sceptic' Tory MPs to wage guerrilla warfare against Major's government and survive the loss of the party whip between 1994 and 1995;[17] it also enabled the controversial Tory Neil Hamilton to remain the official Tory candidate for Tatton in 1997, despite the barely concealed protests of Central Office. If an MP with local party backing wishes to have an adversarial relationship with the party's leaders, then there is generally little those leaders can do. National party officials may be able to set up a 'new improved' party in the constituency concerned, but the electoral effects of such a move could be devastating – and not just in the constituency concerned. As Teresa Gorman (one of the Tory Euro-rebels) pointed out, it is surely better to have an MP who is a semi-detached supporter than one who supports another party.[18]

Since 1981, constituency members of the Labour party have also had the chance to select and deselect its leaders – a power which constituency Tories are also likely to acquire after Hague's accession in 1997. Through Labour's electoral college (see chapter 6), Labour members have contributed to the election of Kinnock in 1983, Smith in 1992 and Blair in 1994 as well as helping the leader and deputy leader beat off challenges to their positions in 1988.[19] Ordinary members now play a part in any challenge to a Labour leader in government. Indeed, it is technically possible for a Labour leader to be replaced by another as Prime Minister against the wishes of most Labour MPs – assuming that the bulk of constituency and affiliated members voted for it.

Ordinary members affect election results
Parties will not do well in elections unless they field the optimum number of candidates and, as explained, the onus for finding candidates rests heavily with local party members; this is particularly true of smaller parties with less sophisticated national bureaucracies. In the 1951 general election, the Liberal party could field only 109 candidates and as a result could only muster 2.5 per cent of the popular vote. The party's recovery ran parallel to its increased number of candidates so that, by October 1974, they were contesting only four fewer seats than the two main parties – earning almost a fifth of the vote in consequence.

During the 1950s, it was conventional wisdom that local parties played little part in the outcome of general elections. Nationwide class voting and uniform swings cemented the idea that elections were won and lost by national party leaders fighting national campaigns through the national media (see chapter 10). Changes in voting behaviour after 1970 prompted a reassessment, however, and the evidence assembled by both Denver and Hands and Seyd *et al.* shows that electoral success depends more and more upon well organised, high-profile local parties.[20] Comparing similar seats in 1992, Seyd's team has shown that Labour did better where it had an above-average number of activists, and that the Tories were better equipped to resist the overall swing to Labour in seats where they spent an above average amount on the local campaign.[21]

All this suggests that parties aspiring to office must in future accord more discretionary power to local members, demands for which took place within both parties after 1992 (see chapters 4 and 6). The revolution in information technology makes this a more realistic idea than it would have been even twenty years ago. As has been noted of constituency Labour parties, 'Desktop publishing has made the publishing of high quality leaflets possible for local activists who feel they can dream up more relevant campaign copy than the professionals at Walworth Road'.[22] Butler and Kavanagh's election studies confirm that computerisation enables local parties to assume many of the responsibilities hitherto left to London-based organisers.[23]

Ordinary members finance the parties
As explained in chapter 9, it is easy to exaggerate the parties' reliance upon 'institutional' donations. In 1992, Labour raised over £2 million from individual members, more than from any single trade union. Likewise, three-quarters of overall Tory revenue normally comes from constituency fund raising and subscriptions. In a democracy where there is only limited state funding of parties, members' efforts in this area are essential to the parties' survival and offer a further assurance that their concerns about policy will be taken seriously.

Ordinary members affect party policy
The impact members have upon policy has been generally overlooked. Much of the responsibility for this lies with R. T. McKenzie, whose book *British Political Parties* (1955) influenced a generation of students. McKenzie argued that both major parties were essentially oligarchic; policy and most other vital issues were the prerogative of the parliamentary leaders, with constituency members playing but a peripheral role.[24] Yet scholars have recently been obliged to amend this traditional, cynical view.

Minkin's study of the Labour party conference in 1978, while conceding that most policy initiatives rested with the parliamentary leadership, stressed that those initiatives were profoundly affected by what conference could be expected to tolerate.[25] Tony Blair's plan to revise clause 4 of Labour's constitution was successful only after a special party conference in 1995 gave its approval – something for which Blair had to campaign vigorously in the preceding six months. It is also worth recalling that Labour's draft election manifesto for 1997 was put to a ballot of over 200,000 party members.

Similar conclusions have been reached (by one of the present authors) in respect of the Tory party, in which, throughout the century, serious party divisions have been resolved by one side commanding more support at conference.[26] During the 1990s, a batch of ministerial initiatives were shaped by an interpretation or anticipation of conference opinion – family and social policy (1993) and custodial sentencing (1994 and 1995) being powerful examples.

In simple terms, no party leader can be effective without the support of the party's rank and file, and the decline of deference in all parties means this cannot be achieved just by the issue of firm commands; leadership now requires an ability to echo as well as mould grass-root concerns.

A superior form of activity?

The diversification, or 'dealignment', of society has placed political parties on the defensive. It is now argued that a wide range of pressure groups is better suited to represent the wide range of interests in society than parties, especially those parties founded upon 'outdated' class differences.[27] With voters now more 'particularistic' in outlook, it is suggested that they are less attracted to the 'package deals' offered by the parties and are drawn instead to the more specific attractions of dynamic, decentralised single-issue groups.

The value of grass-root participation within the parties has also been questioned in recent years. Between 1995 and 1996, for example, Labour's policies on selective secondary education and law and order 'seemed to evolve on a day-to-day basis with little regard for the membership's feelings'.[28] There were similar complaints within the Conservative party after 1992; the vote of no confidence in Major's leadership, passed by members of the Colchester North Conservative association in 1993, reflected a widespread belief among ordinary Tories that 'our fears and concerns are just not being listened to'.[29] Even by 1993, many grass-root Tories were still smarting from the dethronement of Margaret Thatcher in 1990 – a leader with enormous support from ordinary members, who were still excluded from Tory leadership contests. In the 1995 Tory leadership contest, it was noted that Major only just survived, with 34 per cent of Tory MPs failing to support him – despite having support from 92 per cent of local Conservative parties – while Hague's victory in the 1997 contest ignored the fact that constituency party chairs consistently expressed a preference for Kenneth Clarke.[30]

Back in the Labour party, recent events also point to the limitations placed upon constituency Labour parties (CLPs) when selecting their parliamentary candidates. Since 1989, Labour's National Executive Committee (NEC) has reserved the right to impose its own favoured candidate for by-elections. As a result, the Vauxhall CLP had its choice of Martha Osamore overturned in 1989 by an NEC which favoured the subsequent MP, Kate Hoey.[31] Between 1993 and early 1996, thirty-five CLPs were also obliged to select their candidates from women-only short-lists, with some (like Slough) actually having this principle forced upon them by Labour's regional organisers. Even those CLPs which observed the women-only ruling when selecting candidates were still not immune to central interference; the Leeds North East CLP had its choice of Liz Davies overruled by the NEC in 1995 'for reasons that related less to procedure than her personal record as a councillor'.[32]

When linked to the declining power parties have to make a difference in government (see Conclusion), it is unsurprising that there has been a steady decline in party membership and a corresponding growth in membership of pressure groups. Yet, ironically, this development only highlights one of the parties' most traditional and important functions. As McKay notes, 'Even in the most divided society, some conciliation between competing and conflicting interests must occur if government is to operate efficiently. Political parties help this conciliation process by providing united platforms for the articulation of diverse interests'.[33] Although McKay was addressing himself to American politics, the fragmentation of interests in Britain underlines his point. It is all too easy for a new breed of individualistic citizens to pursue particular interests while discarding the trade-offs embodied by large political parties. Yet sooner or later those interests have to be diluted and adjusted in the face of competing demands. Political parties, *simply through the development of their own policies*, remind their members that their own special concerns have to be looked at in a much wider context: otherwise, parties will have little chance of winning elections and members' special concerns will have even less chance of being accommodated by government. A common criticism of pressure groups is that they discourage this wider perspective and encourage a more isolated approach to public policy, one which ignores the need for compromise in a fluctuating liberal democracy.

Parties have often been accredited with the role of 'political education', in that they try to explain to voters the various options available. Yet one of the most effective tools of any educator is the use of example and, by exemplifying how diverse interests can be reconciled within their own ranks, parties can demonstrate how such accommodations can – and must – be reached within modern western societies. In this respect, Britain's political parties are more important than ever to the health of its society.

Notes

1   R. Baggott, *Pressure Groups in Britain Today* (Manchester, Manchester University Press, 1995).

2   S. Neumann, 'Towards a Comparative Study of Political Parties', in J. Blondel (ed.), *Comparative Government: A Reader* (London, Macmillan, 1969), p. 69.

3   P. J. Madgwick, *Introduction to British Politics* (London, Hutchinson, 1984), p. 254.

4   R. Hague and M. Harrop, *Comparative Government and Politics: An Introduction* (London, Macmillan, 1987), p. 139.

5   R. I. A. Martin, 'The Whig Party 1689–1695', unpublished PhD thesis, University of Lancaster, 1978.

6   H. Partridge, 'Italy: An Unusual Democracy', *Politics Review*, November 1995.

7   V. Wright, *The Government and Politics of France*, 2nd edn (London, Hutchinson, 1986).

8   D. Kavanagh, *Thatcherism and British Politics* (Oxford, Oxford University Press, 1987), p. 48.

9   B. Crick, *The Reform of Parliament* (London, Weidenfeld and Nicolson, 1964).

10   P. Norton, *Does Parliament Matter?* (Hemel Hempstead, Harvester Wheatsheaf, 1993).

11   J. Ramsden, *The Making of Conservative Party Policy* (London, Longman, 1980).

12   G. Parry, G. Moyser and N. Day, *Political Participation and Democracy in Britain* (Cambridge, Cambridge University Press, 1992).

13   P. Seyd and P. Whiteley, *Labour's Grass Roots* (Oxford, Clarendon Press, 1992), ch. 3; P. Whiteley, P. Seyd and J. Richardson, *True Blues* (Oxford, Oxford University Press, 1994) ch. 3.

14   P. Norris and J. Lovenduski, *Political Recruitment* (Cambridge, Cambridge University Press, 1995).

15   *Daily Telegraph*, 7 December 1995.

16   A. Ranney, *Pathways To Parliament* (London, Macmillan, 1965).

17   R. Kelly, 'The Left, the Right and the Whipless', *Talking Politics*, autumn 1995.

18   R. Kelly, 'The Whip Hand Tory Rebels Could Hold', *Parliamentary Brief*, February 1995.

19   R. M. Punnett, *Selecting the Party Leader* (Hemel Hempstead, Harvester Wheatsheaf, 1992), ch. 5; R. Kelly, 'Labour's Leadership Contest', *Politics Review*, February 1995, p. 3.

20   D. Denver and G. Hands, 'Constituency Campaigning', *Parliamentary Affairs*, 1992, pp. 528–44.

21   Seyd and Whiteley, *Labour's Grass Roots*, ch. 8; Whiteley, Seyd and Richardson, *True Blues*, ch. 8.

22   R. Heffernan and M. Marquesee, *Defeat From the Jaws of Victory* (London, Verso, 1992), p. 317.

23   D. Butler and D. Kavanagh, *The British General Election of 1992* (London, Macmillan, 1992), p. 238.

24   R. Kelly and S. Foster, 'Power in the Parties: McKenzie Revisited', *Contemporary Record*, February 1990.

25   L. Minkin, *The Labour Party Conference* (London, Allen Lane, 1978), pp. 317–18.

26   R. Kelly, *Conservative Party Conferences* (Manchester, Manchester University Press, 1989).

27   W. Grant, *Pressure Groups, Politics and Democracy in Britain* (Hemel Hempstead, Harvester Wheatsheaf, 1989), ch. 8.

28   K. Livingstone, *Guardian*, 18 January 1996.

29   *Daily Telegraph*, 25 February 1994.

30   R. Kelly, 'Why Can't All Tories Elect Their Leader?', *Parliamentary Brief*, October 1995.

31   Heffernan and Marquesee, *Defeat From the Jaws of Victory*, pp. 265–70.

32   K. Livingstone, *Guardian*, 18 January 1996.

33   D. McKay, *American Politics and Society*, 3rd edn (Oxford, Oxford University Press, 1993), p. 82.

1

The culture of British party politics

In a liberal democracy, it can be argued that the 'culture' of party politics has two dimensions – one superficial, the other substantial. The superficial dimension refers to the spirit or atmosphere in which inter-party debate occurs: is it, for example, marked by scathing and dogged disagreement, or by constructive discussion and a relentless quest for compromise? The substantial dimension refers to the ideological assumptions and policy priorities underpinning such debates: has British party politics been marked by far-reaching and deeply rooted division, with the main parties offering markedly different diagnoses and prescriptions, or by a strong measure of consensus, with the main parties in broad agreement over the principles and objectives of government policy? This chapter tackles these questions from the perspective of post-war British politics and, in so doing, surveys the shifting battle lines of inter-party debate.

An agreement to differ?

Throughout the post-war era, the superficial aspect of Britain's party culture has been one of irreconcilable division. Unlike most European democracies, the tone of party debate in Britain has rarely been set by a desire for cooperation and compromise; for reasons which relate to our electoral system (see chapter 2), adversarial politics has been as much a feature of Britain's political landscape as Westminster, Whitehall and Downing Street. Indeed, supporters of electoral reform often argue that, by ending single-party majorities at Westminster, cooperation and compromise will at last be forced upon party politicians – politicians who have for too long 'talked up' their differences while playing down that which unites them.[1]

During a number of post-war general elections, foreign commentators have been struck by the venomous exchanges between the parties' antagonists, along with their 'eagerness to disagree' on most policy matters.[2]

13

This has often involved exotic and almost libellous forms of acrimony –
from Churchill's claim in 1945 that Labour would introduce a 'Gestapo'
state, to Denis Healey's jibe in 1983 that Margaret Thatcher was (*apropos*
the 1982 Falklands war) 'glorying in slaughter'. Although the tabloid press
has often been criticised for injecting its own notes of bitterness during
election campaigns (the *Sun*'s attack on Labour leader Michael Foot was
particularly cruel in 1983), in general anyone interested in 'knocking copy'
need not have looked much further than the parties' own propaganda.

The next question to be addressed, though, is whether such divisions
really do stem from profoundly different 'world views', or whether they
conceal a potentially embarrassing consensus over major issues. Indeed,
there may be an inverse relationship between the superficial and substantial aspects of a party political culture, with acidic language acting
as a substitute for serious divergence over policy. It is worth recalling that
vitriolic personal attacks are recurrent features of politics in the USA,
where ideological differences between the parties have always been
narrow.

The culture of social democracy (1945–79)

During the 1950s and 1960s, commentators could point to a paradox at
the heart of Britain's party political culture, namely that the adversarial
tone adopted by the two main parties in debate was matched by a striking
similarity in their actual policies.[3] Despite their noisy disagreements in
parliament, it was widely recognised that – in terms of hard policy – what
united the two parties was much greater than what divided them.

This consensus is often referred to as the 'Butskellite' consensus –
'Butskellism' being coined by the *Economist* in the 1950s to denote the lack
of substantive difference between Hugh Gaitskell, Labour party leader
between 1955 and 1963, and R. A. Butler, the Tories' *de facto* deputy leader
for much of the same period. From an academic angle, it is perhaps more
respectable to describe the consensus as social democratic, as its features
and assumptions approximate the various 'social democratic' theories
expounded between 1945 and 1979.[4] Just as Disraeli denounced the
government of Sir Robert Peel (1841–6) as 'Tory men, Whig measures',
more recently it has been common to hear Thatcherites revile the Conservative governments of 1951–64 and 1970–4 as 'Tory men, social
democratic measures' – the implication being that these governments took
the same direction that Labour would have chosen had it been in office.[5]
It must be pointed out, however, that some social democratic theorists take
a more circumspect view, with Marquand complaining that (unlike in West
Germany and Scandinavia) social democracy in Britian was not even
properly attempted, let alone realised.[6]

Features

Despite Marquand's observations, it is still possible to identify a number of characteristics shared by the two main parties between 1945 and 1975 – characteristics which betray a centre-left approach to politics and a view of society normally associated with centre-left politicians.

Egalitarianism/collectivism

The underlying principle of the post-war consensus, and the main reason for it being dubbed 'social democratic', was the parties' belief (held with varying degrees of enthusiasm and explicitness) that society should somehow be made more 'equal', 'just' and 'united'. The language of political discourse after 1945 showed an acceptance that divisions in society – between rich and poor, strong and weak – should be narrowed, and a better society created for 'the people' (*qua* an homogenous entity) rather than a collection of diverse individuals. For most of those in the Labour party, all this seemed fairly logical, given its philosophy and tradition (see chapter 5). Yet these ideals were given further urgency by the make-up of the electorate around this time – roughly 65 per cent working class, living and working in conditions which fostered a collectivist, rather than an individualistic, culture and consciousness.[7] So for the Conservatives, at least, some acceptance of egalitarianism seemed the latest, pragmatic way of assuring their continued relevance in a society whose 'haves' were significantly outnumbered by its 'have nots' (see chapter 3).

Statism

Both parties accepted that the tool with which greater equality should be achieved was state intervention. In other words, 'progressive' social democratic governments – backed by the professionalism of enlightened bureaucracies – should seek and effect a solution to most of the problems afflicting post-war society. For a generation of politicians who remembered the inter-war era, when it was felt that governments had not 'done enough' for the disadvantaged, and for those like Harold Macmillan (Tory Prime Minister 1957–63) who felt that his class had still not repaid the debt owed to the working class from the First World War, the notion of a crusading, proactive state had particular appeal.[8]

The growth of government is actually one of the most crucial features of post-war British politics and society, creating what Thatcher called 'the dependency culture', which her governments sought to erase (see below).

From the viewpoint of British social democracy, the enlarged state had four key manifestations:

Keynesianism

The economic policies of both Labour and Tory governments during this period (1945–75) owed much to the theories of John Maynard Keynes –

a senior Treasury official during the 1930s and 1940s whose *The General Theory of Employment, Interest, and Money* (1936) influenced a generation of politicians, civil servants and academics. As Butler said of Gaitskell (his predecessor as Chancellor), 'We both spoke the language of Keynes, but with different accents'.[9]

Based upon the goal of full employment (justified on both moral and economic grounds), Keynes' prescriptions pointed to a much more interventionist role for government economic policy than hitherto thought tolerable, indicting the old faith in market forces and *laissez-faire* capitalism. Keynesianism required that governments should engage in 'demand management' (through a mixture of taxation, public borrowing and public spending) and ushered in a new age of 'managerial capitalism', where private enterprise was more closely linked to economic direction and planning (*dirigisme*) by central government. This idea was reflected in a series of government agencies set up by Labour and Tory governments – for example, the Department of Economic Affairs (1964), the Industrial Reorganisation Corporation (1966), the Industrial Development Executive (1972) and the National Enterprise Board (1975).

Corporatism

The belief that governments should closely regulate capitalism duly extended into a belief that they should also seek to manage prices and incomes; indeed, the 'prices and incomes policy' became a recurrent feature of the government's anti-inflationary strategy between 1961 and 1979 and led to further examples of bureaucratic invasion in the market (e.g. the Pay Board and the Price Commission, both set up in 1973). These policies naturally gave both trade unions and employers' organisations a vital role in government policy, producing attempts to absorb them into the decision-making process in the classic, corporatist manner – this was, in fact, one of the principal functions of the National Economic Development Council, set up by the Conservatives in 1961.

A 'mixed economy'

Both parties accepted that, in addition to a more regulated form of private industry, significant sections of industry – as well as the major public services – should be owned by the state. The Conservatives thus accepted the 'nationalisation' of coal, railways, gas, water and electricity after 1945 on the basis that their 'special' character made them ill-suited to private enterprise, while the 'social' case for public ownership was applied by a Conservative government itself in 1972 with the nationalisation of the failing Rolls Royce (its eagerness to avoid a further hike in unemployment offering a further indication of Keynesianism's influence).

Although Labour's left was always keen to extend public ownership dramatically, its leaders were inclined to accept Anthony Crosland's theory (expressed in his 1956 book, *The Future of Socialism*) that nationalisation had more or less gone far enough by 1951 and that the cause of equality was now best served by increased public expenditure – mainly financed by a constantly growing, Keynesian-based private sector.[10]

The welfare state

The type of spending Crosland envisaged was exemplified by the National Health Service (set up in 1946), the state education system, the spread of local authority housing, and the network of sickness, unemployment and pension benefits – all paid for out of the public purse and collectively termed 'the welfare state'. These services and benefits reflected a belief in both main parties that the state had principal responsibility for the welfare of its citizens (grounded in the belief that private, and adequate, welfare arrangements were beyond the reach of a largely working-class electorate). Consequently, the parties competed in government to spend more than the other on welfare provision. That the state *should* provide was beyond question: the point of argument was whether such services could be managed more efficiently and financed more generously.

Foundations

This consensus did not spring from any single source, nor did it arise from any clear-cut historical event. Its acceptance sprang from a network of developments occurring over several decades – some spectacular and conspicuous, others incremental and subtle. It is possible, though, to identify five particularly important foundations:

The Attlee governments

There is little doubt that Labour's six years in office after 1945 had an impact lasting much longer. The existence of a mixed economy, for example, owed much to the nationalisation of the Bank of England, coal industry and civil aviation (1946), electricity (1947), railways and gas (1948) and iron and steel (1949). Likewise, the welfare state was shaped largely by the National Insurance and National Health Acts of 1946. It is also clear that the Conservatives' contribution to the consensus had much to do with their own policy developments during these years. Under R. A. Butler, the Tories in opposition underwent a major facelift, which acknowledged many of the government's social and economic reforms.

Tory paternalism

Although the Tories deferred to much of Attlee's agenda, they did not accept that in doing so they were simply raiding rival ideologies (although their heavy electoral defeat in 1945 gave them ample cause to do so).

Butler insisted that the Tories' acceptance of the welfare state, and their repudiation of unfettered capitalism, were throwbacks to 'one nation' Toryism, arguing that Labour after 1945 was only building upon ideas originally pursued by the government of Disraeli seventy years earlier – the Factory Act 1874, Public Health and Artisan Dwellings Act 1875, Education Act 1876 and economic protectionism being cited as examples.[11]

New liberalism

The development of liberalism in the early twentieth century, particularly its rejection of *laissez-faire* as a touchstone, was central to the development of British social democracy (see chapter 7). No history of the welfare state could ignore the reforms instigated by the Liberal government after 1906; Lloyd George's 'people's budget' of 1909 established the principle of welfare benefits financed by progressive taxation, while the National Insurance Act 1911 highlighted the state's responsibility for personal sickness and unemployment.[12] Liberal supporters in the 1950s often blamed their electoral plight upon the two main parties, especially Labour, having cribbed essentially Liberal ideals (both Keynes and William Beveridge – see below – were Liberal party members).

The inter-war years

The 1920s and 1930s were a crucial vindication of social democracy in that they exposed the social and economic shortcomings of minimal government; Harold Macmillan's influential work *The Middle Way* (1938) took its cue from the deprivation he witnessed at the time. Yet the inter-war period was also one in which new forms of state intervention were tentatively practised – mainly by Conservative governments. As Chancellor, Minister of Health and then Prime Minister, Neville Chamberlain introduced a series of statist, social reforms, while the Special Areas Acts of 1935–7 saw the government trying to stimulate regional economic revival – a portent of many similar attempts in the 1960s and 1970s.

The Second World War

During the war, state intervention was practised on a huge scale. Almost no area of civilian life was left untouched by bureaucratic regulation – an heroic exoneration, it was claimed, of state planning. The trials of war also fostered the widespread belief that society afterwards should be inestimably 'better' – that is, fairer – than that which existed before 1939, a belief which Labour articulated to brilliant effect at the 1945 election. In response to this egalitarian mood, the wartime coalition had already taken a number of steps which proved vital to the development of post-war domestic policy, notably the Beveridge report of 1942 (recommending a comprehensive state system of social insurance as well as a new health service), the employment white paper of 1944 (accepting Keynes' goal of 'a high and stable level of employment') and the Education Act of 1944 (ensuring secondary education for all).

It is therefore misleading to argue that the social democratic consensus was simply 'Attlee's legacy'. Yet it would be equally wrong to understate the achievements of the 1945–51 Labour governments. Although they were acting in accordance with long-established trends, they were still responsible for accelerating those trends in a way that would have been unlikely under a Conservative government – or indeed any government with a less robust sense of purpose. Within six years, British politics and society underwent a leftward shift greater than anything it had seen in the previous six decades.

Collapse

During the 1950s, it seemed as if social democracy offered a happy solution to both left-wing and right-wing politicians. Those on the left could assume that greater equality could be achieved without the electoral handicap of massive nationalisation and high taxation, while those on the right saw the mixed economy and the welfare state as a fair trade-off for the retention of a society which still respected private property, hierarchy and hereditary privilege.

This settlement, however, depended heavily upon the sort of economic growth which Keynesianism was supposed to guarantee. When it became clear in the 1960s and 1970s that the supposition was false, it also became clear that social democracy could no longer deliver the best of both worlds: to cope with the demands of a failing economy, it transpired that there would either have to be a further assault upon bourgeois privilege and private enterprise (as radical socialists had always prescribed) or an abandonment of the quest for equality (as apostles of free-market capitalism had always acknowledged).

The Labour government of Harold Wilson, elected in 1964, had promised to pursue Keynesian economics more efficiently, thereby producing enough growth for major increases in welfare spending. Instead, it met intractable economic problems, which led to a restriction of wages and public spending in 1966 and the devaluation of sterling in 1967. Inflation also rose steadily after 1964, while the reflationary ideas pursued by Heath's government following its U-turn of 1971–2 (see chapter 3 and Conclusion) pumped up inflation from 6 per cent in 1971 to over 20 per cent by the mid-1970s.[13] In addition, jobless figures rose from 1.6 per cent in 1964 to 4 per cent by 1976.

The combination of rising unemployment and rising inflation ('stag-flation') cut away the intellectual basis of Keynesianism and, as Labour premier James Callaghan told his party in 1976, the time-honoured Keynesian option of spending the way out of recession no longer existed – and had 'only ever existed by injecting a bigger dose of inflation into the system'.[14] The Labour government, helped by the strict terms of a nation-saving loan from the International Monetary Fund in 1976, thus accepted that economic salvation could lie only in tough control of government spending, an acceptance that was not easily reconciled with the left's egalitarian agenda. Not that the left's critique of capitalism was helped by the record of industry under state control. Indeed, by the end of the 1970s, the record of the nationalised industries was almost legendary in its awfulness – British Leyland (to give just one of many depressing examples) was losing almost £1,000 a minute in October 1976.[15] As a result, neither Keynesianism nor the mixed economy seemed unassailable pillars of British politics by 1979.

Furthermore, the Callaghan government's tough ('monetarist') stance on public spending, allied to its persistence with wage restraint, led to a deterioration in its working relationship with the trade unions, culminating in the 'winter of discontent' strikes of 1978–9. This, in turn, placed another question mark over the social democratic strategy: during a period of recession, the corporatist approach no longer seemed viable. All it appeared to do by 1979 was to make ministers fatally dependent upon certain pressure groups, nurturing the fear that Britain had finally become 'ungovernable'.[16]

A polarised culture (1979–83)

During the late 1970s and early 1980s, it became fashionable to suggest that the two main parties were divided over fundamentals as well as just details, and that British politics was now afflicted with dangerous centrifugal forces.[17] As explained earlier, the consensus after 1945 sprang largely from a centre-left analysis of society and was heavily influenced by the record of the 1945–51 Labour governments. It was therefore unsurprising that, once the consensus failed to deliver economic progress, its assailants would come mainly from the right.

The advent of Thatcherism

The Conservative party had not been slow to question the nostrums of social democracy. The party's 'little local difficulty' of 1958 arose when three Tory ministers resigned rather than put their faith in Keynesian-inspired public spending, while the first six years of Heath's leadership

(1965–71) emphasised a return to *laissez-faire* practices. Heath's U-turn of 1971–2 owed much to the lack of broad intellectual support which then existed for an anti-social democratic approach, but by the mid-1970s the party had far fewer qualms. Stagflation (and the fact that Heath led the party in 1974 to its then lowest share of the vote this century) convinced many Conservatives that the party should redefine its identity and offer an authentically alternative view of Britain's future.

The dethronement of Heath as Tory leader in 1975, and his replacement by Margaret Thatcher, is rightly considered a seminal moment in British politics. Although a member of Heath's government, she shared the view that after 1971 it had made a number of grave errors which obscured Toryism's true purpose. Though no intellectual herself, she was genuinely interested in new ideas and was eager to hear those wishing to give the party a new, and distinctive, intellectual basis.[18]

In the years that followed 1975, the term 'New Right' entered the British political vocabulary. It described a disparate collection of politicians (such as Sir Keith Joseph), economists (such as Alan Walters), academics (such as Roger Scruton) and journalists (such as Paul Johnson) who conveyed to the new leader ideas which questioned the essence of social democracy. The New Right's ideology had three conspicuous, related, themes:

Individualism

The most important of these themes was a renewed emphasis upon individual liberty and personal responsibility. Drawing heavily upon Friedrich Hayek's *The Road To Serfdom* (1944), it was contested that the growth of government – a key feature of social democracy – only made people economically and socially dependent upon the state, a situation which restricted individual initiative and imperilled individual freedom. Liberty could flourish, it was argued, only where government and state intervention were strictly limited.

A contempt for inflation

Linked to this belief in self-reliance and *laissez-faire* was a new, anti-inflationary zeal – fuelled, of course, when Britain's own inflation took it to the brink of bankruptcy in 1976.[19] The corollary of this belief, however, was a rejection of full employment as an economic priority – a priority which often required (as in 1971–2) a boost to public spending and a willingness to stoke up inflation in the short term.

The theoretical basis for this anti-Keynesian approach came largely from Milton Friedman of Chicago University, author of *Capitalism and Freedom* (1962) and widely credited as the author of 'monetarist' economics. Friedman had insisted that low inflation was the benchmark of a thriving economy and the true parent of secure (if not optimum) employment. The key to low inflation was said to be the containment of money circulating in the economy – the 'money supply'. It should be pointed out that monetarism is not theoretically incompatible with a mixed economy and a welfare state; it was after all practised (with a fair degree of success) by the Callaghan government after 1976, which remained otherwise committed to social democracy. Yet many of Friedman's Conservative supporters, particularly at the Institute of Economic Affairs and Centre for Policy Studies, argued that the curtailment of public spending meant the curtailment of the public sector – particularly the loss-making nationalised industries. As a result, the attack on Keynesian-style reflation mushroomed quite easily into an assault upon the very structure of Britain's post-war economy.

Authoritarianism

New Right thinking has occasionally been described as 'libertarian', a neo-anarchic creed where a minimalist state allows its citizens maximum freedom – on condition that it does not impede the freedom of others. There, for many on the New Right, was the rub. It was widely felt in Tory circles after 1975 that the legal and institutional 'freedoms' accorded certain sections of society (notably trade union leaders and those in charge of Labour-run local authorities) *had* injured the rest of society by forcing up public spending (and therefore inflation) while fostering a climate at odds with the free-market, consumer-led vision of the New Right. This vital link between 'the free economy and the strong state' was said to be demonstrated during the 1970s, when Britain was engulfed by its 'crisis of ungovernability'.[20] Having 'overstretched' itself since 1945, principally because it had invaded the economic and industrial spheres, the state had also 'enfeebled' itself, reliant upon and crippled by its corporatist links with producer-based interest groups. As such, governments no longer seemed able to uphold their most vital responsibilities, namely the maintenance of law and order and the protection of individual rights. This charge was given resonance by events in 1970–4 and again in 1978–9, when action by trade unions paralysed much of society and disrupted the lives of countless individuals. Many Conservatives were thus convinced, during the late 1970s, that the next Conservative government should be more concerned with 'the restoration of public order' than with any crusade to 'roll back the frontiers of the state' and 'set the people free'.[21]

The first Thatcher government (1979–83) appeared to synthesise these three ideals, bolstering the idea that modern Conservatism had shifted away from the middle ground. In respect of monetarist rules, the government slashed £3.5 billion off public expenditure in its crisis budget of 1981, while raising interest rates to a record level of 17 per cent. These deflationary measures (the antithesis of Keynesian thinking in a recession), coupled with a refusal to subsidise 'lame duck' industries, resulted in a doubling of unemployment within two years of Thatcher's election as premier. Such drastic medicine was seen by some as a means of softening the trade unions for a new batch of trade union laws after 1980, removing many of the legal immunities they had enjoyed, while 'freeing up' the market.[22] The government's rejection of incomes policies also meant that the unions were no longer central to economic decision making; the age of tripartite corporatism was truly over. In addition, the government began to alter the mixed economy's mixture with the launch of its privatisation programme (admitting varying degrees of market discipline to no fewer than sixteen public industries) and to extend the power of central government in relation to local authorities (the Local Government Planning and Land Act 1980), and sought to give a sharper edge to law and order policy (Police and Criminal Evidence Bill 1982).

Labour's leftward lurch

The notion that Britain's party culture had polarised was underlined by developments inside the Labour party after 1979 (see chapter 5). Among constituency members, there was a strong belief that Labour had lost office because its ministers had 'betrayed socialism'. This belief was powerfully articulated by one of those ex-ministers, Tony Benn, and the Campaign for Labour Party Democracy. Influenced by Benn's analysis of what went wrong and what needed to be done, the Labour conferences of 1980 and 1981 voted for a string of policies which signalled a remarkable shift leftwards – unilateral nuclear disarmament, extensive nationalisation, import controls, withdrawal from the European Community and a near wholesale rejection of the western economic system.[23]

All this was repugnant to a block of moderate Labour MPs, who insisted that Labour was no longer the centre-left, social democratic party they had joined. The outcome was the formation, in early 1981, of a new Social Democratic party, which later entered into the Alliance with the Liberals. The main, initial aim of this new grouping was to fill the 'yawning gap' caused by the 'extremist' tendencies of the two main parties after 1979. That it stimulated such phenomenal interest in its first year, recruiting 60,000 members in a matter of months and pulling off some astonishing by-election wins (as in Crosby and Croydon), suggested an agreement among many voters that the centre ground had been deserted by Labour and the Tories.[24]

The 1983 general election offered voters one of the starkest choices ever witnessed in post-war politics. On the one hand, the Conservatives offered a continuation of the *laissez-faire* economics pursued since 1979 and an even greater stress on the individualistic society, while Labour on the other put forward an adventurously leftist programme of reflation plus extensive state ownership and regulation – in addition to mould-breaking policies on defence, Europe, Northern Ireland, private health, private education and the House of Lords.[25] Labour's manifesto, dubbed by Gerald Kaufman 'the longest suicide note in history', allowed not only the re-election of the Conservatives but also a vote of 25 per cent for the Alliance – a sure sign that Labour was no longer seen as *the* party of the centre-left (its own vote was just 2 per cent greater). Yet Labour's defeat in 1983 was a blow from which its radical left never truly recovered.

Towards a new consensus (1983–92)

When trying to explain Labour's calamitous defeat, it was tempting to cite various short-term factors such as Michael Foot's leadership and the afterglow of the Falklands war. Yet Neil Kinnock, Labour's leader between 1983 and 1992, took a less sanguine view, suspecting that Labour had completely misread the 'new mood' of a dealigned electorate (see chapter 10). That the Conservatives gained a plurality of support from skilled working-class voters, for example, pointed to vital trends which Labour had been slow to grasp. It was also clear that, with the shrinkage of the working class, Labour would have to appeal beyond its natural constituency – as the Tories had done for most of the twentieth century. Just as the Tories had been forced after 1945 to accept aspects of the centre-left agenda, so Labour it seemed would now have to tailor *its* ideals to meet a new, centre-right atmosphere. The culture of party politics after 1983 therefore began to move slowly towards a new consensus. And, just as the post-1945 consensus sprang largely from the achievements of a radical Labour government, the post-1983 accord stemmed largely from the impact of radical Conservatism.

Labour's modernisation

Between 1983 and 1992, 'modernisation' was the watchword of Labour's new leadership, determined to accommodate many of the vital socio-economic changes that were occurring, while carefully re-entering the terrain of centre politics.[26] This strategy involved a purge of the Trotskyite Militant Tendency after 1984, a spirited denunciation of Labour's left at the 1985 conference, the 'Freedom and Fairness' campaign of 1986 – designed to identify the party more closely with consumerism and individualism – and the publication of books by both leader and deputy leader which downgraded nationalisation while hinting at an acceptance of market economics.[27] These consensual tendencies were reflected in the party's 1987 manifesto, a much blander document than its predecessor with fewer specifically controversial pledges (save a continued commitment to unilateral nuclear disarmament).

Despite this moderation of policy, Labour's vote in 1987 (31 per cent) was little better than four years earlier, with none of the 'short-term' excuses that were to hand in 1983. This provoked Kinnock and his allies to take a more urgent look at Labour's priorities and prepare for a more drastic revision of policy. Between 1987 and 1989, the party conducted a policy review, culminating in the document *Meet The Challenge, Make The Change*, representing what was then considered 'the least socialist policy statement ever published by the Party'.[28] It rejected massive renationalisation, unilateralism and continued opposition to Britain's membership of the European Community, while accepting the centrality of private enterprise and much of the Conservative government's own, market-based agenda.

In view of its quantum leap in the late 1980s, it was not altogether surprising that Labour's 1992 manifesto failed even to mention the word 'socialism', amounting in many respects to a promise that existing arrangements would be run more efficiently. Only water and the national grid were to be renationalised, with most of the Tories' trade union reforms retained. Although Labour's proposed tax increases may have cost it dear, it seems that Labour's fourth successive defeat came mainly from its still shaky reputation among voters – but one that was based upon memories of division and extremism ten years earlier rather than any close inspection of its 1992 position.[29]

A more cautious Conservatism

Although the image of radicalism persisted throughout Thatcher's premiership, the government was not without its New Right critics. It was argued that the monetarist experiment had been abandoned as early as 1982, with the government clearly failing to reduce its own spending as a proportion of gross domestic product. The expansionary policies pursued after 1987, and the high interest rates used to cope with the consequences, prompted claims that the government had returned to the old, Keynesian treadmill of 'stop–go' demand management.[30] It must also be recalled that the last vital economic decision made by the Thatcher government was that of entering the European Exchange Rate Mechanism in October 1990, a blatant repudiation of its free-market rhetoric and one which eliminated overnight a key distinction between its own economic policy and that of the opposition.

Any suspicion that the Tories were being affected by centrist forces was naturally endorsed by the fall of Thatcher and her replacement by John

Major in November 1990 – a new leader described by colleagues as a 'social liberal', who promised 'a nation at ease with itself', rather than any continuation of 'conviction politics'.[31] The early direction of Major's government lent credence to the idea that consensus was at last returning.

Within weeks of entering Number 10, Major announced spending increases of over £200 million, made even more poignant by the areas to which it was directed: £81 million for hospitals, £42 million to AIDS sufferers, £96 million for London's homeless, plus increased subsidies to local government. In March 1991, the government also announced that the poll tax – the 'flagship' of Thatcher's third government and symbol of bitter political division since 1988 – was to be scrapped, with its replacement entrusted to Michael Heseltine, the man who instigated Thatcher's downfall. The new 'citizen's charters', said to represent Major's 'big idea', looked suspiciously like ideas already recommended by Labour and the Liberal Democrats, offering an improvement rather than privatisation of most public services.[32] The 1992 budget, which doubled the level of government borrowing, seemed to mark the final break with Thatcher's bold Conservatism; it was small wonder that Thatcherites formed a new pressure group, Conservative Way Forward, to champion the 'threatened ideals' of the former leader.[33]

Consensus restored (1992–7)

Following the 1992 general election, the new demands of electoral success – and the pressures of *realpolitik* – quickened the drive towards a consensual party culture. Once more, this was especially true inside the Labour party.

'New Labour'

Elected Labour leader in 1994, Tony Blair was keen to promote the idea of a 'new' Labour party for a 'new Britain'. In this respect, he was prepared to narrow many of his party's differences with the Conservatives – earning him the nickname of 'Tony Blur' in some Labour circles. Yet, as noted, this was a trend that was already extant inside the party, established by Neil Kinnock and continued by Blair's immediate predecessor, John Smith.

During Smith's short leadership (1992–4), Labour re-emphasised its consensual tendencies in three key areas: Europe, inflation and the trade unions. In respect of the first two, Smith did not conceal his admiration for the anti-inflationary discipline which further European integration (facilitated by the Single European Act 1986 and the 1991 Maastricht Treaty) would enforce upon the British economy. This helped persuade his beaten rival for the leadership, Bryan Gould, to quit Labour politics altogether in 1994, arguing that monetary union precluded Labour's traditional

Table 1.1. *Convergence on Europe: Labour and Conservative policy on European integration, February 1995*

	Tories	Labour
Economic union		
Free-trade bloc	Yes	Yes
Single currency	Decide in 1999	Decide in 1999
Single market	Yes	Yes
Referendum on single currency	Not ruled out	Not ruled out
Social chapter	No	Yes
Political union		
Federalism	No	No
Common foreign and defence policy	No	No
More powers for European parliament	No	Not at the expense of national parliaments
Reform qualified majority voting in Council of Ministers	Yes	Yes
Retention of British veto in Council of Ministers	Yes	Yes
Other European policy		
Enlargement to eastern Europe	Yes	Yes
Reform of Common Agricultural Policy	Yes	Yes

Source: *New Statesman and Society*, 17 February 1995.

commitment to Keynesian-led full employment.[34] In relation to trade unions, Labour resumed its debates about 'one member one vote' (OMOV) within its own organisation, with the 1993 conference voting for a batch of OMOV reforms.[35] For Labour's leadership, OMOV had two major virtues. First, it pointed to a weakening of Labour's union links, which had proved unpopular with many voters. Secondly, it evoked a more individualistic ethos inside the party, attuned to the more individualistic society which had emerged under the Tories.

When Blair succeeded Smith, he was already renowned as a Labour 'moderniser' and, free from much of Labour's historical baggage, instantly quickened the pace of internal reform.[36] Although Labour had long abandoned any genuine faith in nationalisation, he still attached enormous symbolic importance to revising clause 4 of its constitution (see chapter 5) and prompted a six-month debate on the subject. The decision to amend clause 4, made at a special party conference in 1995, was thus a personal triumph and hastened the departure of many 'hard left' elements; the launch of Arthur Scargill's Socialist Labour party in 1996 was dramatic testimony to Labour's shift on public ownership since 1983.

Blair's leadership also activated other, slightly less explosive, reforms of a centre-right character. Shadow Chancellor Gordon Brown pushed Labour away from its usual tax-and-spend position, ruling out in early 1997 any firm spending pledges before the 'harvest' of economic growth, while distancing himself from the middle-income tax increases proposed in 1992. While attacking the 'privatisation' of the National Health Service, Labour also adopted a cautious view of controversial Tory reforms like trust hospitals and fundholding general practitioners; in general, the issue of 'accountability' seemed to supersede that of structure and overall management. Likewise, Blair's decision (in 1994) to send his son to a school which had opted out of the control of the local educational authority exposed Labour's ambivalence on many of the Tories' educational reforms. Indeed, in some areas, like testing and school discipline, Labour seemed to be stealing the Tories' thunder – a charge repeated when shadow Home Secretary Jack Straw denounced 'drop-outs on the streets' in 1995, while courting the idea of 'curfews' for teenagers a year later. On the vital issue of Europe, Labour's offensive tended to highlight Tory divisions rather than the actual content of government policy; as table 1.1 shows, government and opposition policy was surprisingly similar by 1995.

During a visit to the Far East in early 1996, Blair disclosed what purported to be Labour's new 'big idea', the theme which would distinguish it more clearly from post-Thatcher Conservatism. This was the 'stakeholder society', one which involved employers 'treating workers as partners rather than factors of production' and which compelled industry and the City to 'accept a wider social obligation' through (for example) pension funds, compulsory shares for employees and greater workforce involvement in decision making.[37] The notion that this put 'clear water' between Labour and the Tories was substantiated by the Tories themselves, who attacked 'stakeholderism' as a return to 1970s-style corporatism, trade union power and statist meddling in the market. But it could also be argued that it was yet another landmark on the road to a centre-right consensus, with Labour accepting that its perennial goals (greater equality and common ownership) could be achieved only in tandem with private enterprise and a respect for the profit motive – a bold attempt, perhaps, to 'socialise' rather than replace free-market capitalism. There were also strong echoes of the New Right's approach to welfare, which had already been harnessed by the radical Labour MP Frank Field in his 'welfare into work' ideas.[38] The stress upon company pensions, for example, reflected Field's argument that traditional state provision was now outflanked by the demands of a more diverse society.

Centripetal Conservatism?

Mindful of Labour's dash for the centre, John Major made a number of efforts after 1992 to reassert his and his party's centrist credentials. In so doing, he incurred the wrath of many right wingers, who pointed to a betrayal of the radical Thatcher legacy. The leadership challenge of John Redwood in 1995 was inspired largely by a belief that the government had lost its cutting edge, with voters no longer sure of what distinguished it from the opposition.[39] This was particularly true of Europe, which sparked a series of bitter Conservative divisions after 1992.[40]

Ever since 1990, when the new premier declared his wish to see Britain 'at the heart of Europe', the party's Euro-sceptic elements had viewed Major with distrust – even though his predecessor allowed far more power to pass from Westminster to Brussels (through the Single European Act of 1986 and membership of the Exchange Rate Mechanism in 1990). The frequent demands for a referendum on Europe (from erstwhile Euro-rebels like Teddy Taylor and Teresa Gorman – as well as Lady Thatcher) arose from a belief that on Europe the main parties were indistinguishable, giving voters no opportunity to reject 'creeping' Euro-federalism.[41]

In other areas too there were fears (cogently expressed by Lady Thatcher in the House of Lords in early 1996) that the government – beset by a dwindling majority – had lost its ideological nerve. Following a revolt by centre-left Tory MPs, it abandoned the privatisation of the Post Office in 1994, while Clarke's budget of the same year showed a willingness to raise taxation rather than cut expenditure. In early 1995, Major also shocked his party's right wing by accepting Blair's suggestion that governments had 'a duty to reduce inequality', while later adding to Labour's complaints about pay rises for senior executives (even hinting at preventative legislation).

Full circle

In the run-up to the 1997 general election, it would have been facile to claim that there were no serious differences between the two main parties. Although Labour had accepted much of the post-1979 privatisations, its 1997 manifesto did not propose any further episodes; the Major government, meanwhile, had prepared the railways, coal mines and the nuclear industry for free-market disciplines, while the 1997 Tory manifesto promised to privatise London Underground and Parcelforce (see table 1.2). In relation to welfare and the public services, Labour continued to stress the need for formal, structured 'accountability', while the Tories remained more concerned with the concept of 'consumer choice' for patients, parents and tenants. In respect of the way Britain is governed, the two parties were further apart than at any stage since the war, with Labour taking a significant interest in constitutional reform – an issue which Tories continued to treat with profound distrust.

Underpinning the 1997 campaign was also a serious divergence over the role of the state in society; whereas Labour retained its Hegelian view that the state was an ally of freedom and a force for good, the Conservatives

Table 1.2. Conservative and Labour manifestos, 1997

	Conservative	Labour
Education	School performance targets, with action taken to bring under-performers up to the mark. Inspection of local education authorities, with remedial action when required. More delegation to schools, more specialist schools and a grammar school, if wanted, in every major town. Nursery vouchers, education or training credits to be introduced.	Nursery places to be provided for all four-year-olds. Class sizes to be cut to 30 or fewer for all pupils aged 5, 6 and 7, financed by phase-out of assisted places scheme. Ministers to close and restart failing schools. Open University-style University of Industry.
Jobs	Exemption from European Working Time Directive to be demanded. Project Work, 'workfare', programme to be extended, if economically viable, to cover long-term unemployed nationwide. Developing scheme to use private and voluntary sectors to get people off welfare and into work.	Windfall tax to finance welfare-to-work scheme for 250,000 under-25s, unemployed for more than six months. Six-month tax rebate for employers taking on long-term unemployed. Special Employment Zones to coordinate benefits, training and job-hunting. Special help for lone parents.
Environment	'Tough but affordable' targets to improve air quality. Sustained improvement in water quality, at affordable pace. Encouragement of low-pollution vehicles. Continuing exploration of polluter-pays principle. Product labelling to show environmental impact of how goods are made.	All departments to promote environmental policies, with parliamentary audit. Integrated transport policy. Review of vehicle excise duty to promote low-emission vehicles. Tough regulation of water industry. Tax penalties for pollution. Moratorium favoured on 'large-scale sales' of Forestry Commission land.
Economy	Tight control on public spending with five-year goal of reducing government expenditure to below 41 per cent of national income. Maintaining inflation target of 2.5 per cent or less. Aim to virtually eliminate public borrowing by 2000. Maintain lowest European tax burden.	Inflation target of 2.5 per cent or less. Greater independence for Bank of England. Public debt at 'stable and prudent level', borrowing only to invest 'over economic cycle'. Review of Whitehall assets. Maintenance of current two-year spending plans. High and stable employment.
Unions	Public protection from 'abuse' of union power by removal of legal immunity from court action for strikes which	Union legislation of 1980s to stay on ballots, picketing and industrial action, but where majority of relevant workforce vote for representation, union should be

	have 'disproportionate or excessive effect', allowing public and employers to seek injunctions to stop such strikes. Strike ballots to be repeated at regular intervals.	recognised. 'Full consultation on the most effective means of implementing this proposal.' Minimum wage to cut taxpayer subsidy to low-pay employers.
Crime	Mandatory prison sentences for persistent burglars and drug dealers; automatic life terms for anyone convicted of second serious sexual or violent crime. Extra 10,000 public-place CCTV cameras by 1999. Voluntary ID cards. Speedy court sanctions for young offenders, including electronic curfews and parental control orders.	Halving of time to get persistent young offenders from arrest to sentence. Parental responsibility orders, to make parents face up to children's misbehaviour, community safety orders for bad neighbours, and child protection orders for youngsters left out too late at night. Free vote on total handgun ban.
Health	Annual increases in real resources for NHS. Hospital league tables to inform patient and GP choice. Practice-based cottage hospitals. Nurse prescribing to be extended. No long-stay mental hospitals to be closed without adequate community-care alternative. Private finance initiative to 'unleash' modernisation funds.	First £100 million saved on ending internal market bureaucracy to take 100,000 off waiting lists. No-wait cancer surgery. Annual real-terms increase in NHS spending. Action on mixed-sex wards. Ban on tobacco advertising. Independent food standards agency. New Minister for Public Health.
Pensions	All youngsters entering work to get personal pension fund, with rebate on National Insurance contributions. More flexibility for personal pension holders to continue investing even if they subsequently join company schemes. Easier set-up for small-employer personal pension plans.	Basic state pension to be increased 'at least in line with prices'. Private, state-approved second pension scheme proposed, offering high value-for-money standards. Action to stop pension mis-selling. Help mooted for million pensioners not claiming income support entitlement.
Transport	Complete 'successful transfer' of British Rail, followed by plans to privatise London Underground, with recycling of proceeds to modernise network within five years, and regulation of fares to ensure no rise above inflation for four years. Road-building programme to be sustained.	More effective regulation of privatised railways, with new rail authority back-up. Unpersuaded on case for 44-tonne lorries. Strategic review of roads programme. New public–private partnership for London Underground, with no sell-off. Proper, local regulation of bus services.
Constitution	Evolutionary, rather than revolutionary, change. Plan to give parliament more time to consider legislation by extending Queen's speech programme to cover firm programme for year ahead and provisional programme for the year after.	Referendums offered on Scottish, Welsh and London assemblies, and proportional representation for general elections. Abolition of hereditary peers' rights in Lords. Reform of party funding. Freedom of Information Act. More freedom for councils. Human rights guarantee.

Table continues overleaf

Table 1.2. Continued

	Conservative	Labour
Tax	Around 2 million one-taxpayer families to get extra £17.50 from transfer of married partner's unused tax allowance to working spouse, where partner is looking after dependants. Five-year parliament 'aim' to reduce basic-rate income tax to 20p. Cuts in burden of capital gains tax and inheritance tax 'as prudent'.	Five-year pledge of no increase in income tax rates. Long-term objective of 10p starting-rate income tax. VAT on domestic fuel and power reduced to 5 per cent. No extensions of VAT to food, children's clothes, books, newspapers or public transport fares. Windfall tax on privatised utilities.
Housing	Aim to raise £25 billion over decade for run-down housing estates where tenants agree to switch to private-sector landlords. Rough-sleeper initiative to be extended from London to other big cities. Aim for at least 60 per cent of all new homes to be built on derelict urban sites.	Phased release of council house sale receipts to be reinvested in housing. Action on gazumping. Tenant agreement to be sought for private-finance improvement of public housing. Commonhold ownership of blocks of flats, and easier purchase of freehold by leaseholders. New council duty to protect homeless.
Europe	Positive vision of partnership of nation states; no further extension of qualified majority voting, or erosion of veto. Strong defence of frontier controls. Demand exemption from Working Time Directive. Will not join fudged Euro currency. Membership only by referendum approval.	Rapid completion of single market, high priority enlargement, urgent reform of CAP, greater democracy in EU bodies, retain national veto over key national interest issues, and signing of Social Chapter. Triple lock on single currency membership: cabinet, parliament and referendum.
Privatisation	London Underground and Parcelforce. Preserve national identity, universal service and distinctive characteristics of Post Office Royal Mail while considering options – including 'different forms of privatisation' – for providing private capital and management.	'We will ensure that self-financing commercial organisations within the public sector – the Post Office is a prime example – are given greater commercial freedom to make the most of new opportunities.' Privatisation not mentioned.
Defence	Encouragement of further development of cadet forces. No need for defence spending review. Will resist attempts to bring Western European Union under control of EU.	Retention of Trident, though nuclear weapons to be included in multilateral negotiations 'when satisfied with verified progress towards our goal of global elimination'. Strategic defence, security, and spending review promised.

Source: Observer, 12 April 1997.

remained much more suspicious. This was shown up clearly by the parties' positions on the purpose of economic growth: for Labour it would finance further public spending, allowing the state to 'do more', while for the Tories it would allow further cuts in personal taxation, giving greater 'choice' to individuals. It should also be recalled that, by 1997, two Tory MPs (Alan Howarth and Emma Nicholson) had defected to other parties on the grounds that the Conservative party was no longer the 'moderate' party they once believed in.

Yet the 1997 manifestos still implied strongly that Britain's party culture was essentially consensual – even more consensual, perhaps, than it had been in the 1950s. If the first post-war consensus was 'social democratic', then its successor could be (and has been) described as a 'social market' consensus.[42] To summarise, this accord seems to have seven notable features:

(1) An acceptance that individual freedom, rather than equality or social justice, is the philosophical backdrop to modern political activity. There is still some argument about the extent to which state provision can bring this about. Yet even Labour now accepts that the state's role here can be nothing like as great as the left once imagined.

(2) An acceptance that a modern economy must be based upon capitalist criteria, market practices and consumer choice. During the 1950s, the question for Conservatives was how to make the welfare state and an expanding public sector compatible with private property and middle-class privilege. Today, the question for Labour is how to make consumerism and a market economy compatible with the provision of social services and a practical concern for society's 'losers'.

(3) An acceptance that the mixed economy of the 1970s has been remixed, irreversibly and justifiably, in favour of private enterprise.

(4) An acceptance that the trade unions should be mainly concerned with the needs of individual members, and that any return to the status they enjoyed in the 1970s would be inappropriate.

(5) An acceptance that the state retains vital responsibilities for the public's welfare (particularly health and education) but that they should be reworked to give more importance to consumer choice, cost-effectiveness, managerial efficiency and value for money. There is a linked acceptance that public services cannot be improved simply through increased expenditure, and that the electorate is in any case unwilling to endorse the large increases in taxation this would involve.

(6) An acceptance that macro-economic management has been curtailed by European integration and a globalised economy. An opposition party is now much less likely to offer radically different prescriptions on economic and industrial policy for one simple reason: such policies are likely to prove impracticable given the rapid internationalisation of markets since the 1970s.

(7) An acceptance that the social and economic shake-up of the 1980s may have weakened social cohesion and that steps should now be taken to rekindle a certain type of collectivism – variously depicted as 'citizenship', 'community values', 'stakeholder society', 'back to basics' and 'one-nation Toryism'. The new relevance of think-tanks like the Social Market Foundation is linked to their attempts to make capitalism and individualism somehow less divisive in their effects upon society.

This last feature became particularly marked towards the end of Conservative rule. The 1996 Queen's speech promised a range of restrictions – from gun ownership to 'anti-stalking' devices – designed to produce a more 'moral' society, restrictions which produced wide cross-party support. The demands made by Frances Lawrence (the widow of a murdered headmaster) for 'a moral crusade ... healing our fractured society and banishing violence' were approved loudly by all the main party leaders, while Straw claimed that the new Labour government would be judged 'not so much on the economy as upon the expectation that we will be the agents of a different ethical order'.[43]

Politicians are quick to claim that any change in political culture was forged by their own efforts, a claim made by Thatcherites and 'New Labourites' alike. Yet it must be pointed out that much of this new culture has been forged by developments that would have occurred almost regardless of party activity – the decline of heavy industry and the *embourgeoisement* of society being obvious examples. Furthermore, the changes in Britain's political culture is only a reflection and result of trends worldwide. It was difficult, for example, to argue for the 'abolition of capitalism' following the seismic changes in eastern Europe in the late 1980s. Little wonder that Fukuyama's 'end of history' thesis has attracted so much critical acclaim – even though its echoes of Bell's *End of Ideology* (published three decades earlier) should make us wary of deterministic, end-game analyses.[44]

Consensus, however, cannot be enforced. If a party wishes to ignore the *Zeitgeist* and polarise debate it can of course do so – as did Labour in 1983 and, to a lesser extent, the Conservatives in 1945. But a party which does this is likely to marginalise itself as a potential party of government – a fear which dogged John Redwood's campaign for the Tory leadership in 1997. As Richard Rose argued, consensus normally presages a variety of party governments (as the 1997 general election demonstrated) while polarisation normally indicates hegemony – as occurred in Britain during the 1980s.[45] In other words, the culture of party politics is vital to the shape of its party system. This point is developed in the following chapter.

Notes

1   See S. E. Finer, *Adversary Politics and Electoral Reform* (London, Wigram, 1975).

2 D. Butler, *British General Elections Since 1945*, 2nd edn (Oxford, Blackwell, 1995), ch. 2.
3 D. Kavanagh and P. Morris, *Consensus Politics From Attlee To Major*, 2nd edn (Oxford, Blackwell, 1994), pp. 5–18.
4 Kavanagh and Morris, *Consensus Politics*, chs 2–5.
5 J. Ranelagh, *Thatcher's People* (London, Fontana, 1992), ch. 5.
6 D. Marquand, *The Unprincipled Society* (London, Cape, 1988).
7 R. McKibbin, *The Ideologies of Class* (Oxford, Oxford University Press, 1990).
8 A. Horne, *Macmillan*, Vol. 2 (London, Macmillan, 1989), pp. 137–44.
9 R. A. Butler, *The Art of the Possible* (London, Hamish Hamilton, 1971), p. 160.
10 E. Shaw, *The Labour Party Since 1979* (London, Routledge, 1994), pp. 5–6.
11 R. Kelly and J. Cantrell (eds), *Modern British Statesmen 1867–1945* (Manchester, Manchester University Press, 1997), Introduction.
12 D. Fraser, *The Evolution of the British Welfare State* (London, Macmillan, 1973), ch. 7.
13 S. Foster and R. Kelly, 'Keynesians or Monetarists?', *Talking Politics*, summer 1989.
14 Quoted in Foster and Kelly, 'Keynesians or Monetarists?'.
15 *Listener*, 15 September 1976.
16 A. King (ed.), *Why is Britain Becoming Harder To Govern?* (London, BBC, 1976).
17 W. Kennett (ed.), *The Rebirth of Britain* (London, Weidenfeld and Nicolson, 1982), ch. 3.
18 P. Riddell, *The Thatcher Era* (Oxford, Blackwell, 1991), pp. 5–6.
19 D. Healey, *The Time of My Life* (London, Penguin, 1990), ch. 18.
20 A. Gamble, *The Free Economy and the Strong State* (London, Macmillan, 1988).
21 M. Cowling (ed.), *Conservative Essays* (London, Cassell, 1978), pp. 141–55.
22 J. McIlroy, *The Permanent Revolution?* (Nottingham, Spokesman, 1991), ch. 2.
23 Shaw, *The Labour Party Since 1979*, pp. 11–15.
24 I. Crewe and I. King, *SDP: The Birth, Life and Death of the Social Democratic Party* (Oxford, Oxford University Press, 1995).
25 J. D. Derbyshire and I. Derbyshire, *Politics in Britain* (Edinburgh, Chambers, 1990), pp. 109–15.
26 M. Smith and J. Spear (eds), *The Changing Labour Party* (London, Routledge, 1992), ch. 2.
27 N. Kinnock, *Making Our Way* (Oxford, Blackwell, 1987); R. Hattersley, *Choose Freedom* (London, Michael Joseph, 1987).
28 I. Crewe, 'The Policy Agenda', *Contemporary Record*, February 1990.
29 D. Butler and D. Kavanagh, *The British General Election of 1992* (London, Macmillan, 1992), pp. 275–8.
30 A. Sherman, *Sunday Telegraph*, 28 August 1988.
31 S. Hogg and J. Hill, *Too Close To Call* (London, Little Brown, 1995), ch. 1.
32 R. Kelly, 'After Margaret: The Conservative Party Since 1990', *Talking Politics*, summer 1993.
33 *Daily Telegraph*, 18 January 1991.
34 B. Gould, *Goodbye To All That* (London, Macmillan, 1995), pp. 265–8.
35 R. Kelly, 'Labour's Leadership Contest and Internal Organisation', *Politics Review*, February 1995.
36 J. Sopel, *Tony Blair* (London, Michael Joseph, 1995).
37 *Guardian*, 17 January 1996.
38 F. Field, *Making Welfare Work* (London, Institute of Community Studies, 1995).

39   B. Jones, 'The Conservative Party Leadership Contest 1995', *Talking Politics*, autumn 1995.

40   R. Kelly, 'The Left, the Right and the Whipless', *Talking Politics*, autumn 1995.

41   T. Gorman, *The Bastards* (London, Pan, 1993).

42   D. Kavanagh and A. Seldon (eds), *The Major Effect* (London, Macmillan, 1994), pp. 3–17.

43   *New Statesman*, 25 October 1996.

44   F. Fukuyama, *The End of History and the Last Man* (London, Hamish Hamilton, 1992).

45   R. Rose, *Do Parties Make A Difference?* (London, Macmillan, 1984).

2

The party system

Definitions and varieties

As explained in the previous chapter, the 'culture' of party politics stems largely from the ideological assumptions and policy priorities underpinning debate between the main parties. The party 'system', on the other hand, stems largely from the electoral context in which such debate occurs.

Defining the *sort* of party system which exists therefore depends upon the electoral opportunities voters have and the amount of electoral support parties obtain. If, for example, only one party presents itself to the electorate (as was the case in most of the Soviet Union's elections) then a one-party system obviously prevails. If a number of parties present themselves, but only one seems capable of attracting enough support to govern, then a dominant-party system may be said to exist – as was the case until recently in Japan, where the Liberal Democratic party governed continuously between 1955 and 1993.[1] Britain's two-party system (discussed below) stemmed from the existence of just two parties with substantial support, each capable of winning elections outright. If there are three parties with enough support to attain office (as with the Social, Christian and Free Democrats in West Germany in the 1960s and 1970s), then a three-party system seems a fitting description. If, on the other hand, there is a variety of parties capable of influencing the course of government and politics – usually through governing coalitions – then a multi-party system is considered to be in operation (after 1994 the Irish coalition government led by John Bruton contained no fewer than four different parties).

Party systems and party culture

There is often a close link between party systems and party cultures. A two-party system, for example, often exists where there is a consensual party culture, where the bulk of voters' views are reflected by two competing parties and where it is difficult for other parties to offer much that is both distinctive and relevant – a situation which, as we have seen, existed in

37

Britain for much of the post-war period. Conversely, a more varied party system can begin to develop if that consensus is seen to break down: in Britain in the early 1980s, the Alliance between the Liberals and the Social Democratic party (SDP) profited from a sense that 'moderate' voters had been abandoned as a result of 'extremism' within the two main parties.

However, it is not simply the case that a party culture determines the shape of a party system; the reverse can often apply. During the heyday of Britain's two-party system (1945–70 – see below), both parties saw the strong chance of securing an overall majority of seats in parliament and an uncompromising place in government. This, in turn, encouraged them to tailor their policies to win the support of 'moderate' floating voters, thus having a centripetal effect upon the culture of party politics. As Anthony Downs observed in 1957, competition between the two main parties entailed 'both situating themselves towards the middle of the political spectrum to maximise their market share'.[2]

The emergence of a three- or multi-party system, and the corresponding likelihood of hung parliaments, can again affect party culture. Hung parliaments offer a fertile environment for smaller parties representing small sections of public interest. The guarantee of hung parliaments, such as that provided by proportional representation, may deter such parties (indeed *any* party) from diluting core beliefs in the interests of maximising electoral support. This can then lead to a more diverse, and possibly centrifugal, party culture, both within and outside Westminster. Indeed, one of the staple arguments for proportional representation – usually the midwife of a multi-party system – is that it would encourage a more varied tone of political debate and allow a wider range of views and interests to be heard in parliament.[3]

The emergence of a dominant-party system can have equally important consequences for a democracy's political culture, a point developed by Heywood in respect of Britain after 1992.[4] Within the dominant party itself, it can encourage a certain arrogance and disregard for public opinion in its approach to government policy, based upon the belief that, no matter how unpopular the party may be at the time, come the next election voters will again 'cling to nurse'.[5] For the non-dominant parties, meanwhile, permanent opposition can engender an inhibited and cautiously consensual approach to policy, based upon a belief that voters will consider them only if they echo many of the dominant party's own themes. In short, dominant-party systems can create a political culture which is fatalistic and intellectually lazy, or – much worse – open to allegations of self-serving corruption by those in power (as demonstrated in Japan during the Lockheed bribery scandal of 1976).

Britain's two-party system: features

Recent argument about the nature of Britain's party system represents a sharp contrast with the situation until 1970, when Britain was widely thought to host the classic example of a two-party model. Writing in 1962, Ivor Jennings suggested that the two-party system was a 'cornerstone' of the British constitution, while Malcolm Punnett agreed in 1968 that such a system was the logical outcome of both the Westminster model of democracy and the pattern of political debate in Britain.[6] This system could be said to have five key characteristics:

A parity of power

As indicated earlier, the most important feature of any two-party system is the existence of two dominant parties, equally capable of governing alone. It would be careless to state that the parties alternated in office, for between 1951 and 1964 there was an uninterrupted period of Tory rule. Nevertheless, it is significant that in the twenty-five years between 1945 and 1970, the Tories governed for thirteen years, while Labour governed for twelve.

Table 2.1. *British general election results, 1945–97: numbers of seats won (percentage share of vote)*

	Conservative	Labour	Liberal[a]	Others[b]
1945	213 (39.8)	393 (47.8)	12 (9.0)	22 (3.4)
1950	298 (43.5)	315 (46.0)	9 (9.1)	3 (1.4)
1951	321 (48.0)	295 (48.8)	6 (2.5)	3 (0.7)
1955	344 (49.7)	277 (46.4)	6 (2.7)	3 (1.2)
1959	365 (49.4)	258 (43.8)	9 (5.9)	1 (0.9)
1964	304 (43.4)	317 (44.1)	9 (11.2)	0 (1.3)
1966	253 (41.9)	363 (48.0)	12 (8.5)	2 (2.6)
1970	330 (46.4)	287 (43.0)	6 (7.5)	7 (3.1)
1974 (Feb.)	297 (37.9)	301 (37.1)	14 (19.3)	23 (5.7)
1974 (Oct.)	277 (35.9)	319 (39.2)	12 (18.5)	26 (6.4)
1979	339 (43.9)	268 (36.9)	11 (13.8)	17 (5.4)
1983	397 (42.4)	209 (27.6)	23 (25.4)	21 (4.6)
1987	375 (42.3)	229 (30.8)	22 (22.6)	24 (4.3)
1992	336 (41.9)	271 (34.4)	20 (17.8)	24 (5.9)
1997	165 (30.7)	418 (43.2)	46 (16.8)	30 (9.3)

[a]The 'Liberal' total denotes that of the Liberal party until 1979. In 1983 and 1987, it denotes that of the Alliance between the Liberal and Social Democratic parties. In 1992 and 1997, it denotes that of the Liberal Democratic party.

[b]Since 1974, 'Other' parties include the main Ulster Unionist parties, which until then had been included in the Conservative total.

A parity of support

This balance of power sprang from a balance of support; in the eight post-war elections before 1974, the average gap between the two parties' share of the vote was a mere 4 per cent, with neither party (apart from the Tories in 1945) ever failing to secure less than 43 per cent of votes cast (see table 2.1).

A duopoly of support

The figures just mentioned clearly point to the electoral dominance – or 'duopoly' – of two parties, with the vast majority of voters consistently supporting either Labour or the Conservatives. In 1951, almost 97 per cent of votes cast went to the two parties and, until 1974, the two-party vote never fell much below 90 per cent. By contrast, the support obtained by third parties during this period was derisory, prompting speculation after 1951 as to whether the Liberals could even survive as a distinct political entity.[7]

A duopoly of representation

Helped by the electoral system (to be discussed below), the two parties therefore duopolised seats in the House of Commons, with well over 90 per cent of MPs having allegiance to either Labour or the Tories. It was even suggested that the rectangular shape of the House of Commons, in contrast to that of most other democratic legislatures, reflected its two-dimensional nature, looking less like a debating chamber than a battleground for two political armies.[8]

A nationwide pattern

The two parties' dominance at Westminster was reflected in most individual constituencies. In no more than 10 per cent of all British constituencies could any other party expect to achieve even second place when the votes had been counted: for the bulk of voters it was a straightforward choice between the Labour and Tory candidates. This was reflected in the fact that both parties, though obviously stronger in some regions than others, could still count on substantial levels of support nationwide. At the 1955 general election, which it lost, Labour still won forty-two seats in southern England (not including seats won in Greater London), while the Conservatives won thirty-six seats in Scotland – two more than Labour. In major cities like London, Manchester, Liverpool and Glasgow, it was quite common to find the two parties holding a similar number of seats. Students from Liverpool may be surprised to learn that, as late as 1959, Toxteth was a seat won by the Conservatives.

Britain's two-party system: causes

Between 1945 and 1970, Britain's two-party system was founded upon four related factors – constitutional, sociological, political and economic.

Constitutional

When seeking explanations for the two-party system, the nature of Britain's electoral system is an obvious target, particularly if one's view of a party system is influenced mainly by the composition of a national parliament. It is undeniable that, during this period, the first-past-the-post electoral system gave the two main parties disproportionate representation in parliament while compounding the plight of the Liberals. In 1964, for example, the Liberals' share of the vote doubled to 11 per cent, yet its share of seats remained what it had been at the previous election – less than 2 per cent. Conversely, Labour's 44 per cent of votes in 1964 translated into over 50 per cent of seats, while the Tory vote of 43 per cent produced a 48 per cent share of seats. It was small wonder that the Liberal party's interest in electoral reform predated the change in voting behaviour after 1970 (see below).

Sociological

It must be emphasised, though, that first-past-the-post and a two-party system are not inseparable. During the inter-war years (following the emergence of Labour and the fission of the Liberals), Britain's electoral system did allow multi-party voting patterns to produce a multi-party parliament. Success under the British electoral system requires concentrated support and, as table 2.2 demonstrates, it is not unprecedented for more than two parties to meet this criterion.

That only two parties managed to meet it after 1945 points to the most important sociological feature of the period, namely *class alignment*. This was the phenomenon whereby most voters felt a strong and lasting identity with one of the two major social classes: the working class (those reliant upon manual or blue-collar occupations, living mainly in rented property in urban areas) and the middle class (those reliant upon non-manual or white-collar employment, living mainly as owner occupiers in suburban and rural areas).

The causes of class alignment were complex, and relate to the structure of the British economy and its material and psychological effects upon the workforce.[9] Yet its political effects were quite simple: about two-thirds of working-class voters identified with and habitually supported the Labour party – a party founded by the organised working class and rooted in working-class culture – while about three-quarters of the middle class did

Table 2.2. *The first-past-the-post system and multi-party politics, 1918–23*

Party	Share of total vote (%)	MPs elected
1918 general election		
Coalition Unionist	32.6	335
Coalition Liberal	13.5	133
Coalition Labour	1.5	10
Conservative	3.4	23
Liberal	12.1	28
Labour	22.2	63
1922 general election		
Conservative	38.2	345
National Liberal	11.5	62
Liberal	17.5	54
Labour	29.5	142
1923 general election		
Conservative	38.1	258
Liberal	29.6	159
Labour	30.5	191

Source: D. Butler and G. Butler, *British Political Facts 1900–1994* (London, Macmillan, 1994).

likewise with the Conservatives, a party historically linked to property, privilege and hierarchy. Class alignment dealt a double blow to 'classless' parties like the Liberals. First, it left them with very few voters to pursue. Secondly, the demographic division of Britain into largely working-class and largely middle-class areas gave the two main parties the concentrated support needed to prosper under first past the post, while denying it to parties without clear class connections.

Political

As explained in chapter 1, after 1945 both major parties upheld a centre-left consensus which was arguably Liberal in origin. Keynes had been a prominent Liberal party supporter, while the Liberals under Lloyd George (1926–31) were the first mainstream party to propagate Keynesian theory. William Beveridge, architect of the post-1945 welfare state, also had a Liberal pedigree, while many of Attlee's reforms had echoes of the 'New Liberalism' practised by the Liberal government of 1906–11. As a result, the post-war Liberal party was again delivered another body blow: what could have made Liberalism both popular and distinctive had been plagiarised by its rivals. In a political market that was saturated with centre-left policies, there was simply no room for another centre-left party.

Economic

The social democratic consensus, and by implication the two-party system, were further upheld by the relative health of the British economy and the steady growth of living standards during the 1950s and early 1960s – epitomised by Harold Macmillan's claim in 1958 that voters had 'never had it so good'. Election results in the 1950s lent weight to Macmillan's view, while those voters who were more circumspect simply put faith in the wisdom of Her Majesty's Opposition rather than any group of 'untried' politicians.

Britain's two-party system: effects

In addition to reinforcing the consensual character of party debate (in the manner described above by Downs), the two-party system had other consequences for the culture of British politics – most notably giving it a 'two-tone' character. By this, we mean that political debate inside and outside Westminster – indeed, inside and outside the parties themselves – was a two-dimensional reflection of the ongoing, two-party battle. On television and radio current affairs programmes, it was customary to pit Labour and Tory spokespeople against each other, with little interest being shown in the views of other parties. Likewise, the criticism and calumnies coming from one of the parties would inevitably have just one direction, third or fourth parties again being deemed unworthy of attention. Party manifestos also failed to acknowledge more than one 'enemy', while from an academic angle it is noteworthy that McKenzie's seminal study of *British Political Parties* in 1955 relegated analysis of the Liberal party to its appendix.[10]

Yet by far the most important effect of two-party dominance was *single-party government*: it could be assumed that, even when the two parties 'drew' an election in terms of votes (as in 1951 and 1964), one of them would still obtain an overall majority of seats. Of course, this owed much to the character of Britain's electoral system, for never did either party score an overall majority of votes. Yet the electoral system itself is no guarantee of avoiding hung parliaments, as the elections of 1910, 1923 and 1929 had already demonstrated. To deliver single-party majorities in parliament, the electoral system relied heavily on a low level of support for third and fourth parties – something which had been missing at the aforementioned elections but which was present throughout the 1945–70 period.

Single-party governments distinguished Britain from most other European democracies and had a profound effect upon the character of British politics. For example, the fact that Her Majesty's Government consisted solely of one party's representatives, while Her Majesty's Opposition consisted solely of the other's, deterred constructive argument between the parties, fostering instead *adversary politics* – a situation whereby the party in government would instinctively reject most of what was proposed by the opposition, while the opposition would instinctively reject most of what was done by the government. For many liberal observers, adversary politics had a foul effect not just upon the conduct of government but upon the whole tenor of society. Bogdanor lamented that 'it overstates what divides us and understates the strong national desire for consensus', while for Finer it underlined the case for replacing the first-past-the-post system with one which (by producing hung parliaments) would force parties to have a more cooperative relationship.[11]

Adversary politics had an undisputed effect upon the House of Commons, forging a gladiatorial atmosphere which most foreign correspondents found remarkable.[12] Yet a more telling consequence was that it spawned the *doctrine of mandate*, a concept crucial to the evolution of British government this century. Having won an overall majority of seats, the leaders of the governing party were emboldened to claim a licence, or 'mandate', to effect the policies on which they had fought the general election. The importance of this doctrine was strengthened in the post-war era by the increased content of manifestos, an effect of the statist consensus governing main-stream politics at this time: parties in government were now expected to 'do more' and therefore promise more to voters at election time. The point about this doctrine is that it loses its cogency in a three- or multi-party system of hung parliaments, where governments are stitched together after elections before pursuing a hybrid programme of policies based upon a *combination* of manifestos – for which no one, of course, directly votes.

This doctrine profoundly affected the conduct of most MPs. Quite apart from the 100 or so who belonged to an ever-expanding government team (and who were therefore bound by collective responsibility), the remaining 200 or so from the governing party were also vulnerable to the argument that they were elected to parliament not to act as quasi-independent legislators – scrutinising, delaying and blocking government policy – but to allow the implementation of the policies on which they fought the election. As such, governments with decent majorities had little trouble imposing their will upon parliament, while the prospect of a government defeat in the House, on even the most minute aspect of policy, was now thought to represent a vote of no confidence – so rare had such defeats become.[13] This, of course, made MPs on the government side even more reluctant to frustrate it, giving them the reputation of 'lobby fodder' and parliament that of being a 'rubber stamp' for governments.[14] In brief, the two-party system – by allowing single-party governments and the doctrine of mandate – arguably led to the emasculation of parliament, leaving Britain without any institutional check upon executive power.

These particular effects of the party system naturally existed beyond 1970; indeed, they have come to play a more central part in the study of contemporary British politics. But it took a series of developments after 1970 to highlight their importance.

The changing party system: features

Since 1970, it is been widely agreed that Britain's party system has been in a state of flux. This has been prompted by the emergence of four particular features which represent a signal change from the 1950s and 1960s:

Party support is more conditional

No longer are most voters firmly wedded to a particular party. Whereas 43 per cent identified strongly with either Labour or the Conservatives in 1964, this had fallen to less than 20 per cent by 1992. ICM's eve-of-poll survey in 1997 found that only 19 per cent of Labour's potential voters were 'reliable' supporters of the party.[15] The two parties can thus no longer assume automatic support from huge blocks of voters.

Party support is more fragmented

Increased voter volatility has produced more interest in other parties. The combined two-party vote fell to below 80 per cent in 1974 and just 70 per cent by 1983 following increased support for centrist and nationalist parties. In 1997, SNP support in Scotland was greater than that of the Tories, with the Liberal Democrats cementing their position as the main anti-Tory party in the south-west of England.

Party support is more regionalised

The old, nationwide pattern of voting behaviour which gave elections a uniform swing (and the parties healthy representation everywhere) has gone. After 1987, Labour was left with only three seats in southern England, while the Tories in 1997 won no seats in Scotland or Wales.

Party support is less equal

After 1992, it was no longer possible to assume that a spell in office for one party would soon be followed by a spell for the other. Indeed, there was a fear in some quarters that only the Conservatives had enough credibility to win elections.[16] Also notable was the disparity of support between the two main parties. The votes gap between Conservatives and Labour was as wide as 13 per cent in both 1983 and 1997, with three of the last four general elections producing a double-figure lead in votes for the winning party.[17]

The changing party system: causes

Just as sociological, economic and political factors once solidified Britain's party system, these same factors threw it into chaos after 1970 and account for most of the changes outlined above.

Sociological

Sociological change, in the form of class dealignment, has had a critical impact upon British party politics. Owing to changes in the nature of the economy (chiefly the shift to a more diverse, or 'post-Fordist' mode of production) and the spread of mass communication, the class basis of society has steadily diminished.[18] An increased number of voters no longer define their interests in class terms; they express their ambitions in a more individualistic fashion (see chapter 10). As voters feel less affinity with either of the two main social classes, so they feel less of an affinity with the two class-based parties. As a result, they have been more prepared to vote for parties with no clear class affiliation and show a great deal more volatility between elections (the national average swing to Labour in 1997 was a record 10.3 per cent).

Economic

Yet class dealignment does not explain entirely the contraction of support for the two main parties after 1970. Fewer voters may have felt inclined to vote Labour or Tory out of habit, yet this does not explain why fewer voters were also unprepared to vote for those parties on even a short-term, conditional basis.

This touches on the failure of both parties in government to meet the economic expectations of their voters. After 1959, neither party proved able to sustain earlier improvements in voters' standards of living, a problem compounded by later failures to avoid industrial unrest and the disruption of essential services (consider the 'three-day week' of 1973–4 and 'winter of discontent' of 1978–9). This inevitably created a sense of 'plague on both your houses' among voters.

Political

The two parties were themselves aware of growing public disenchantment, yet the course of action they took to remedy the problem only made the prospects of other parties look brighter still – especially the parties of the supposed centre. The radical analyses which both parties adopted between 1975 and 1983, leading both to reject in various ways the old Butskellite consensus, fuelled the idea that politics had polarised between a Thatcherite Tory party and a Bennite Labour party – one of the principal reasons behind the surge of support for the SDP–Liberal Alliance after its formation in 1981 (see chapter 7). Thatcherism, of course, was far from inimical to concurrent shifts in public opinion and although Tory support after 1970 never achieved the levels it reached in the 1950s, its loss of support was not particularly drastic (48 per cent in 1951, around 42 per cent over 1979–92) and did not, of course, prevent it winning elections. This was due to political ineptitude on a grand scale within the Labour party. For Labour, abandoning the old centre ground proved an unmitigated disaster, largely because it ignored the social trends which inspired a similar shift from the Tories. Labour's lurch to the left after 1979 left voters unimpressed and prompted a near-fatal split in its own ranks. At ensuing elections, the centre-left vote duly divided and, from a high of nearly 49 per cent of votes in 1951, Labour plunged to less than 28 per cent in 1983.

Evidently, three of the pillars which sustained the old two-party system – class alignment, economic growth and consensus politics – had been eroded by the 1980s, with obvious effects upon voting patterns. However, the fourth pillar of the two-party system – the electoral system – could not be so easily dislodged. And, with third- and fourth-party support being largely diffuse, the first-past-the-post system could not translate its rise into House of Commons seats: the Alliance's 25 per cent of votes in 1983 yielded a mere 3 per cent of seats, while Labour's own share of votes (just 2.2 per cent greater) gave it 32 per cent of the seats. As a result, the permanence of Britain's electoral system concealed from Westminster the sea change which had taken place outside. This impact of this is considered below.

Britain's changing party system: effects

Legitimacy of government undermined

Those who oppose the Conservative party tend to argue – not incontestably – that the crucial effect of increased third-party voting (under first past the post) was a split in the anti-Tory vote, which led in turn to a prolonged period of Tory rule.[19] This ties in with the less arguable fact that, when a fragmentation of votes is not reflected in seats, it is possible for single-party governments to be elected on a much smaller minority vote.

Whereas under the party system of the 1950s a party needed 48–9 per cent of votes to guarantee an overall majority in seats, by October 1974 just 39 per cent of votes was sufficient. From 1983 to 1997, the Conservatives governed with a lower share of votes than in 1964 when they lost – a crisis of legitimacy worsened by the shamefully low level of Tory support in areas like Scotland and Wales (see chapter 10). Labour's landslide of 1997 was also won with a lower share of votes than in the 1950s, when Labour was in opposition, with the new government only polling 32 per cent in the south-east of England – the most densely populated part of Britain. This has naturally fuelled complaints about the legitimacy of modern British government, putting strains on the old 'unitary' structure (see chapter 8).

Interest in constitutional reform widened

The claim that a government elected on less than 43 per cent of votes used its Commons majority ruthlessly – bulldozing a series of provocative reforms with little (effective) institutional resistance – focused further attention on the British constitution, especially its lack of any bold second chamber or any codified protection of individual rights.[20] Developments since 1970 have sparked particular interest in reform of the electoral system, an interest which, since 1983, has exercised growing numbers in the Labour party. Prompted by a succession of emphatic defeats, influential Labour figures like Robin Cook and Frank Field argued that Labour no longer had a vested interest in the first-past-the-post system. This erosion of bipartisan support for the constitution in general, and the electoral system in particular, is inevitable when only one party feels advantaged by present arrangements. But it is not yet clear that victory in 1997 has fully restored Labour's faith in first past the post.

Prospect of hung parliaments increased

In view of the three landslide majorities between 1983 and 1997, it may seem odd to talk about the likelihood of hung parliaments. Yet changed voting patterns have wrecked the old 'cube law', which normally ensured that a party with a certain lead in votes would have a much bigger lead in seats, thus granting it a Commons majority.[21] The decline of class-based voting, and the rise of third- and fourth-party support, have reduced the number of marginal seats which in any case no longer 'swing' together; in 1992, the north-west Tory marginal of Pendle showed a 4.5 per cent swing to Labour, while the neighbouring Tory marginal of Bolton North East showed virtually no swing at all.

    This means that a party needs a much larger national lead in votes if it is to be sure of a majority in parliament. It is striking that the Tory vote lead over Labour in 1992 (7.5 per cent) produced a non-durable majority of just twenty-one seats – the lowest Tory majority since 1951, when the party polled fewer votes than Labour. Given the variable pattern of voting in 1992, it is possible to extrapolate that eight of the previous twelve post-war general elections (excluding February 1974) would have produced hung parliaments.[22] John Curtice has calculated that, on the basis of voting patterns in 1997, the Conservatives will need nothing less than a 9 per cent vote lead over Labour to be sure of gaining a majority of seats at the next general election.[23]

Those old enough to remember the 1974–9 Labour government will not be unfamiliar with the effect of hung parliaments. For most of that period, the usual rhythms of British government and politics were disturbed, mainly as a result of the new voting patterns which had first surfaced in February 1974. The hung parliament resulting from that election meant a government was not formed, as per usual, within a day of polling; neither was it clear at one stage that it would, as usual, involve the party with the most seats. After 1977, the Labour government was overtly dependent for its survival upon smaller parties, and was unable to avoid a string of embarrassing defeats over individual items of policy – highlighting the resurgence of back-bench power on the government's side of the House (the government was even unable to secure a majority for its budget in 1977). Eventually, the government was brought down by a motion of no confidence in 1979, the first time this had happened since 1924. There were clear echoes of this period during the Tory government of 1992–7. It too had its majority whittled away after by-elections. It too became reliant upon small parties (in this case the Ulster Unionists). It too suffered from the magnified power of backbenchers when there is no large majority, forcing it to recast policy on Europe, privatisation and taxation.[24]

Such events would not seem extraordinary in countries where proportional representation and multi-party politics are customary. They seemed so in Britain only because the old two-party system had usually ensured single-party governments with solid parliamentary majorities.

The strong possibility of hung parliaments brought into doubt many of the key assumptions affecting British government and politics. Parties would have to enter a less adversarial dialogue for governments to be formed and sustained. Back-bench opinion would have to be courted more assiduously, with MPs perhaps less willing to vote with their front bench if it was seen to be diluting the party's manifesto commitments; regular government defeats in parliament would therefore need to be accommodated. The notion that the House of Lords had little right to obstruct the government's programme would also lose its force if that programme (having been created by post-election deals) had no direct endorsement from voters. Indeed, many of the arguments for constitutional reform could be vitiated if governments were unable to act in the 'bombastic' manner cited by critics of traditional, single-party government.

The problem of description: a quartet of ideas

The changes to Britain's party system have caused a 'crisis of definition', with scholars unable to agree about what sort of system we now have. A number of ideas have been advanced, but none is without difficulties.

A three-party system?

Academics like Berrington have written about the emergence of a three-party system since 1979, usually on the basis of votes cast.[25] In 1983, for example, the Alliance vote (25 per cent) was just 2 per cent smaller than Labour's, with Labour until 1992 eclipsed by the third party in southern England; in 1992, Labour's vote in the South West was only 19 per cent, compared with 31 per cent for the Liberal Democrats. By-election results between 1992 and 1994 – notably those of Newbury, Christchurch and Eastleigh – seemed to confirm that the Liberal Democrats were now the main anti-Tory party in southern England.[26] This development had prompted Benyon to argue that in England there were 'two two party systems', with the Tory–Labour battle in the north running parallel to a Tory–Liberal Democrat battle in the south.[27] This theory has since been weakened, not least by Labour's solid performance in southern England at the 1997 general election, where it won over fifty seats outside London (including some remarkable gains in places like Hastings and Rye and the two Brighton constituencies). Yet Benyon's idea was also damaged by the fact that in Scotland and Wales the Liberal Democrats after 1997 held more seats than the Tories (not difficult given that the Tories did not hold any), claiming the right to speak as the official opposition in parliamentary debates concerning those two countries. Although the Liberal Democrats' performance in 1997 was again hampered by the British electoral system (gaining only 7 per cent of seats for 17 per cent of votes), their seat tally of forty-six was the largest for any third party since 1929 and naturally reinforced their parliamentary profile. Beyond parliament, too, there was further evidence to support a three-party system: by 1995, the Liberal Democrats controlled 11 per cent of local authorities in Britain and had 21 per cent of councillors – more than the Conservatives.[28]

A multi-party system?

Although the Liberal Democrats had reason to be pleased with their progress across Britain in 1997 (gaining three seats in Scotland and

Wales), the situation does become more complex when Scotland, Wales and Northern Ireland are brought into the picture.

Following the start of direct rule in 1972, Ulster's voters had to wait twenty years before mainland parties even *sought* votes in the province; the Tory vote there in 1992 (6 per cent) suggested that they had not been sorely missed (see chapter 8). In Scotland and Wales, there has – as in England – been increased support for centre parties (reaching 19 per cent and 18 per cent in 1987). But the real third force in Scotland has been the SNP, which, in October 1974, polled 30 per cent of Scottish votes – more than the Conservatives. In 1997, the SNP vote was still polling 22 per cent, again more than the Tories. In many of its Scottish seats, Labour has also had to acknowledge the SNP as its main opponent; in 1997 the SNP came second in thirty-two of Labour's forty-six seats. In the non-Westminster elections, SNP strength is also in evidence – polling 33 per cent of Scottish votes in the 1994 Euro-elections and 29 per cent in elections to the new unitary local authorities in 1995, well ahead of either the Tories or Liberal Democrats.[29]

All this has encouraged Scottish-based academics like Kellas and Drucker to assert that Scotland, *ergo* Britain, has a multi-party system – a thesis demonstrated perfectly by the 1992 general election result in Inverness, Nairn and Lochaber, won by the Liberal Democrats with just 27 per cent of votes cast.[30]

In Wales, too, nationalist votes cannot be discounted. In both 1992 and 1997, all four of the seats on Wales' western seaboard were held by Plaid Cymru, making it by 1997 Wales' second party in terms of seats. (In an extraordinary contest in Ceredigion in 1992, the Liberal Democrat MP was ousted by Plaid Cymru, fighting in alliance with the local Green party.) Plaid also claimed second place in the 1994 Euro-elections (with 17 per cent of votes) and the 1993 county council elections (winning forty-one seats, compared with the Tories' thirty-two and the Liberal Democrats' thirty-one).

The obvious problem with both the three-party and multi-party theses is that, owing to the electoral system, such support is still not being converted into parliamentary representation: after 1997, the two main parties still occupied 88 per cent of Commons seats. Although the likelihood of hung parliaments means that meagre representation could still allow small parties some influence (such as that enjoyed by the Ulster Unionists following the decline of John Major's majority during 1992–7), a much greater presence in the Commons needs to be secured if a hung parliament is to be brought about. Indeed, Labour's 179 majority after 1997 left the minor parties with significantly less bargaining power than they had before. This has lent encouragement to the third theory of Britain's current party system.

Still a two-party system?

This theory was propounded by Finer, based on the reality that parliament was still dominated by two parties.[31] The idea was reinforced by the steady decline of the third party's popular vote at each of the three elections since 1983 and Labour's concurrent recovery as a governing party. The existence of two parties capable of winning a handsome Commons majority is a *sine qua non* of any return to a two-party system, and was amply realised in 1997. Yet to claim a return to the 'old' two-party system would be bizarre. Labour's 1997 victory does not overturn the enormous changes in voting patterns since the 1960s, nor can it detract from the legacy of prolonged Tory government. This leads to the fourth theory.

A dominant-party system?

The idea of a dominant-party system became fashionable in the aftermath of the 1992 general election.[32] It was not just that the Tories won an unprecedented fourth term, nor was it due simply to another wide margin in votes (7.5 per cent). What gave the idea resonance were the circumstances in which that epochal victory was achieved – during a recession, after the introduction of a ferociously unpopular poll tax and during a period when Labour had moderated and modernised its approach.

The 1992 result thus encouraged the belief that only one party was trusted to run a modern capitalist economy; research confirmed, in fact, that many people had reluctantly voted on this basis.[33] The dominant-party thesis was underlined by the fact that, by 1997, three decades had elapsed since any other party had won a general election convincingly, while it was over twenty-five years since any other party won even 40 per cent of the votes.

At first glance, Labour's return to power, with the biggest majority this century, appears to make the dominant-party thesis redundant. Yet the thesis was not based solely upon electoral data: it was embellished by ideological, sociological and bureaucratic elements which allowed its proponents to claim that although the Conservatives were rejected in 1997, Conservatism was not and remains entrenched in the governance of Britain.

The Tories' electoral success meant that their policies became rather infectious. As explained in the previous chapter, Labour under Blair reaffirmed its new-found sympathies for market economics, consumer choice and the 'remixed' economy. So, as Moran noted in 1994, 'if Conservative ideological assumptions have been accepted by their opponents, even electoral defeat may not end Conservative dominance: whichever party is in office, the Conservatives will always be in power'.[34]

Much of this could be attributed to modern, sociological realities. Those reliant on white-collar jobs had risen from 48 per cent of voters in 1974 to 67 per cent in 1996, while home owners had increased from 55 per cent in 1974 to over 70 per cent in 1996. Furthermore, there has been a steady demographic shift from Labour's northern, urban heartlands to suburbia and the south, while in the 1980s the number of shareholders exceeded the number of trade unionists.[35] Much of New Labour's project was based upon a recognition that, to win votes, a party must now offer a variant of contemporary Conservatism.

Almost two decades of Tory rule have also left their mark upon the character of the government machine. Conservative rule after 1979 was marked by the erosion of elective local government and the growth of appointed quasi-government bodies ('quangos'), which accounted for over a fifth of public spending by 1993. The leadership and composition of these quangos stoked fears that Conservative partisanship had permeated the official state machine, making it all the more difficult for non-Tory ministers to redirect the course of government.

Research carried out by the *Independent on Sunday* proved especially valuable in this respect.[36] It was found, for example, that among 185 National Health Service trust chairs, 62 had clear personal links with the Conservative party. The Funding Agency, responsible for monitoring opt-out schools, comprised four businessmen whose companies had all made hefty donations to Tory funds, plus the Conservative leader of Wandsworth council and the chairman of the South East Area Conservative Associations. These 'quangocrats' have considerable influence over public administration, which they may well choose to exercise in a partisan way. Yet there is no way they can be deselected by the public, thus entrenching Conservative values within the governance of Britain.

Against this grim thesis, it has to be said first that quasi-government in particular, and bureaucracy in general, are 'so vast and ramshackle that it is unlikely that the Conservatives have done more than acquire control over a small part of the structure'; furthermore, that which they do control could be hijacked without too much difficulty by supporters of other parties should they win an election.[37] Indeed, within weeks of assuming office, Labour was attracting the charge that it was 'Americanising' the central administration by flooding it with advisors and consultants openly sympathetic to the Labour party.[38]

The Tories' ideological 'hegemony' also looks overstated. In 1992, voters may well have trusted the Tories most to run the economy, but their preference did not extend to every part of the Tory agenda; 55 per cent, for instance, preferred a society which 'emphasises the social and collective provision of welfare' to one where 'the individual is encouraged to look after himself'.[39] The electorate's fondness for social democracy was arguably – some would say triumphantly – vindicated by polls during the 1997 campaign, which showed a rather progressive attitude towards higher taxation.[40]

Conclusion: a defunct party system?

The word 'system' usually denotes a degree of certainty – and, thirty years ago, when voting behaviour had that degree of certainty, it was possible to identify a particular type of party system. But with the disappearance of such psephological reliability, any quest to define a new party system is fraught with difficulty, carrying the risk that remarkable phenomena – such as the fourth Tory victory in 1992 – will be confused with something more long term and established. The 1997 general election offered further, startling proof of the electorate's volatility, with a nationwide swing of 10.3 per cent being accompanied by swings of over 18 per cent in certain constituencies (as the defeated Michael Portillo found to his cost). Such fickleness on the part of voters makes it impossible to speak with much assurance about the shape of Britain's party system as the century draws to a close: it is therefore tempting to conclude that the British party system today is best described as a volatile one. However, if the 'systematic' aspects of party competition have been replaced by trendless fluctuations, then a more accurate conclusion might be that the British party system has actually ceased to exist.[41]

Notes

1   A. Heywood, 'Britain's Dominant Party System', in L. Robins, H. Blackmore and R. Pyper (eds), *Britain's Changing Party System* (London, Leicester University Press, 1994), p. 12.
2   Quoted in R. Leach, *Turncoats* (Aldershot, Dartmouth Press, 1995), p. 67.
3   See V. Bogdanor, *The People and the Party System* (Cambridge, Cambridge University Press, 1981), pp. 40–55.
4   Heywood, 'Britain's Dominant Party System'. See also A. Heywood, *Talking Politics*, winter 1993, p. 2.
5   H. Young, *Guardian*, 11 April 1992.
6   I. Jennings, *The British Constitution* (Cambridge, Cambridge University Press, 1962), p. 62; R. M. Punnett, *British Government and Politics* (London, Heinemann, 1968), p. 101.
7   M. Baines, 'A United Anti-Socialist Party?', *Contemporary Record*, February 1991.
8   J. P. Mackintosh, *The Government and Politics of Britain* (London, Hutchinson, 1977), ch. 10.
9   See R. McKibbin, *The Ideologies of Class* (Oxford, Oxford University Press, 1991).
10   R. T. McKenzie, *British Political Parties* (London, Heinemann, 1955).
11   S. E. Finer, *Adversary Politics and Electoral Reform* (London, Wigram, 1975); Bogdanor, *The People and the Party System*, p. 41.
12   R. Hague and M. Harrop, *Comparative Government* (London, Macmillan, 1982), ch. 7.
13   P. Norton, 'The Pattern of Backbench Dissent', in M. Burch and M. Moran (eds), *British Politics: A Reader* (Manchester, Manchester University Press, 1987).

14   See B. Crick, *The Reform of Parliament* (London, Weidenfeld and Nicolson, 1964).
15   D. Denver, *Elections and Voting Behaviour* (Hemel Hempstead, Harvester Wheatsheaf, 1994), pp. 33 and 54; *Guardian*, 3 May 1997.
16   M. Harrop and A. Shaw, *Can Labour Win?* (London, Unwin, 1990).
17   See H. Margetts and G. Smythe (eds), *Turning Japanese? Britain with a Permanent Party of Government* (London, Lawrence and Wishart, 1996).
18   See S. Hall and M. Jacques, *New Times* (London, Lawrence and Wishart, 1988).
19   See M. Foot, *Another Heart and Other Pulses* (London, Collins, 1984).
20   R. Holme and M. Elliott, *1688–1988: Time for a New Constitution* (London, Macmillan, 1988).
21   See J. Curtice and M. Steed, 'The Results Analysed', in D. Butler and D. Kavanagh, *The British General Election of 1992* (London, Macmillan, 1992).
22   Curtice and Steed, 'The Results Analysed'.
23   J. Curtice, 'Anatomy of a Non-landslide', *Politics Review*, September 1997.
24   R. Kelly, 'Conservative Divisions Since 1992', *Talking Politics*, autumn 1995.
25   *Sunday Telegraph*, 5 May 1985.
26   See *Politics Review*, November 1993.
27   J. Benyon, 'The Enduring Two Party System', *Social Studies Review*, November 1988.
28   See *Politics Review*, September 1995.
29   See *Talking Politics*, autumn 1994; *Politics Review*, September 1995.
30   J. G. Kellas, *The Scottish Political System* (Cambridge, Cambridge University Press, 1989); H. M. Drucker (ed.), *Multi-Party Britain* (London, Macmillan, 1977).
31   S. E. Finer, *The Changing British Party System* (New York, American Enterprise Institute, 1980), pp. 3–4.
32   Heywood, 'Britain's Dominant Party System'.
33   I. Crewe, 'Why Did Labour Lose?', *Politics Review*, September 1992.
34   M. Moran, 'Britain: A One Party State?', *Talking Politics*, autumn 1994.
35   I. Crewe, *Guardian*, 17 April 1993.
36   *Independent on Sunday*, 3 April 1994, 22 May 1994.
37   Moran, 'Britain: A One Party State'. See also F. F. Ridley and D. Wilson (eds), *The Quango Debate* (Oxford, Oxford University Press, 1996).
38   *New Statesman*, 12 June 1997.
39   A. King *et al.*, *Britain at the Polls* (Chatham, NJ, Chatham House Publishers, 1992), pp. 20–1.
40   Gallup, *Daily Telegraph*, 16 April 1997.
41   For a development of this idea, see P. Norris, *Electoral Change since 1945* (Oxford, Blackwell, 1997), and D. Leonard, *Elections in Britain Today* (London, Macmillan, 1996).

3

The Conservative party:
theory and practice

Flexibility and the pursuit of power

Conservative Century was a fitting title for a recent history of the Conservative party since 1900.[1] By 1997, the party had been in office (either alone or as the dominant coalition partner) for all but twenty-nine years of the twentieth century. When one considers the enormous changes that the century has witnessed, this is by any standards an almost incredible achievement. What makes it all the more remarkable is that the party has been historically associated with wealth and privilege, while for most of the century (certainly after the franchise extension of 1918) the electorate has been dominated by propertyless, working-class voters. Yet the party always managed to attract at least a third of such voters at general elections and was in fact the most popular party among working-class voters in the inter-war period.[2]

This electoral durability has been attributed to the party's ideological flexibility and its reluctance to be burdened by weighty doctrines. Indeed, it has been asked whether Conservatives have *any* ideology or fixed principles, being bound instead to the pursuit of power *per se*.[3] Gilmour, himself a Conservative, claimed that the party had 'emotions but no doctrine'; White believed that Conservatism was 'less an ideology than a frame of mind'; Grimond argued that Conservatives 'do not conserve any principles, merely the state of affairs they happen to inherit'.[4]

Such charges are both unfair and simplistic. A party that has spent most of its history running a fluid liberal democracy must inevitably trim its priorities if the state is to be even remotely effective; the governance of a complex, dynamic society just does not lend itself to any rigid ideology and, even if the Tories had lost office more often as a result of failing to recognise this, it is likely that such trimming would then have fallen to other parties – as post-war Labour governments have all discovered.

Furthermore, it *is* possible to detect certain recurrent themes in Conservative politics throughout the last two centuries which, taken together, add up to as much of an ideology as anything offered (in practice) by the

Labour party: first, the conservation of socio-economic inequality; secondly, broad support for existing constitutional practices; thirdly, a faith in certain Judaeo-Christian principles like free will, the encouragement of individual responsibility and the centrality of the family.

If we accept, as most scholars do, that a determination to govern has been stronger among Conservatives than among their rivals (who have often displayed an 'oppositional' mentality), it is not immediately clear why the principles outlined above should be more conducive to such a determination than, say, a belief in socialism. Both, after all, require governmental power to guarantee their effect. But an important clue is that, for much of the century, Conservatives have been pessimistic of the future, sensing that 'history' was not on their side and that they were fighting a rearguard action against the forces of egalitarianism – an understandable reaction given the urbanised, trade unionised, blue-collar nature of society for most of the century, and the intellectual hegemony of centre-left ideas.

This made Conservatives much less confident about the 'inevitability' of their ideals than their opponents were about theirs. For most of the democratic era, Conservatives have felt that the preservation of inequality required a supreme act of political will: in other words, an absolute commitment to winning and keeping office. This shines through the writings of Conservatism's most influential scholars. Paul Smith noted that 'Change is irresistible, but a Conservative can moderate and delay what of it he finds repugnant'; Quentin Hogg argued that Conservatism's 'indispensable role' was to 'mould the latest heresy in the name of tradition'; R. A. Butler observed that the party's duty was to 'maintain the old order by appeasing and accommodating the forces which threaten it'.[5] For all these aims, office was the *sine qua non*. But – and it is necessary to restate this in view of Davies' recent, cynical study – it would be wrong to assume that Conservatives wanted office for its own sake.[6] As much as those in other parties, Conservatives have always had their own ideological agenda – based largely upon the retention of existing power structures. It was the social and political climate of industrialised Britain which made Conservatives the more fearful of opposition.

During its history, the Tory party has pursued power in a variety of ways – emphasising those parts of its ideology which are, at the time, electorally expedient, concealing those which are, at the time, electorally damaging, embracing policy themes which seem popular, and ditching those which are difficult or electorally hopeless. Conservatism, however, has not been a static or homogeneous philosophy, derived from some quasi-biblical text. Instead, it has emerged from the party's long history, an organic rather than mechanically constructed creed.

Although events and historical currents have been crucial to this process, it is still possible to identify three crucial figures in the development of Conservatism – men whose legacy still resounds in Conservative thought, with the influence of each one rising and falling according to the party's changing circumstances: Burke, Peel and Disraeli.

Tradition, order, hierarchy: the legacy of Burke

It is impossible to discuss the roots of Conservatism without reference to a non-Conservative politician – Edmund Burke, an eighteenth-century Whig MP whose *Reflections on the Revolution in France* (1790) assailed both events in France and received opinion in England. Burke's writings sowed the seed of three vital Conservative themes: piecemeal change, the importance of authority and elite rule.

The starting point of Burke's thesis was a pessimistic view of human capability and a belief that the imperfections of human society were the inevitable result of an imperfect human nature. The utopianism of the French revolution was therefore derided as futile and dangerous. Government, like so much of everyday life, was about choosing lesser evils, making the best of a difficult situation, accommodating rather than eliminating problems. It was a profoundly pessimistic view, which dismissed any idea that politicians could effect dramatic improvement in people's lives – a view which has since been used by countless Conservatives in retort to the idealism of the left.[7]

Yet Burke's dim view of politics as an activity did not lead him to dismiss the importance of government. Echoing Thomas Hobbes' *Leviathan* (which had argued in 1651 that life without government would be 'nasty, brutish and short'), Burke saw government as a vital corrective to dark, human forces. There was, within Burke's arguments, a clear authoritarian streak which clashed with the unfettered liberty promised by the early French revolutionaries – an obvious link with Conservatism's perennial interest in law, order, police power and stern punishment (Michael Howard's zeal for custodial sentencing being a recent example).

Though wary of change, Burke recognised that it must occur and his claim that 'a state without the means of change is without its means of conservation' has been the cynosure of most Conservative governments. Yet Burke insisted that change must be cautious, gradual and respectful of traditional practices and institutions – partly out of respect for humanity's imperfections, partly out of a belief that society was a mysterious organism which evolved in a subtle, complex way. Burke argued that those practices and institutions should be respected precisely because they have survived the test of time and embrace the collective wisdom of ages, which chimes with his key assertion that society should proceed according to experience rather than experiment. To govern on the basis of abstract theory or doctrine, rather than empirical reality, was anathema to Burke and his later devotees.

Finally, Burke provided later Conservatives with a rationale for hierarchy, claiming that the best society was one where 'the wiser, the more expert and the more opulent conduct ... the weaker, the less knowing and the less provided'.[8] Yet the ruling class Burke commended was to be underpinned by a clear sense of *noblesse oblige*, having benevolent obligations towards the less fortunate – a paternalistic ethos which later appealed to a string of aristocratic Tory leaders, struggling to defend an unequal society in a democratic age.

Laissez-faire, individualism, expediency: the legacy of Peel

It is often observed that Conservatism is a curious blend of libertarian and authoritarian instincts. As just explained, the latter instinct may be traced back to the influence of Burke. But to explain Conservatism's less Hobbesian elements, it is useful to recall the career of Robert Peel, usually seen as the first 'Conservative', as opposed to 'Tory', Prime Minister. (As Blake points out, Peel became premier in 1834, shortly after 'the "Conservative Party" became ... the normal expression for the party of the right'.[9])

Peel might be thought an unusual icon for the party, as his premiership proved disastrous for it. His support for *laissez-faire* economics and his subsequent disdain for the Corn Laws occasioned a seismic split and almost thirty years in opposition. Yet Peel's leadership established three crucial precedents for modern Conservatism.

First was its appeal to the new middle class (merchants, traders, industrialists), customarily seen as the preserve of the party's Whig opponents. Though initially at odds with party unity (owing to the influence of Tory aristocrats), this brought into Conservative thinking a new set of 'bourgeois' ideals – like self-reliance, individualism, thrift, frugality and probity – which supplemented its traditional stress upon authority and tradition. Secondly, it established the notion that Conservatism should be the natural creed for all society's 'haves' – new money as well as old, middle as well as upper class – and the principal advocate for those with something material to conserve. Thirdly, Peel's assault upon established, aristocratic interest stemmed from the cool calculation that Conservatism's traditional base was no longer enough in a changed social climate. This was the first example of a certain utilitarian ruthlessness in Conservative politics: a willingness to make remarkable and audacious changes in the interests of electoral survival.

The decline of the Liberal party after 1918 gave the Conservative party a batch of new, middle-class recruits whose views were to strengthen Conservatism's marriage of libertarian and authoritarian ideals. These recruits (who included Thatcher's father – a man whose views she revered) were generally supporters of traditional, Gladstonian Liberalism and its stress upon limited government and self-improvement; that they found the party such an obvious refuge is a tribute to Peel's legacy.

About fifty years later, that legacy was again evident when the party embraced Thatcherism – an interesting fusion of Burke (with its stress upon law, order and 'governability') and Peel (with its faith in capitalism, market forces and individual enterprise). Thatcherism is discussed at greater length later in the chapter. But note here that the title of one particular study of the Thatcher governments – *The Free Economy and the Strong State* – reflects perfectly the union of Peelite and Burkean ideas.[10]

Statism and patriotism: the legacy of Disraeli

Having led the party out of the electoral wilderness by 1874, it was almost inevitable that Benjamin Disraeli was a stern critic of Robert Peel – widely seen as the man who put it there in 1846. Yet the two actually had much in common as political animals, both being committed to the election of Tory governments through the accommodation of threatening electoral trends. But whereas for Peel such threats had come from the emergent middle class, for Disraeli they came from the enfranchised working class. And whereas for Peel such threats invited an acceptance of *laissez-faire* politics, for Disraeli they demanded the embrace of state intervention and collective provision – symbolised by his promise in 1872 to 'elevate the condition of the people' and demonstrated by a string of social reforms passed by his 1874–80 government.[11]

For certain Conservatives, Disraeli's ministry saw the beginning of 'one nation' Conservatism, one which accepts that statist, social reform is the reasonable price for a stable and cohesive society.[12] After 1945, when the Tories hurried to accept much of the popular Labour government's agenda (like nationalisation and the welfare state), Disraeli's legacy allowed them to rebut the charge that they were unprincipled and plagiaristic. Recalling Disraeli's record in office, the Conservative MP L. S. Amery wrote in 1946 that 'Conservatism has always recognised that *laissez faire* unchecked can destroy freedom and individuality', while Anthony Eden claimed in 1950 that 'Conservatives have historically rejected unrestrained capitalism and minimal government'.[13] Such claims evidently demand a narrow version of party history. Yet, remembering its determination to govern, the point is that – even by 1945 – Conservatism had enough variety to adapt quite easily to shifting electoral requirements.

Disraeli's promise to 'elevate the condition of the people', outlined in his famous Crystal Palace speech of 1872, was accompanied by two others, equally important to the development of Conservatism: these were to 'maintain the institutions of the country' and 'uphold the empire of England'. By elucidating the concept of nation and empire – and by linking the party closely to it – Disraeli bequeathed to Conservatives the patriotic ideal, one which has helped attract voters from the working class in particular. McKenzie and Silver's study of working-class Conservatism found that, by appealing to the xenophobic and nationalistic sentiments of many working-class voters, other parties were made to seem 'utterly distrusted where the fate of the nation's institutions are concerned'.[14] McKibbin also argued that trade union militancy in the late nineteenth and early twentieth centuries was much attenuated by Disraeli's 'jingoistic' legacy.[15]

Since then, the party has regularly 'wrapped itself in the flag' and 'played the patriotic card', placing upon its opponents an uncomfortable obligation to match its patriotic credentials.[16] As a Tory nationalist herself, whose reputation was forged largely by the Falklands war, Margaret Thatcher is a conspicuous example of this legacy. As such, it may be argued that her Conservatism – far from being the 'aberration' some Tory opponents claim (see below) – is in fact an interesting synthesis of the party's three most important traditions: the Burkean, the Disraelian and the Peelite.

Towards a new Conservatism (1965–75)

For most of this century, the Disraelian, statist, 'one nation' element has been dominant in Conservative thought. This is unsurprising given the predominantly working-class electorate created by the franchise reform of 1918, allied to the party's perennial determination to govern. As explained in chapter 1, the social democratic consensus after 1945 owed much to the Tories' acceptance of Labour's own, interventionist agenda in both industrial and welfare policy. Tory minister R. A. Butler is reputed to have remarked, 'if the people want that sort of life, they can have it – but under our auspices', an idea which neatly typifies both Conservatism's flexibility (or opportunism) and its preoccupation with power.[17]

After 1965, however, there was a greater willingness to initiate policy themes instead of cautiously following those of other parties. That year saw the election of Edward Heath as party leader, one whose 'meritocratic' background distinguished him from most of his predecessors (see chapter 4). Heath promised a 'quiet revolution' which restated the party's Peelite liberal tradition; Keynesian-style intervention would give way to a more *laissez-faire* economic policy, harnessed to a new emphasis upon individualism over collective provision. As Heath told the 1970 Tory conference, 'Our purpose is to make our fellow citizens realise that ... nobody will stand between them and the results of their own free choice'.[18]

During Heath's premiership (1970–4), this particular feature of Conservatism was quickly eclipsed by more familiar aspects, namely a willingness to act expediently in the name of political survival, followed by a return to statist territory in the name of social cohesion (and, again, political survival). Mounting unemployment, industrial unrest and a political culture still locked to social democracy pushed Heath's government into a series of policy U-turns after 1971. As a result, a government which came to power contemptuous of state intervention became one of the most statist this century.[19]

Had Heath's government been re-elected, it would have doubtless been hailed by the party as a reward for its 'pragmatism', a shining vindication of its lack of heavy, ideological baggage. Instead, the Tory vote in 1974 plunged to its then lowest level this century. This paved the way for the 'alternative' Toryism of Margaret Thatcher.

Thatcherism in perspective

During Thatcher's leadership of the party (1975–90), it was common to hear her Tory opponents arguing that she was not really a Conservative at all.[20] Much of this was related to her enthusiasm for free-market economics and a 'rolling back' of the state in both economic and industrial policy; for Tory MP Julian Critchley, this threatened to 'cut the Party off from its past ... [for] the Tories are not the natural champions of the minimalist state and a market economy'.[21] Mindful of Burke's 'organic' theory of the state, Thatcher's contempt for many established institutions – like the BBC, the universities, the Church of England and the public corporations – was also judged odd for a Conservative leader.

This critique required a somewhat selective view of both Conservative history and the record of Thatcher's governments. As this chapter has already explained, there is nothing unprecedented about Conservative support for market capitalism and an individualistic slant upon politics (consider Peel). In addition, it is absurd to argue that Thatcherism was nothing more than a libertarian crusade, at odds with Toryism's former emphasis on law, order and the constraining hand of government. The Tory victory in 1979 owed much to the party's argument that Britain was collapsing into disorder (trade union action during the 'winter of discontent' being cited as an example) and that there was a paramount need for strong, decisive government – a sentiment with which Burke could easily have agreed given the civil unrest of the 1970s. After 1979, indeed, the most controversial legislation was that which *strengthened* central authority in the interests of greater 'governability' – most notably in respect of trade union rights (reduced), civil liberties (reduced), the autonomy of local councils (reduced) and police power (increased).[22] As Simon Jenkins reveals, the Thatcher years saw not so much the rolling back of the state as the 'nationalisation of power in Britain'.[23]

Not that Thatcherites saw any contradiction between their economic libertarianism and their social authoritarianism; the shedding of the state's economic and industrial responsibilities was justified on the grounds that it would enable government to concentrate on its 'proper' task, namely the maintenance of public order and the protection of private property – a task which had been jeopardised by the 'overload' of government during the social democratic era.[24] Again, these aims were scarcely at odds with the Tory tradition, though Jenkins points to several discrepancies between aspiration and achievement (public spending as a portion of gross domestic product actually rose between 1979 and 1994).[25]

Furthermore, Thatcher's patriotic-imperialist aspect was not just demonstrated during the Falklands war but also during her regular skirmishes in Europe, where the supposed assailant of national institutions became one of their most robust defenders – her emotive defence of parliamentary sovereignty (in a speech in Bruges in 1988) being a well recorded example. On the other hand, it must be remembered that the Thatcher government – through its support for the Single European Act 1986 and its enrolment in the European Exchange Rate Mechanism in 1990 – also committed two of the greatest erosions of national sovereignty since 1972, proving that Thatcher was yet another Tory leader prepared to sacrifice principle for expediency when circumstances required it.

Yet Thatcherism did represent a new type of Conservatism, for three conspicuous reasons. First, in Margaret Thatcher the party had a leader who (cf. Burke) was genuinely committed to certain abstract doctrines. Unlike Heath (before his U-turn), her faith in market economics and individual responsibility was grounded not simply in a desire to 'modernise' Britain or make it more efficient. Accepting the premise of Friedrich Hayek's *The Road To Serfdom*, she felt that such ideas had a strong philosophical justification which would lead to the moral enrichment of society. Similarly, her economic ideas were also much influenced by the heady monetarist theories of Milton Friedman and the 'Chicago school' of economics.[26] Critchley's diatribes on Thatcherism should be treated cautiously; yet he is right to argue that Thatcher had an 'implacable zeal' for Hayek's theories in particular and a resulting 'ideological fervour' for certain government policies like privatisation and a 'hands-off' view of unemployment.[27]

This leads to the second of Thatcherism's distinguishing features. Although Conservatives, from Burke onwards, have accepted the need for reform, the *pace* of reform under Thatcher's governments was still remarkable.[28] The relentless flow of reformist legislation was a supreme example of how governments, adhering to a meticulous and detailed programme of policies, can effect staggering changes to society (see Conclusion) – a far cry from the cautious, piecemeal approach to change identified with 'normal' Conservatism. Local government, for example, was subjected to over fifty reforming acts of parliament in just over a decade, leaving its structure and functions dramatically different from 1979. The trade unions, too, were emasculated by a raft of increasingly hawkish reforms after 1982, when the consensual approach of James Prior gave way to the less patient strategy of Norman Tebbit.[29] In short, Conservatism in the 1980s became *iconoclastic*, a term that would be difficult to apply to any previous period of Tory government.

Related to this is the third hallmark of Toryism under Thatcher: a readiness to defy the *Zeitgeist*. Throughout its history, the party has generally sought power by reflecting public opinion and by adapting its core beliefs to the prevailing public mood. Although this strategy was again in evidence during Thatcher's leadership of the opposition, when calls for trade union reform and lower taxation echoed the complaints of voters, after 1979 there was a clear effort to *shape* public opinion on a wide range of issues, adapting public opinion to the government's core beliefs rather than vice versa. In respect of unemployment, privatisation and local government reform, there were numerous examples where the government consciously defied opinion poll evidence and apparent public sentiment. Not only that, it made political capital out of doing so, claiming it underlined its 'resolute approach', its rejection of U-turns, and its contempt for short-term politics.[30]

This new, talismanic version of Conservatism was reluctantly applauded by many on the left who bemoaned the 'excessive caution' of recent Labour governments. Martin Jacques (editor of *Marxism Today*) argued that the Tory party under Thatcher was the major purveyor of 'adventure politics' in Britain, while Ken Livingstone had lamented that, for the first time in their history, Tories were setting the ideological agenda.[31] As Crewe noted, Thatcherism's attempt to change the culture of the electorate, weaning it away from public spending and state provision, was very much 'A Crusade that Failed'.[32] Yet it still represents a startling contrast to the party's traditionally defensive and reactive character, and the time when Conservatism could chiefly be understood 'only by reference to the policies of its opponents'.[33]

To understand these distinctive features of Thatcherite Conservatism, it is necessary to recall the distinctive circumstances in which the party found itself after 1974. To begin with, there was strong evidence that Conservatism's traditionally cautious and 'reactive' character – most recently its embrace of statist social democracy – was not producing electoral dividends. By 1974, the party had lost four of the last five general elections, with its vote in October 1974 falling to as low as 36 per cent; claims that Conservatives were now the 'natural party of opposition' did not seem fanciful. For a party obsessed with office, this in itself was enough to warrant a new and more challenging strategy.

Secondly, it was felt that Britain by the mid-1970s had moved an alarming distance from essential Conservative beliefs. The fall of the Heath government had fuelled a dread that trade union power was now the decisive force in British politics, a notion that was fashionable well beyond

Conservative circles. Books published around this time, like *The Death of British Democracy* and *Why is Britain Becoming Harder To Govern?*, reflected a widespread belief on the right that traditional British society – based upon private property, individual responsibility, family structures and the rule of law – was on the verge of collapse.[34] When allied to fears that the post-Vietnam, post-Watergate west had lost its nerve in the cold war, claims that Britain was 'ripe for Marxist conversion' were rife in Tory circles.

All this convinced the new leadership that, to restore the society they believed in, the party would have to radicalise itself; otherwise it would merely sustain a status quo which most Conservatives found offensive. So, for the first time in their history, Conservatives felt they had little to gain from being conservative. Yet Conservatives also sensed that, by the late 1970s, the public mood was changing in a way that might assist their 'radical restoration'.

As pointed out at the start of this chapter, Conservatives have traditionally been fearful of the future, largely on account of society's working-class composition and the prevalence of centre-left ideas. By the late 1970s, the latter had already been undermined by the poor record of social democratic governments, while there was clear evidence of new and compelling social trends, namely the decline of heavy industry, the fragmentation of blue-collar employment, the growth of white-collar employment, the demographic shift from urban to suburban areas and the general *embourgeoisement* of society. The Thatcher governments were to accelerate these trends, but their existence before 1979 encouraged among Tories a much braver approach to politics. As a result, the party by 1979 again found itself in unusual territory, sensing that 'history' was at last on its side and that public opinion could now be fashioned to suit Conservatism's interests.

Conservatism in crisis

For many, the party's fourth successive victory in 1992 marked its new intellectual dominance in British politics.[35] Although there had been a slight rhetorical change after Thatcher's fall in 1990 (hence Major's talk of 'a nation at ease with itself'), and a slight concession to statism and collectivism (hence the citizens' charters of 1991), there was also enormous continuity. Indeed, the 1992 manifesto was said by some to 'out-Thatcher Thatcher', promising even bolder privatisation and an even lower rate of personal taxation.[36] Thatcherism's legacy therefore seemed intact and the hegemony of Conservatism assured. In the event, the period after 1992 was to reveal a deepening crisis of Conservatism, stemming from an ancestral conflict of Conservative values, heightened by the peculiar circumstances of contemporary Britain and culminating in the party's worst electoral defeat since 1832.

As explained earlier, Conservatism since the nineteenth century has evolved into an odd mixture of ideals – collectivist and individualist, authoritarian and libertarian. Self-evidently, the potential for conflict between these ideals is considerable and actually produced two calamitous splits inside the party – in 1846, over the Corn Laws, and in 1905, over tariff reform. Both occasions saw the eruption of a bitter dispute between, on the one hand, 'Whig' or 'neo-liberal' Conservatives, who prioritised free trade, *laissez-faire* and individualism, and, on the other, 'Tory', 'one nation' Conservatives, who prioritised state provision and economic protectionism – usually in the name of social harmony, public order and the utility of British institutions (both Disraeli and Baldwin tied their support for protectionism to a somewhat romantic view of English society).

This uneasy coalition of ideas was held together for most of the present century by the perception of a common, dual menace: state socialism at home and Soviet communism abroad. This dual menace made the party's innate differences over how to live with capitalism seem almost irrelevant, freeing its energies for the pursuit of power in a 'cold' climate. By the end of the 1980s, this dual menace had disappeared with the ending of the cold war, the electoral triumphs of Thatcherism, the marginalisation of Labour's left and the *embourgeoisement* of society. Yet, far from assuring Conservatism's future, these developments have merely allowed its historic tensions to resurface, threatening the coherence of both party and ideology (see appendix). It is telling that those who were once considered allies (or 'fellow dries') within the party – such as Howe and Thatcher, Tebbit and Lawson – have since become implacable adversaries in the face of new political challenges.

The triumph of capitalism – what Fukuyama terms 'the end of history' – poses two particular problems for today's Conservatives: one constitutional, the other social.

The constitutional problem

This is at the heart of the party's chronic division over European integration. The Maastricht treaty of 1991 confirmed fears that the European project which Britain joined in 1973 was not primarily commercial (as the Heath government alleged) but the blueprint for a supra-national, federal state – in effect, a United States of Europe, complete with single currency and common foreign policy.[37] The arguments inside the Conservative party over Europe, between Euro-philes like Clarke and Euro-sceptics like Redwood, were in many ways a rerun of the 1846/1905 battles between protectionists and free-traders: the Euro-philes are today's protectionists, believing that British capitalism will prosper best if protected by an exclusive European market, while the Euro-sceptics are self-confessed free-traders, arguing that British capitalism will only be stifled by such European protection.

Yet the split over Europe also shows marked differences to those of 1846/1905. Previously, it was the protectionists – like Disraeli and Baldwin – who exalted parliamentary sovereignty and Britain's governmental institutions; free-traders seemed mainly interested in economic advancement. Yet today's protectionists (Clarke, Heseltine, Dorrell) believe that the British state cannot give adequate protection to an increasingly internationalised British economy; they therefore seek a wider form of protection through the structures of a nascent European state, with the formal dilution of parliamentary sovereignty as the trade-off. By contrast, it is today's free-traders (Redwood, Portillo, Lilley) who are defensive of parliamentary sovereignty and sceptical of European union. The free-traders, however, are themselves faced by a dilemma: how can they support a nationalistic creed of politics while supporting an economic creed that is, if anything, globalistic? As Andrew Marr has written, the main threat to the integrity of British politics comes not from Europe but from an increasingly international market.[38] More and more British workers, for example, depend upon multi-national forces and multi-national employers over which British governments have little control.

At the time of going to press, this Euro-sceptic dilemma is yet to be resolved, along with this latest division between free-traders and protectionists: the superficial remedy offered during the 1997 Tory leadership contest – a 'dream ticket' involving Clarke as leader and Redwood as deputy – earned derision from across the parliamentary party. In the meantime, 'Europe' has demolished what used to be the party's 'secret weapon' – loyalty to the leader and unity in the ranks.

The social problem

This also has a certain timeless quality. Marx argued over a century ago that capitalism was a dynamic system, no friend of stability, no respecter of traditional institutions and, eventually, self-destructive. Scholars like John Gray claim that modern capitalism is even more inimical to Conservative values.

The breakdown of old, class-based communalism, the fragmentation of family life, the escalation of urban tension and the growth of various (and often violent) sub-cultures all stem, Gray argues, from a society which promotes competitive individualism and self-fulfilment – ideals which are now at the heart of British Conservatism. The party's central problem, he claims, is that its 'lauding of the free-market leaves unmet the human needs for security and community which were once its chief concern ... the traditions and institutions it claims to defend are undermined by the market principles it seeks to extend'. Proposed reforms of the police service, for example, 'threaten its ethos of public service, replacing it with the meagre contractual morality of Securicor', while the introduction of market forces to the National Health Service and Civil Service 'wreck their traditions of probity and altruism'. In all these areas, Gray notes, 'the need for continuity in our institutions – in other words for old Conservatism – are sacrificed to economic dogmas'.[39]

Acknowledging the crisis

The Conservative party began to appreciate this dilemma shortly after the fall of Thatcher, when it was already clear that the political themes of the 1990s would be more communitarian and less economic. Chris Patten's appointment as party chairman in 1990 was thought by many to signal a shift away from the abrasive individualism championed in the 1980s; Patten was seen to be on the left of the party, having described himself as a Christian democrat, with particular concern for Conservatism's social dimension.[40] As Patten explained in 1991, 'people express their individuality best in groups larger than themselves ... the collective and the social are more important to the working out of individualism'.[41]

More recently, cerebral Tories like David Willets and John Patten have tried to develop a 'civic Conservatism' which stresses the need for social harmony without regretting the reforms of the 1980s.[42] While accepting that market forces create particular social problems, they have also leapt to their defence in the social context, arguing that in the old Soviet Union (where market forces were suppressed) crime, greed and moral paralysis reached a scale far greater than anything yet seen in the west. Neither is it the case, they add, that British society was somehow more 'moral' before 1979; the number of people involved in philanthropic voluntary organisations, for example, is much greater now than it was then. True morality and civility, they claim, rest upon the individual choice and responsibility which Thatcherism extended. They concede, nonetheless, that free-marketeers must now give more thought to the old Tory nostrums of community and the maintenance of the social fabric.

Along with the need to boost its failing popularity, such thoughts propelled the government towards an initiative of its own in 1993 – the ill-starred 'back to basics' campaign.[43] Unveiled at the 1993 Tory conference, and eagerly received by activists, 'back to basics' was tied to Major's own conference speech – 'an across the board attack on the decline of community, family, tradition and responsibility'.[44] It is well known that 'back to basics' had become a shambles by early 1994, after revelations of 'sleaze' among the party's own MPs. As the *Daily Telegraph* remarked, 'Every time a Tory spoke of unmarried mothers, the press produced a Tory love child'.[45]

Yet the brief and fated life of 'back to basics' concealed a more serious deficiency in terms of serious politics. There was little effort, for example, to match cosy rhetoric about the 'traditional' family with practical action (such as introducing tax breaks for stay-at-home mothers); neither did it answer charges that the decline of 'basic' values was caused by the government's own economic policies – demanding, for example, that the modern labour market should be bound not by community ties but by geographic mobility.

In any case, the communitarian ideal inherent to 'back to basics' did not enthuse all senior Conservatives, many fearing it would blur the party's former appeal to voters. Right-wingers like Portillo therefore responded with their own vision designed to put 'clear blue water' between Conservatives and their opponents – a vision involving an even greater stress upon privatisation, consumer choice and market solutions.[46] Far from solving the 'social' dilemma of modern Conservatism, 'back to basics' had merely highlighted it.

A grim outlook?

The Tories' 1997 manifesto did little to hide their deep-seated ideological confusion and it is unclear how they will respond to such an emphatic defeat. The choice of William Hague as new party leader – an inexperienced politician whose views were somewhat elliptic at the time of his election – confirmed the party's own uncertainty as it stumbled through the early stages of opposition. Peter Lilley, charged by Hague to review all aspects of party policy, seemed aware of the difficulties which Tories would face in the run-up to the general election of 2001/2. A further push to the right – towards markets, individualism and Euro-scepticism – invites the charge of 'ostrich politics', ignoring the realities of global economics and communal disintegration. Yet a movement in the opposite direction makes a distinctive and popular message all the more difficult to present as the century draws to a close.[47]

Meanwhile, many Conservatives are again worried that 'history' is against them. With hindsight, it can be argued that Conservatism in the late nineteenth and early to mid-twentieth centuries offered an attractive and indispensable package to voters, one which harnessed social stability to the irresistible – yet potentially destructive – forces of democracy and egalitarianism. The 'historic' task of governments in the early twenty-first century could be that of harnessing social stability to today's irresistible and potentially destructive forces – market values and dynamic individualism. It is still unclear whether contemporary Conservatism is equipped for this challenge, or whether its traditional zeal for social stability has been eclipsed by its modern zeal for markets.[48]

If it is the latter scenario, then Margaret Thatcher's legacy would be supremely ironic and a rich example of *hubris* leading to *nemesis*. For, having proved the most electorally effective brand of Conservatism in the twentieth century, Thatcherism would have left the Conservative party unable to govern the volatile market society of the twenty-first. William Hague's inheritance is scarcely a comfortable one.

Appendix: Conservative factions

It must be stated that the term 'Conservative faction' is considered a misnomer by many authors. Given the organisational incoherence of many of the groups listed below, there tends to be a preference for the term 'tendencies', which implies a much looser and less formal approach. It should be noted that within these groups it is rare to find membership cards or lists, let alone a regular timetable of meetings. Neither is membership mutually exclusive; there is a clear overlap, for instance, in the membership of No Turning Back (described below) and bodies like the 92 Group and Salisbury Group, which have similar ideological leanings. In other words, the debate about Conservative factions must always bear in mind the party's dislike of rigid, formalised organisation and its preference for *ad hoc* arrangements. One of William Hague's first decrees after becoming leader in 1997 was that overt membership of the following groups was incompatible with membership of his shadow cabinet.

The Bow Group

One of the most enduring of party groups, the Bow Group was formed in 1951 and claims to have about a thousand members. Until the 1980s, it was seen to support extensive state intervention and collective provision and was normally regarded as being on the left of Conservatism. More recently, however, its pronouncements have been more eclectic, giving qualified support to the economic liberalism of the Thatcher governments. Its luminaries have included Lord Howe and Douglas Hurd.

The Monday Club

Formed in 1961, to combat the Macmillan government's 'softness' on race and nationhood, the Club may be regarded as representing the 'old right' of the party, emphasising order, discipline and authority within society alongside the centrality of national sovereignty. It also claims to have invented Euro-scepticism inside the party, having been opposed to Common Market entry and constantly critical of the European project. Its MPs have included John Carlisle and Terry Dicks, with Enoch Powell a frequent guest of honour at its gatherings.

No Turning Back Group

A more modern version of right-wing Conservatism is provided by No Turning Back, founded in 1983 by some of Margaret Thatcher's most ardent back-bench supporters (including Peter Lilley and Michael Portillo). Its main concern is the promotion of free-market economics and the extension of privatisation, although since 1983 its pamphlets have increasingly dwelt upon the constitutional problems posed by European integration, fearing it will impede the sort of economic ideas favoured by the Group's members.

Conservative Way Forward

Many of No Turning Back's members would have applauded the formation of Conservative Way Forward shortly after Thatcher's downfall in 1990. Dedicated to the defence of her ideals, and endorsed by a gallery of ex-ministers (like Parkinson and Tebbit), it was described in 1991 as a 'sunset home for superannuated Thatcherites'. Six years later, there seemed some truth in this comment: as its principal members became more aged, the frequency of its meetings and publications markedly waned. Nonetheless, many of its themes were taken up by the think-tank Conservative Foundation 2000, set up by John Redwood after his leadership challenge of 1995. By 1997, the Foundation was considered sufficiently controversial for William Hague to demand Redwood's dissociation from it in return for joining the new shadow cabinet.

The Tory Reform Group

The Tory Reform Group was formed in 1975 and claimed to embody the 'one nation' Conservatism despised by Thatcherites and supposedly upheld by most previous Tory leaders. Unconvinced of the virtues of market economics, it has sought to defend the values of 'community' and 'society', fearing that much of Thatcher's agenda would create dangerous social divisions. With its principal supporters including Michael Heseltine and Kenneth Clarke, it is no surprise that the Group takes a more relaxed view of European integration. Since 1995, it has shared its role as champion of left-wing Toryism with the revived *Macleod Group* (though many Tories question whether Iain Macleod, who died shortly after becoming Chancellor in 1970, would have shared its suspicion of Thatcherite economics). Though small and – like most of the other groups mentioned – rather disjointed in its activities, the Macleod Group attracted extra media attention on account of John Major's professed admiration for its eponymous hero. The centre-left was also meant to be complemented by the *Positive European Group*, formed by MPs like Peter Temple-Morris in 1995 as an intended counterblast to the party's Euro-sceptics, and *Conservative Mainstream*, formed by ex-minister David Hunt in 1996. However, the intellectual credibility of all four groups has been undermined in recent years by the absence of any clear policy differences between them and 'New Labour', while the overtures made by its supposed leading lights – notably Stephen Dorrell and Chris Patten – to the free-market nostrums of the party's right wing suggest that 'pre-Thatcher' Conservatism is still a minority taste within the parliamentary party.

The Charter Movement

From the angle of party organisation, the Charter Movement is by far the most interesting: its sole aim is to bring more formal democracy to the party's structure. This would include a more influential role in policy making for the National Union's central council, and the election of party chair by all party members. Set up by activists in Kent in 1981, it has generally been regarded as a maverick outfit inside the party, although it was instrumental in the publication of Central Office accounts after 1985. After the election defeat of 1997, however, when even leading MPs began to recognise the need for more party democracy, Charter's reputation has increased, with its members claiming to have trail-blazed many of the ideas now popular with the leadership.

Sources: V. McKee, 'Conservative Party Factions', *Contemporary Record*, autumn 1989; E. Pearce, *Guardian*, 18 March 1991. See also V. McKee, 'Factions and Tendencies in the Conservative Party Since 1945', *Politics Review*, April 1996; J. Barnes, 'Ideology and Factions', in A. Seldon and S. Ball (eds), *Conservative Century* (Oxford, Oxford University Press, 1994).

Notes

1   A. Seldon and S. Ball (eds), *Conservative Century* (Oxford, Oxford University Press, 1994).
2   R. Waller, 'Conservative Electoral Support and Social Class', in Seldon and Ball, *Conservative Century*.
3   A. J. Davies, *We, The Nation: The Conservative Party and the Pursuit of Power* (London, Little, Brown, 1995).
4   J. Grimond, *The Liberal Challenge* (London, Hollis and Carter, 1963), p. 14; I. Gilmour, *Inside Right* (London, Hutchinson, 1977), p. 109; R. J. White, 'The Conservative Tradition', in P. Buck (ed.), *How Conservatives Think* (London, Penguin, 1975), p. 174.
5   P. Smith, *Disraelian Conservatism and Social Reform* (London, Routledge and Kegan Paul, 1967), p. 106; *New Statesman Profiles* (London, Phoenix House, 1958), p. 66.
6   Davies, *We, The Nation*.

7   See R. Eccleshall, *English Conservatism since the Restoration* (London, Unwin Hynman, 1990); M. Francis and I. Zweiniger-Bargielowska (eds), *The Conservatives and British Society* (Cardiff, University of Wales Press, 1996); B. Evans and A. Taylor, *From Salisbury to Major: Continuity and Change in Conservative Politics* (Manchester, Manchester University Press, 1996).

8   Buck, *How Conservatives Think*, p. 52.

9   R. Blake *The Conservative Party From Peel to Thatcher* (London, Fontana, 1985), p. 6.

10 A. Gamble, *The Free Economy and the Strong State: The Politics of Thatcherism* (London, Macmillan, 1988). See also K. Baker (ed.), *The Faber Book of Conservatism* (London, Faber, 1993).

11 Buck, *How Conservatives Think*, p. 70; S. Weintraub, *Disraeli: A Biography* (London, Macmillan, 1995).

12 W. Waldegrave, *The Binding of Leviathan* (London, Hamish Hamilton, 1980), p. 34.

13 Buck, *How Conservatives Think*, p. 142. See also J. Charmley, *A History of Conservative Politics* (London, Macmillan, 1996), ch. 7.

14 R. T. McKenzie and A. Silver, *Angels in Marble* (London, Heinemann, 1968), p. 48.

15 R. McKibbin, 'Deference and Democracy', *Times Higher Educational Supplement*, 15 February 1985.

16 See J. Barnes, 'Ideology and Factions', in Seldon and Ball, *Conservative Century*, pp. 336–9.

17 D. Kavanagh, *Thatcherism and British Politics* (Oxford, Oxford University Press, 1987), p. 191.

18 *Conservative Party Conference 1970: Report of Proceedings* (London, Conservative Central Office, 1970), p. 131.

19 D. Hurd, *An End to Promises* (London, Collins, 1979).

20 J. Critchley, *Westminster Blues* (London, Futura, 1985); I. Gilmour, *Dancing with Dogma* (London, Simon Schuster, 1992).

21 Critchley, *Westminster Blues*, pp. 125–6.

22 See J. McIlroy, *Trade Unions in Britain Today* (Manchester, Manchester University Press, 1988); K. D. Ewing and C. Gearty, *Freedom Under Thatcher: Civil Liberties in Modern Britain* (Oxford, Clarendon, 1990); J. A. Chandler, *Local Government Today* (Manchester, Manchester University Press, 1996).

23 S. Jenkins, *Accountable to None: The Tory Nationalisation of Britain* (London, Hamish Hamilton, 1995).

24 See P. Hutber (ed.), *What's Wrong with Britain?* (London, Sphere, 1978).

25 Jenkins, *Accountable to None*, p. 104.

26 J. Ranelagh, *Thatcher's People* (London, Fontana, 1991), pp. 8–9.

27 Critchley, *Westminster Blues*, pp. 125–6.

28 P. Riddell, *The Thatcher Era* (Oxford, Blackwell, 1991), pp. 1–14.

29 McIlroy, *Trade Unions in Britain Today*.

30 See H. Young, *One of Us* (London, Macmillan, 1989).

31 S. Hall and M. Jacques (eds), *The Politics of Thatcherism* (London, Lawrence and Wishart, 1983), p. 6; *Tribune*, Labour party conference issue, September 1990.

32 I. Crewe, 'Values: A Crusade That Failed', in D. Kavanagh and A. Seldon (eds), *The Thatcher Effect* (Oxford, Oxford University Press, 1989).

33 S. Ingle *The British Party System* (Oxford, Blackwell, 1987), p. 28.

34 S. Haseler, *The Death of British Democracy* (London, Elek Books, 1976); A. King (ed.), *Why is Britain Becoming Harder to Govern?* (London, BBC, 1976).

35 A. Heywood, 'Britain's Dominant Party System', in L. Robins, H. Blackmore

and R. Pyper (eds), *Britain's Changing Party System* (London, Leicester University Press, 1994).

36   *New Statesman and Society*, 2 October 1992.
37   See A. Geddes, *Britain in the European Community* (Manchester, Baseline, 1993), pp. 57–71.
38   A. Marr, *Ruling Britannia* (London, Penguin, 1995).
39   J. Gray, *The Undoing of Conservatism* (London, Social Market Foundation, 1994); see also *Independent*, 11 October 1994; and introduction to K. Minogue (ed.), *Conservative Realism: New Essays in Conservatism* (London, Harper Collins, 1996).
40   C. Patten, *The Tory Case* (London, Longman, 1983).
41   *Marxism Today*, February 1991.
42   D. Willets, *Modern Conservatism* (London, Penguin, 1992); J. Patten, *Things to Come* (London, Sinclair Stevenson, 1995); J. Patten, 'The Deepening of Conservatism', *Talking Politics*, winter 1994.
43   See S. Ludlam and M. J. Smith (eds), *Contemporary British Conservatism* (London, Macmillan, 1996), pp. 276–7.
44   M. Durham, 'Renewing Conservatism', *Talking Politics*, autumn 1995.
45   M. Durham, 'Family Values and the Tories', *Talking Politics*, autumn 1994.
46   M. Portillo, *Clear Blue Water: A Compendium of Speeches and Interviews* (London, Conservative Way Forward, 1994).
47   *Sunday Telegraph*, 22 June 1997.
48   This idea is explored in a provocative way in T. Evans, *Conservative Radicalism* (Oxford, Bergahn, 1996).

4

The Conservative party:
organisation, membership and authority

During the 1997 Conservative leadership contest, all five candidates promised that, if elected, they would review and reform the party's organisation. Commentators responded by questioning the very existence of a 'Conservative organisation', pointing instead to a series of disparate and ramshackle arrangements.[1]

This may explain one of the most curious features of British political science, namely, the lack of detailed attention given to the structure of Britain's most successful political party. Although Labour's organisation has been comprehensively assessed in a number of distinguished studies during the last twenty years, the Conservative organisation has not received any exhaustive treatment since McKenzie's *British Political Parties* of 1955, making it (in Bulpitt's words) 'one of the least studied political organisations in Britain'.[2]

As a result, the mechanisms of the party remain – *in the words of its own members* – 'governed by secrecy and confusion'.[3] This impression was fortified by the party's 1995 leadership contest, when even Tory MPs seemed unsure of proceedings; it was later disclosed, for example, that Major would have thought twice about causing the contest had he realised that a challenger would need the backing of only two Conservative MPs to stand and not thirty-three as Major's advisers thought.[4]

The arcane nature of Conservative organisation has much to do with the fact that the party has no official constitution from which to compare theory with reality, functioning instead mainly on the basis of convention and *ad hoc* procedure. Indeed, no such body as the 'Conservative party' actually exists. Literature from Conservative Central Office (CCO) confirms that the party consists of 'three separate components' (see below), leaving the outsider to infer what organisational relationship exists between them. As the party's former Director of Organisation explained: 'There are virtually no absolute rules, that's why – unlike Labour – we do not get bogged down in procedural wrangles. We have family squabbles instead'.[5]

The 1993 reorganisation, supervised by Sir Norman Fowler, was designed to amend this fractured structure by creating the Board of Party Management (see below); yet demands for reorganisation after 1997 indicated that the problem remained.

The 'three separate components' cited by the party are:

(1) the party in parliament (MPs and peers);
(2) the voluntary extra-parliamentary party (the National Union of Conservative and Unionist Associations);
(3) the professional extra-parliamentary party (CCO and its regional satellites).

In common with most other textbooks, we shall begin by exploring the party in parliament, for the simple reason that it is considered pre-eminent both inside and outside Tory ranks.

The parliamentary party

As explained in the previous chapter, the first Conservative government is widely assumed to be that of Sir Robert Peel formed in 1834. Yet, as we shall see, no Conservative organisation existed outside parliament until 1867. The extra-parliamentary Conservative party was therefore created by Conservative MPs to serve their interests without challenging in any way their autonomy and supremacy inside the party.

That supremacy has allegedly remained throughout the party's history; having secured their election to the Commons, Tory MPs are assumed to expect loyalty and support from their extra-parliamentary colleagues rather than dissent and instruction. But, as will be shown later, that assumption has been shaken in recent years.

The Conservative leader

Much of the parliamentary party's supremacy is supposedly concentrated in its leaders. It should be emphasised, though, that the term 'Conservative party leader' is a colloquialism, for the leader has no formal authority, particularly over the party outside parliament. Like much else in the Conservative tradition, the term derives largely from convention.

The Conservatives have been widely seen as a leader-dominated party. McKenzie claimed that 'the most striking feature of Conservative Party organisation' was 'the enormous power which appears to be concentrated in the hands of the leader'.[6] Richard Rose compared the leader to a pre-constitutional monarch, surrounded by a personal court of advisers, but pursuing ultimately his own course.[7] Even some of the more outspoken elements inside the party go along with this analysis:

> Power in the Conservative Party is still excessively centralised and concentrated in one person.... We place huge responsibilities on that person – to run the government, to choose its members, to be the sole author of policy and to be in ultimate control of the Party's central organisation.... It [the Tory organisation] is not only undemocratic, it is feudal.[8]

In comparison with Labour leaders, Tory leaders certainly seemed to enjoy a large amount of freedom from institutional constraint. Professor Harold Laski, a Labour activist, argued that the 'autocratic' character of the party merely reflected the roots of its philosophy, one which emphasised leadership, hierarchy, deference and discipline – Labour leaders, by contrast, being the victims of a doctrine exalting revolt and a contempt for existing authority.[9] Modern Tory leaders still have the exclusive right to make front-bench appointments without reference to any party ballot (cf. Labour), and do not have to work with an independently elected deputy leader; indeed, there does not have to *be* a deputy Tory leader (cf. Labour).

Tory leaders also have the freedom to make policy without being encumbered by a party conference or any other body with official policy-making powers (cf. Labour); all the party's assemblies and committees are purely advisory. Butler and Kavanagh's study of the 1992 general election showed a lack of party democracy in the way the Tories' election manifesto was constructed, it being written largely by Sarah Hogg (head of the Prime Minister's Policy Unit) after consultation with ministers and other Policy Unit members.[10] Major's description of the finished product to journalists – 'It's me, it's all me' – could have acted as the classic portrayal of power in the party. Although there was a formal consultation of grass-roots members over policy between 1995 and 1996, it was judged little more than a cosmetic exercise, with the construction of the 1997 manifesto again involving only a small group around the leader.

Neither does the leader's influence pervade only the parliamentary party. Through the appointment of party chairman (the post has never been held by a woman), the leader exercises a critical influence over the shape and path of the party bureaucracy. One of the first steps taken by both Thatcher and Major after becoming leader was to appoint to the chairmanship a close and trusted ally (Thorneycroft in 1975, Chris Patten in 1990). Conversely, if the leader is unhappy with the performance of CCO (or the chairman himself) then the leader can make a replacement, as the luckless Jeremy Hanley found in 1995 and Brian Mawhinney in 1997.

It could be argued that the 'feudal' powers of a Tory leader stem from the party's lack of any grand or historic statement of values, something which might compel leaders to give at least the impression that the party was moving in a direction not just of their choosing. Yet this vacuum is typical of a deeper characteristic. As discussed in the previous chapter, the Tories have always given prime emphasis to the election of Tory governments. There has also been a general belief that the best way to secure this goal – rather like an army trying to win a battle – is to allow the leadership discretion and flexibility and to give unqualified support to whatever decisions the leadership makes.

Yet this in itself is symptomatic of a certain, conservative approach to politics. Apart from a few general themes like the defence of private property, constitution and nation state, most activists have been unconcerned with the minutiae of policy and content to support whatever ideas the leadership thought conducive to electoral success. Party structures which spell out in detail a party's policies and procedures often spring from an impatient membership, keen to change society in specific ways and keen to ensure that the party follows specific prescriptions. For much of its history, the Tory party has been a more languid creature than its principal opponents and therefore content with a Micawberish organisation.

Leadership elections

Until 1965, the arcane nature of the Tory party was illustrated by the way in which it chose its leaders. When the leadership fell vacant (as in 1955 and 1957) it was customary for a new leader to 'emerge' after clandestine discussions among Tory MPs.[11] This had the merits of concealing from the public obvious party divisions and the extent of opposition to the new leader. The pre-1965 system, however, was geared to finding a leader who *did* have near-unanimous support, although it tended to produce leaders who sparked a lack of hostility rather than massive enthusiasm. Given the party's preoccupation with unity, it would have been difficult for an MP vigorously opposed by, say, 30 per cent of Tory MPs to emerge as leader, even if the other 70 per cent vigorously backed that candidate. As a result, this *sans ballot* arrangement made a key contribution to the consensual character of most Tory leaders this century.

The arrangement foundered upon the resignation of Harold Macmillan in 1963, when there was no clear and uncontroversial successor. The result was that that year's Tory conference, which coincided with Macmillan's resignation in October, turned into an American-style party convention where the various contenders touted for support, highlighted divisions and thereby killed one of the old system's supposed advantages. The party's embarrassment was compounded by the eventual accession of Lord Home, a rather unlikely figure in whose government two prominent ministers under Macmillan (Macleod and Powell) refused to serve. In a *Spectator* article shortly afterwards, Macleod derided the old system for the power it placed in what he termed 'The Magic Circle', a group of senior MPs (mainly educated at Eton and Harrow) who orchestrated the process of consultation. That the patrician Home looked so ill at ease when faced with the 'classless' Labour leader Harold Wilson convinced Macleod that reform of leadership selection was overdue.

The Tories' defeat in 1964 quickened the pace of change. Home himself presided over an inquiry recommending that new leaders be chosen in a ballot of Tory MPs and his own resignation in 1965 provided a swift opportunity for the new procedure to be used. Heath duly became the first Tory leader to be elected in a formal party ballot (see box 4.1).

The 1965 reform made no provision for an incumbent leader to be challenged, assuming perhaps that an unsuccessful or divisive leader would have the sensitivity to resign. Heath's determination to stay on after losing two elections in a year showed the flaw in this arrangement and at the end of 1974 the rules were altered by the 1922 Committee (see below). After that, a leader could be challenged annually if certain, not particularly tough, conditions were met (see box 4.2).

Heath became the first Tory leader to be challenged in a ballot in early 1975, and was surprisingly passed on the first ballot by Margaret Thatcher. She was duly elected on the second ballot, defeating those who entered

---

Box 4.1. Tory leadership elections, 1965–97: the results

1965
First ballot: Heath 150, Maudling 133, Powell 15, abstentions 6 *(Heath failed to secure a technical victory, but was elected after rivals withdrew)*

1975
First ballot: Thatcher 130, Heath 119, Fraser 16, abstentions 11
Second ballot: Thatcher 146, Whitelaw 79, Howe 19, Prior 19, Peyton 11, abstentions 2 *(Thatcher elected)*

1989
First ballot: Thatcher 314, Meyer 33, abstentions 16 *(Thatcher re-elected)*

1990
First ballot: Thatcher 204, Heseltine 152, abstentions 16
Second ballot: Major 185, Heseltine 131, Hurd 56 *(Major failed to secure technical victory, but elected after rivals withdrew and further ballots declared unnecessary by executive of 1922 Committee)*

1995
First ballot: Major 218, Redwood 89, abstentions 22 *(Major re-elected)*

1997
First ballot: Clarke 49, Hague 41, Redwood 27, Lilley 24, Howard 23
Second ballot: Clarke 64, Hague 62, Redwood 38
Third ballot: Clarke 70, Hague 92, abstentions 2 *(Hague elected)*

Box 4.2. Tory leadership elections 1965–97: the procedures

Any challenge to be announced within fourteen days of a new
Commons session or three months of a new parliament. Challenger
requires backing from (unnamed) 10 per cent of Tory MPs[a]

MPs consult constituency associations

First ballot of Tory MPs
Victory involves one candidate achieving overall majority plus 15 per
cent lead over nearest rival.[b] Otherwise ...

Second ballot of Tory MPs
Those not initially candidates may now enter contest. Victory involves
one candidate achieving overall majority of votes cast. Otherwise ...

Third ballot of Tory MPs
Involves the two leading candidates from second ballot[c]

Winner (after whichever ballot)[d] confirmed at party meeting comprising
MPs, peers, MEPs, parliamentary candidates and members of National
Union Executive

[a]A 'challenge' is deemed to occur only if there is no vacancy for the leadership
(as in 1975, 1989 and 1990). If such a vacancy exists, a contestant requires
backing from only two MPs (as did a 'challenger' until 1991). As the 1995
contest was sparked by Major's resignation, Redwood did not need to fulfil the
10 per cent ruling – much to the shock of many Major supporters.
[b]Since 1974, this has been based upon those entitled to vote.
[c]Until 1991, there was no formal provision for the contest to end as a result of
the leading candidate's rivals withdrawing. Neither did the rules envisage a
third ballot involving fewer than three candidates.
[d]Since 1991, the rules allow for a fourth ballot should the third end in a dead
heat.
NB Although rules for Tory leadership ballots have existed since 1965, there
was no provision for a challenge until after the October 1974 general election
(when Heath showed no inclination to resign).

Source: R. M. Punnett, *Selecting the Party Leader* (Hemel Hempstead, Harvester
Wheatsheaf, 1992).

the fray only after Heath's departure (the ability of candidates to skip the first ballot being a peculiar feature of the Conservative system).

Nearly fifteen years were to elapse before the system was to be used again. Taking advantage of the lax preconditions, the self-confessed obscurity Sir Anthony Meyer challenged Thatcher in 1989. Though easily defeated, it still dented the Prime Minister's authority and made the more momentous challenge of Heseltine a year later more credible. This led to Thatcher's resignation after an inconclusive first ballot and her replacement by John Major after the slightly less inconclusive second ballot: Major failed to secure the required majority of votes, but a third ballot was avoided after his two rivals conceded defeat.[12]

In the wake of the 1990 contest, the procedures were again amended by the executive of the 1922 Committee and these amended rules governed both the 1995 and 1997 contests. Only in 1997 did they make a notable difference – the third ballot now being restricted to two challengers only (see box 4.2).

These changes to Conservative rules, particularly those of 1965 and 1974, had enormous implications not just for the leader but for the very nature of the party. To begin with, the post-1965 procedure (with its various 'democratic' elements, such as ballots, publicised campaigns, and the breakdown of voting figures) paved the way for a less consensual type of leader. In simple terms, a victor no longer needed either near-unanimous approval or an absence of passionate opposition, only more votes than any rival. Hague demonstrated in 1997 that it was possible to become leader while conspicuously lacking support from seventy Tory MPs – not the ideal start, perhaps, for a leader seeking to impose unity upon the party.

It has also become easier for the party to saddle itself with a leader who, far from even trying to unite it, seeks to 'convert' it to a certain brand of Conservatism. This was shown vividly during the Thatcher era and even by the election of Major, who was then assumed to be her torch-carrier. It is no coincidence that since this new type of 'meritocratic' and 'abrasive' leader first appeared in 1965, the incidence of dissent in the parliamentary party has soared: during two parliamentary sessions in the 1950s, not a single dissenting vote was cast by a Tory MP, whereas 137 MPs cast 416 dissenting votes during the 1983–4 session alone.[13] The advent of leaders less concerned with consensus than the development of their own personal agendas naturally begs division inside a political party.

This culture of dissent, fostered inadvertently by the 1965 reform, was fuelled by the follow-up reform of 1974. The rules governing a challenge to a Tory leader have always been more inviting than those concerning a challenge to leaders of the Labour party (see chapter 6). Between 1974 and 1991, a challenger needed the support of only two MPs and, even after the rules were tightened up in 1991, still required only half the parliamentary support (10 per cent of Tory MPs) needed by anyone challenging a Labour leader. That Tory leadership contests have involved only MPs also made them more likely, as they could be swiftly organised and dispatched (during a six-year period, 1989–95, the leader faced a challenge on no less than three occasions).

These 'challenge-friendly' rules have heightened the probationary nature of a Tory leader's position. For much of 1993, 1994 and 1995, there were rumours of an impending leadership challenge, which naturally weakened Major's authority. (Eventually, these rumours had a self-fulfilling quality by precipitating the 1995 contest.) Moreover, it is not just the preconditions but the mechanics of a contest which made the leader's overthrow likely. *Pace* Redwood's challenge in 1995, it is unusual for any party leader to be openly challenged by a feasible replacement, for such a replacement is normally part of the leader's front-bench team. But by voting for a 'stalking horse', Tory MPs could activate the leader's resignation and thus allow the 'respectable' contestants to enter on the second ballot. This was in the mind of many who initially voted for Thatcher in 1975 (hoping to pave the way for Whitelaw) and may have influenced some of Major's opponents in 1995 (hoping to instigate the candidacies of Portillo or Heseltine). As a result, a leader could be unhorsed by the most implausible of challengers.

Recent contests also remind us that publicised voting figures can further undermine a leader's position. Thatcher, for example, saw off Meyer's 1989 challenge easily enough but was still wounded by the knowledge that nearly sixty Tory MPs failed to support her. Likewise, Major's victory in 1995 was compromised by the amazing fact that a third of his MPs refused to endorse his leadership. On the other hand, the existence of such ballots can actually shore up a leader's position. Before 1974, any leader who forfeited the confidence of a third of parliamentary colleagues would have certainly resigned. Yet, as Major showed, a tenacious leader can now face down such substantial opposition by 'toughing out' a leadership contest, claiming victory as long as the technical requirements are met. As Hugo Young commented, 'the contest redefined what a Tory leader can get away with as proof that he is boss'.[14]

The 1974 reform allowed the party to set two constitutional 'firsts': until 1989, no Prime Minister had been challenged in a party ballot and until 1990 none had been ousted by one. It may seem ironic that the party responsible was the Conservatives, not a party noted for internal democracy and the extensive use of ballots. Yet the 1974 reform merely highlighted what has been a perennial feature of Conservative organisation – that the power of the leader rests entirely upon the party's expectation of electoral success. In essence, this is the trade-off for the leader's freedom from the institutional restraints found in the Labour party: in return for almost exclusive responsibility for policy and strategy, the leader must accept exclusive responsibility for electoral failure. Yet, as has been shown, the situation has changed in one crucial respect. Tory MPs are no longer prepared to defy their leader only when they want a change of leadership. After 1992, it was clear that they are now prepared to question regularly a leader's policies rather than question periodically overall competence.[15] Dissent, in other words, no longer occurs only when the party wants to exchange one 'omnipotent' leader for another, although events of 1975 and 1990 show that the party's taste for *coup d'états* is undiminished.

More than any other leadership contest, that of 1997 drew attention to the undemocratic flavour of current arrangements; whereas the 1994 Labour leadership contest had enfranchised all party members (of whom nearly a million voted), the election of William Hague involved only 164 Tory MPs. The party outside parliament was again only 'consulted' before the ballots at Westminster. To add insult to injury, this 'consultation' only involved members of the European parliament (MEPs), constituency chairs and 179 other officials – thus excluding the bulk of constituency members – while Hague's victory showed how little weight it carried anyway (those consulted had consistently expressed a preference for Kenneth Clarke). In showing such disdain for grass-roots opinion in this matter, Tory MPs were at least being consistent: the dethronement of both Heath and Thatcher was also in defiance of what ordinary Tories had said during these farcical periods of 'consultation'.[16]

During the 1997 contest, all five candidates seemed to recognise that it would be the last to take place under existing rules and that future elections would grant a more formal and definite involvement to constituency Tories. Hague was particularly insistent on this point, seeing it as vital to the recruitment of new members and the Blair-esque modernisation of the Conservative party. The rather undignified tone of the 1997 contest only provided further impetus to reform.

Backbenchers

It has been suggested that the decline of deference among Tory MPs has something to do with changes in their social background.[17] Though not as great as sometimes assumed (two-thirds are still public-school educated), there has been a shift towards the commercially employed, grammar-school-educated meritocrat (see tables 4.1, 4.2, 4.3, 4.4). It should also be noted that, among those with a business background, there has since 1945 been a sharp fall in the number of company owners and a rise in the number of executives and middle managers.[18]

The generation of Tory MPs elected since 1983 have proved unusually rebellious, scotching the old idea that a party's new recruits were among its most obedient and pliable (a third of the sixty-nine MPs signing the controversial 'Fresh Start' motion in 1992, attacking Major's approach to Europe, had been in the Commons only a few weeks). Burch and Moran argue that such MPs, having made it to Westminster through talent and

Table 4.1. *Occupation of Conservative MPs, 1945–97*

Year	Professions[a] (%)	Business[b] (%)	Miscellaneous[c] (%)	Manual (%)	Total MPs (N)
1945	48	27	25	–	210
1950	43	41	16	–	298
1951	41	37	22	–	321
1955	46	29	24	–	345
1959	46	31	23	–	365
1964	48	26	25	1	304
1966	46	30	23	1	253
1970	45	30	23	1	330
1974 (Feb.)	45	32	23	1	297
1974 (Oct.)	46	32	21	1	277
1979	45	34	20	1	339
1983	45	36	19	1	397
1987	42	37	20	1	376
1992	39	38	22	1	336
1997	37	39	23	1	165

[a]Barristers, solicitors, doctors, architects, surveyors, engineers, accountants, military officers, civil servants, lecturers and teachers.
[b]Company directors and executives in commerce, finance and industry.
[c]Farmers and landowners, publishers and journalists, political organisers and housewives.

Sources: for information up to 1997, B. Criddle, 'Members of Parliament', in A. Seldon and S. Ball (eds), *Conservative Century* (Oxford, Oxford University Press, 1994); for 1997, D. Butler and D. Kavanagh, *The British General Election of 1997* (London, Macmillan, 1997).

commitment alone, are less likely to be team players than those who profited from the 'old-boy network'. They may find loyalty and discipline less instinctive than the traditional 'knights of the shire', whose background often emphasised service and duty rather than competition and achievement.[19] It has also been argued that the ideology of Thatcherism – iconoclastic, individualistic, irreverent – is also difficult to square with centralised party discipline.[20] Many of the troublesome MPs from the 1992 and 1997 intakes (such as Iain Duncan-Smith and John Bercow) have indeed been dubbed 'Thatcher's children', MPs for whom promotion at Westminster is secondary to the advancement of their own 'conviction politics'.

The decline of deference, however, also has earthier explanations. The large Tory majorities after 1983 and 1987 made dissent seem an affordable luxury, one that could easily be soaked up by the party's huge numerical advantage at Westminster. Yet having blooded themselves as rebels in the 1980s, many Tory MPs then had the 'bottle' to rebel after 1992, when the consequences for the government were much more serious; in 1994 nine of those rebels were prepared to have the party whip taken away from them on account of their opposition to 'Europe'. All this must concern a new leader like William Hague, somewhat lacking in gravitas and less

Table 4.2. *Education of Conservative MPs, 1945–97*

Year	Public school				University				Public school and Oxford or Cambridge (%)	Total MPs (N)
	Eton	Harrow	Other	All	Oxford	Cambridge	Other	All		
1945	29	6	41	76	29	22	11	62	48	210
1950	26	6	43	75	31	21	10	62	50	298
1951	24	7	43	74	31	21	10	62	49	321
1955	23	6	47	76	31	22	10	63	50	345
1959	20	5	47	72	28	22	10	60	46	365
1964	22	6	47	75	30	22	11	63	48	304
1966	22	6	53	81	33	24	10	67	51	253
1970	18	4	52	74	30	22	12	64	45	330
1974 (Feb.)	18	4	52	74	29	24	14	67	48	297
1974 (Oct.)	17	4	54	75	29	27	13	69	47	277
1979	15	2	55	72	27	23	19	69	43	339
1983	12	3	55	70	26	22	23	71	42	397
1987	11	2	55	68	24	20	26	70	37	376
1992	10	2	50	62	25	20	28	73	32	336
1997	11	0	55	66	27	22	32	81	51	165

Sources: for information up to 1997. B. Criddle, 'Members of Parliament', in A. Seldon and S. Ball (eds), *Conservative Century* (Oxford, Oxford University Press, 1994); for 1997, D. Butler and D. Kavanagh, *The British General Election of 1997* (London, Macmillan, 1997).

Table 4.3. *Education of new Conservative MPs, 1945–97*

Year	Public school (%)	Eton (%)	Public school and Oxford or Cambridge (%)	Total new MPs (N)
1945	84	28	41	71
1950	70	23	45	119
1951	75	25	46	41
1955	75	14	50	49
1959	73	16	35	71
1964	85	15	56	41
1966	61	16	44	18
1970	63	10	37	100
1974 (Feb.)	81	15	45	53
1974 (Oct.)	60	–	33	10
1979	61	13	30	86
1983	52	6	25	101
1987	59	6	30	53
1992	55	5	33	63
1997	56	7	29	41

Sources: for information up to 1997, B. Criddle, 'Members of Parliament', in A. Seldon and S. Ball (eds), *Conservative Century* (Oxford, Oxford University Press, 1994); for 1997, Ben Elton, research paper, Manchester Grammar School.

experienced in parliament than most of his fellow Tory MPs. His exhortations to unity are not easily reconciled with the recent behaviour patterns of Tory backbenchers.

The 1922 Committee

The most famous Tory committee in parliament is the 1922 Committee. Students often assume that the 1922 takes its name from a fateful meeting at the Carlton Club in October of that year. In fact, it was formed in 1923 as a self-help group for all those Tory MPs elected in the 1922 general election (thus excluding all those at the Carlton Club meeting). Since 1943, its doors have been open to all backbenchers when the party is in government and all Tory MPs when it is not. As such, it is one of the main channels through which Tory MPs check their leader's power.

The 1922 meets weekly and considers all matters affecting the party in parliament. It has a sixteen-strong executive and a chair (currently Sir Archibald Hamilton). It is often thought to be a rather sinister body, skilled in the black arts of political manoeuvre. In fact, it is 'entirely reactive, often disjointed in discussion and with attendance ebbing and flowing'.[21] Yet through its regular contacts with the whips and leadership, it does have

Table 4.4. *Social background of parliamentary candidates, 1992*

	Con.	Lab.	Lib. Dem.	Nat.	Green	All
Male	85	74	78	79	72	78
Female	15	26	22	21	28	22
White	99	96	98	100	97	98
Non-white	1	4	2	0	3	2
Middle class	99	92	98	97	92	96
Working class	1	8	2	3	8	4
Graduate	67	72	70	76	66	70
Non-graduate	33	28	30	24	34	30
Mean age completing education	20	20	20	21	20	20
Older age (50+)	22	21	23	15	11	20
Middle age (40–50)	39	42	34	30	31	38
Younger age (18–39)	39	37	43	54	58	42
Mean years of age	39	43	44	41	40	42
Religion	85	33	62	53	26	53
None	15	67	38	47	74	47
Union member	14	96	38	55	39	51
None	86	4	62	45	61	49
Income less than £10,000	2	8	4	8	29	8
Income £10,000–£20,000	15	26	25	27	36	25
Income £20,000–£30,000	22	28	30	28	19	26
Income £30,000–£50,000	31	31	31	32	13	29
Income over £50,000	31	7	11	5	3	12
Non-married	32	36	29	33	49	35
Married	68	64	71	67	51	65
N	209	312	311	76	141	1,048

Percentages are reported for all categories except mean ages.

Source: P. Norris and J. Lovenduski, *Political Recruitment* (Cambridge, Cambridge University Press, 1995).

the power to end ministerial careers – simply because no minister can function without the confidence of the party's backbenchers. Lord Carrington's resignation at the start of the Falklands crisis came after a grilling from the 1922, while the resignations of Edwina Currie (1988), David Mellor (1992), Neil Hamilton (1994) and Rod Richards (1996) were all supposedly encouraged by words of warning from the 1922 chairman.

The controversy generated by the 1922 tends to eclipse the range of 'specialist' Tory committees on which many MPs also serve and whose influence (according to Norton) is 'difficult to overstate'.[22] Criticism by the Education Committee in 1984 forced the shelving of student loans, while the Trade and Industry Committee helped delay the pit-closure programme in 1992. A poor performance in front of these committees can again damage a minister's prospects (Leon Brittan's departure from the cabinet during the 1986 Westland crisis followed a row with the Trade and Industry Committee). In view of all this, it seems odd that fewer MPs are now prepared to serve on such committees; in 1990 the whole committee system was said to be 'withering on the vine', attributed by Norton to increased constituency business and the distractions of parliamentary lobbyists.[23]

Association of Conservative Peers

Finally, it would be remiss to discuss the parliamentary party without mentioning the Association of Conservative Peers, the Lords' equivalent of the 1922 Committee. This is the largest grouping in the upper house and, given its willingness to defeat the government after 1979 (on more than 200 occasions) has obvious influence upon policy decisions.

The voluntary extra-parliamentary party

The sub-national structure

It is impossible to understand changes in the nature of the parliamentary party without reference to those who are its gatekeepers, namely those who choose the party's parliamentary candidates. Before 1949, there was an element of self-selection to the parliamentary party. Harold Macmillan was fond of recalling how, in the 1920s, one constituency chair asked candidates to write their names on a piece of paper along with the amount they were prepared to donate to the local party: the most generous candidate was immediately selected, by no means an uncommon occurrence at that time.

Since the party's Maxwell-Fyfe report of 1949, this practice has been forbidden. This encouraged local parties to increase their own fund-raising activities and achieve a large measure of financial self-sufficiency, with big consequences for the spread of power in the party. As Ball has commented, 'In the Conservative Party the flow of influence is rarely opposite to the flow of funds', and many local parties have since achieved considerable autonomy *vis-à-vis* national party organisers.[24]

The constituency Tory party is known as an 'association' and was described by the party's Chelmer report of 1973 as 'the vital unit of organisation inside the Party'. The selection of parliamentary candidates, especially in safe or winnable seats, is obviously their most important task (the procedures are outlined in box 4.3). Since 1988, the associations have accepted a curb on their autonomy by choosing only candidates approved by national party officials. This was seen by the associations as the deal for superior vetting and the avoidance of red faces at election time (activists recalled the mess at Stockton South in 1983 when it was discovered, during the campaign, that their candidate had fought previous elections for the National Front). Yet activists retain much autonomy in their final choice and any attempt to impose candidates may backfire; it was the suspicion that black barrister John Taylor had been 'parachuted in' which split the Cheltenham association in 1992 and contributed to the loss of the seat.

The associations' residual autonomy is a source of frustration to national organisers in three particular areas:

Box 4.3. The selection of Tory parliamentary candidates, 1992–7

National procedures
(1) National Union Standing Advisory Committee recommends most applicants to ...
(2) National Union Parliamentary Selection Board, which recommends c. 60 per cent of applicants to ...
(3) National Union Approved List of Candidates (c. 800)

Local procedures
(1) Sub-committee of constituency association's executive short-lists then interviews about twenty, then reduces short-list to no less than three candidates[a]
(2) Association's executive interviews remaining candidates, then recommends at least two to general meeting of association[b]
(3) General meeting makes final selection[c]

[a]The sub-committee comprises about twenty association officials. All candidates must be drawn from the approved list or have approval of Standing Advisory Committee before selection procedure continues.
[b]The executive comprises about sixty association officials.
[c]Entitled to attend the meeting are all those who have been association members for at least six months. This enabled almost 1,000 members of the Kensington and Chelsea association to participate in the selection of Alan Clarke in January 1997.

Source: *National Union Model Rules 1993*. See also R. Kelly, 'Selecting Parliamentary Candidates', *Talking Politics*, autumn 1996.

---

(1) *Candidate selection.* It is well known that CCO would like to see the party field more black and women candidates, the declared aim of the Conservative Women's Organisation in the mid-1980s and the driving force behind the creation of its One Nation Forum in 1990. As table 4.4 shows, the numbers remain small but would probably be greater if there was more central control of candidates. During the 1997 leadership contest, this was deemed desirable by nearly all the candidates (Redwood being the exception), and following Hague's victory it was suggested that it might occur in return for constituency members having a vote in future leadership contests. There were signs, however, that constituency members would be uneasy with such an agreement.[25]

(2) *Funds.* In 1993, the party chairman confirmed that, in an average (non-election) year, about 70 per cent of party revenue is raised at association level – yet only about 10 per cent of this (£745,000 in 1994) finds its way into national coffers. This makes it difficult for CCO to ensure that party resources are deployed in the most effective manner; the wealthier associations tend to be found in safe Tory seats rather than marginal constituencies. Since 1994, this problem has been alleviated somewhat by the central employment of constituency agents, which means that CCO can now direct these professionals to the seats where they are most needed. The 1994 reform, though, put further strain on CCO's debts, which stood at £19 million in 1993. These debts could be cleared quite easily by the combined wealth of the associations, but the legal independence of the associations precluded any central raid upon their funds. Former Asda executive Archie Norman (brought in by Hague to 'rationalise' the Tory machine) said that closing this loophole would be a priority.[26] But again, a large measure of local cooperation would be needed for this and it was unclear whether it would be forthcoming.

(3) *Discipline.* After his election as leader, Hague announced that he wanted a more disciplined and united party in parliament – in sharp contrast, it seemed, to what his predecessor had had to endure. Yet unless something is done to weaken the autonomy of local parties, discipline may prove no easier to impose than under previous regimes. Parliamentary leaders would certainly be strengthened, for example, if they had the power to threaten maverick MPs with deselection as parliamentary candidates before the next general election. Yet Conservative rules state that only the MP's association can debar that MP from restanding as the official Conservative candidate.[27] It was this, indeed, which emboldened the whipless nine during the Euro-battles of 1994–5 – MPs like Teresa Gorman would have almost certainly thought twice about incurring the wrath of the leadership had they not had the backing of their associations to safeguard their political future.[28] Constituency autonomy again embarrassed the leadership during the election campaign of 1997. Deputy Prime Minister Michael Heseltine let it be known publicly that two of the Tory MPs then

besmirched by scandal – Neil Hamilton and Piers Merchant – were a liability to the party and should not stand as candidates. Yet their local parties (Tatton and Beckenham) thought otherwise, and were able to deliver a damaging rebuff to the Tory hierarchy. CCO was later able to claim that, in the case of Tatton, this type of local independence clearly led to the loss of a seat.

However, MPs do not always benefit from a relatively autonomous and increasingly assertive rank and file. The associations are no longer so respectful towards their MPs, and disputes between MPs and their activists are no longer brought about solely by an MP's personal, or 'apolitical', conduct (such as that which led to the deselection of Sir Nicholas Scott, in Kensington and Chelsea, in 1996). The culture of dissent spawned by Tory MPs has rubbed off on the associations, who are now not so easily subdued by a leader's call for unity at all costs. If an MP can justify criticism of the leadership on the grounds that it will benefit the party, then an association can likewise justify criticism of its own MP.

This was apparent after Tory MPs forced the resignation of Thatcher in 1990, in brazen defiance of the associations' wishes. It was not altogether surprising that about a dozen of the MPs who had publicly supported Heseltine's bid faced reselection battles afterwards, while Sir Anthony Meyer (the stalking horse candidate in 1989) was actually deselected by his Clwyd North West association in 1989. In early 1997, Sir George Gardiner was also deselected by the Reigate association, following his persistent attacks on the party leadership.

In early 1994, there was a new illustration of the associations adopting a less than respectful attitude towards MPs. Tim Yeo, a junior minister, was forced by his Suffolk South association to quit the government after details of his private life surfaced in the press. This episode was given added poignancy by the support Yeo had earlier received from Major, making it a rare occasion when a minister had been forced from office by activists against the will of the Prime Minister. It reinforced the impression that, if Tory activists perceive weak leadership, they themselves will try to fill the vacuum, at least within their own territory. Such a perception was quite common after 1992; a BBC *On the Record* survey in June 1993 found that a third of association chairs thought Major should resign, while the Mistley branch of the Colchester North association passed a motion of no confidence in Major's leadership shortly afterwards.

The importance of constituency party activity was highlighted in a pair of reports prepared by Seyd *et al.* in the early 1990s.[29] Their central message was that 'an active party membership is absolutely vital to electoral performance ... since it is clear that local campaigning plays a big part in influencing election outcomes'.[30] Yet 'an active membership' is exactly what the Tories now appear to lack. Seyd's team found that Tory membership plunged from 2.8 million in 1952 to less than half a million by 1992, that 66 per cent of its members were over fifty-six years old, that only 5 per cent were under thirty-five and that 68 per cent had not attended a single party meeting in the previous year.[31]

The old axiom that the Tories' grass roots are more energetic than Labour's is no longer tenable and helps explain why, in 1992, a 7.5 per cent lead in national votes gave them only a narrow parliamentary majority: Labour's local organisation was simply superior in many marginal areas.[32] By 1997, it was clear that Tory activists had simply ceased to exist in many constituencies, while the party's largely abandoned grass-roots structure is thought to have contributed to the loss of about forty marginal seats – the Tories being unable to combat the Labour/Liberal Democrat campaign for tactical voting in the constituencies concerned.[33]

The decline of party membership is common to most democracies and is in many ways inevitable given social, economic and cultural changes (see Conclusion). Yet Seyd's study takes a less deterministic view, putting much of the blame on the Conservatives' own policies since 1979 – notably the erosion of local government. They argue that, with local councils starved of real power, there is less incentive for the Tory-minded either to seek election as councillors themselves or give active support to those who do – both of which would lead to membership of the local party. The decline of membership can be reversed, they argue, only by offering ordinary Tory members the chance of real political power. A good place to start might be the party's own national organisation.

The national structure

All Conservative associations (along with other aspects of the voluntary extra-parliamentary party, like the Young Conservatives and Conservative Women's Organisation) are enfolded by the National Union of Conservative and Unionist Associations. It was set up in 1867 in response to the new electoral challenges posed by the second Reform Act and was designed to 'support, not question or control, the Party in Parliament'.[34] That original purpose is still central to any assessment of its role today.

The governing body of the National Union is the Central Council, a yearly gathering of about a thousand constituency officials which discusses policy and any proposed changes to its rules and structure. Its responsibilities are delegated to some extent to the National Union Executive Committee, containing about 200 members and meeting about three times a year, which in turn passes on some of its duties to the General Purposes Committee. Fowler's reforms of 1993 reduced the size of the latter to about thirty-five members, meeting about four times a year alternate to meetings of the National Union Executive Committee.

When considering these two committees, it is wise to remember the observation of the Maxwell-Fyfe report that the National Union is 'primarily deliberative and advisory', with no power to bind the leader. Yet Maxwell-Fyfe also recognised that the National Union 'enables the collective opinions of the Party to find expression' and for that reason alone cannot be ignored by a leader wishing to lead a united and effective party.[35] Thatcher, when premier, began the practice of holding two or three meetings a year at Downing Street with National Union officials, and the number of meetings increased under her successor.

Conservative conferences

One of the most important tasks falling upon the National Union's leadership is to organise the party's conferences. With a potential attendance of 8,000–9,000, it is in theory one of the largest political gatherings in any western democracy. It is attended by representatives, not delegates, who communicate (but are not bound by) the views of their associations and various National Union sections. Most of the motions debated are bland and uncritical, and most are passed overwhelmingly on a show of hands. The motions are not, in any case, binding and do not constitute official party policy.

Tory conferences have not been taken very seriously by academics, who have been inclined to dismiss them as revivalist meetings rather than 'serious' political assemblies. A journalist once observed that 'Tory conferences are intended to be, and are, the dullest things that ever happened'.[36]

This traditional view has been challenged, from both an historical and a contemporary perspective, by one of the present authors. The conference has in fact played a pivotal role at several moments in the party's history – like Suez in 1956 – while most Tory leaders have at some stage endured stormy conferences which questioned their leadership qualities.[37] More recently, it is argued that the main October conference should not be seen in isolation from the sixty or so other Tory conferences which precede it each year – what may be termed the 'Conservative conference system'. Debates at these 'secondary' conferences tend to be shockingly frank and critical, yet there is evidence that the ovations most ministers receive at the main conference spring not (as is supposed) from blind loyalty, but from a recognition that they had responded to the frank criticism heard at previous party conferences that year.[38] Neither has the main conference been free of embarrassment to the leadership; the decision to phase in the poll tax was abandoned after a revolt at the 1987 conference, while the decision to field official Tory candidates in Northern Ireland was forced upon a reluctant leadership by the conference of 1989.

The *embourgeoisement* of society gave Tory leaders an added incentive to listen to the conferences' message. With the spread of white-collar employment and home ownership, the vested interests of Tory activists came close to being those of an electoral majority. This also served to encourage a bullish tone among representatives; sensing they may embody the views of the new average voter, they became more reluctant to accept meekly the leadership's advice and impatient with those leaders who did not heed their own opinions.

After 1992, the conference was used by Euro-sceptics like Lord Tebbit to advertise the support their views had among the membership, hoping to knock the leadership off its existing course and encourage more back-benchers to defy it back at Westminster. Aware of mounting grass-roots criticism, ministers also became anxious to impress conference with their own ideas and initiatives. The 'back to basics' policy was unfurled at the 1993 conference to counter activists' unease over the direction of policy, while Portillo's outburst of Euro-phobia at the 1994 conference ('stop the rot from Brussels') was designed to raise both his profile and his leadership prospects. When factionalism is rife among a party's MPs, the views of its rank and file gain in significance. The conference thus becomes a vital arena in which support is mobilised and differences resolved.

The professional extra-parliamentary party

Conservative Central Office, set up in 1870, represents the headquarters of the party's civil service. It employed 183 staff in December 1993 and, since Fowler's reforms of that same year, is supported by seven regional offices in England and Wales, plus a quasi-independent Scottish Central Office.

Central Office is under the day-to-day management of the chairman of the party organisation, appointed by and accountable to the leader. Indeed, CCO could be seen as the leader's personal machine, as through the chairman leaders can insist that the party's bureaucracy acts in the way they would wish. One of Hague's first decisions as Tory leader was to recall Lord Parkinson to the chairmanship, under clear instructions to reorganise the party machine (which Hague had identified as a priority during the leadership election campaign). Yet the chairman's job is not purely organisational, having a big part to play in the marketing of the party generally. This was exemplified by Sir Norman Fowler, who, in 1992, was left to give the media 'an almost single-handed defence of Britain's abandonment' of the Exchange Rate Mechanism.[39]

Central Office is widely considered inefficient by Tory insiders, who in 1997 drew painful comparisons with the slickness of Labour's own national operation. Hague quickly sought to address this problem after becoming leader by revitalising CCO's propaganda wing, creating a Mandelson-style 'instant rebuttal' unit under the direction of MP Alan Duncan. Yet for many Tories, CCO's problems will remain as long as its structure remains undemocratic.[40] Although it is supposed to serve the constituency parties, many of its critics – particularly those in the Charter Movement – believe that it 'acts as if it were master rather than servant' and that this is caused by its lack of formal accountability to the membership.[41] Fowler's 'Board of Party Management' (set up in late 1993) did nothing to alleviate this criticism. Its key figures were to be its Director General, appointed by the chairman, and the chairman himself (still appointed by the leader); furthermore, only three of its thirteen members were to have any elective connection with the associations.

Many in the Party believe that the Board's true purpose was to eliminate CCO's horrendous debts, by at last giving CCO access to the associations' funds.[42] Hitherto, this had been impossible owing to the legal separation of the voluntary and professional extra-parliamentary wings (as confirmed by a judicial ruling involving CCO and the Inland Revenue in 1982). The new Board, however, could have been a way of squaring the circle: by giving the National Union nominal representation on a body supposedly responsible for the whole extra-parliamentary party, its associations may also have been landed with shared responsibility for its whole debts – or, more specifically, the huge bills run up at CCO. The associations, in short, may have been given responsibility without much power.

The Board, in fact, was only the latest example of CCO trying to usurp the associations' powers. Yet none of it could have taken place without the collusion of the National Union's own hierarchy, who share CCO's dislike of the associations' autonomy. Through CCO's large *ex officio* presence on the National Union's Executive and General Purposes Committee (the chairman sits on both), the party's London-based officials have pushed through a series of centralising reforms since 1993.[43] These reforms may well relieve the strain on the party's central finances. But with voting behaviour becoming more localised, suggesting the need for party structures which are less centralised, the Tories may have only caused themselves the more serious problems which emerged at the last two general elections.

Conclusion

Since 1979, there have been clear, attitudinal changes inside the Conservative party which have injected greater democracy into its culture and code of conduct. Yet, by 1997, there had been no similar changes to the party's formal structure, which was still rooted in a nineteenth-century, paternalistic approach to politics.

Even before the last general election, there were signs that this was a source of growing annoyance to party activists, with a large number of critical motions submitted to Tory conferences.[44] But, as the party reorganisation of 1993 showed, such stirrings did not detain the party hierarchy; the Tories entered the 1997 election still looking like 'one of those armies that rely overmuch on its dashing and daring commanders'.[45]

William Hague assumed the leadership promising not just another reform of CCO, but a 'root and branch' review of the whole Conservative structure, offering to do for the Tory machine what Kinnock, Smith and Blair did for Labour's after 1987 (see chapter 6). As with Labour, it seems likely that Hague's plans involve recruiting more constituency members by giving them more say in national party affairs, such as policy making and leader selection, in return for national organisers having more control over constituency business, notably membership recruitment campaigns. Such deals, however, require the consent and trust of the associations. Following the defeat of 1997 – which so many activists attribute to a sclerotic CCO plus misconduct on the part of the parliamentary party – this may not prove easy to secure. Indeed, the 1997 Tory conference proved one of the stormiest this century, with grass-roots members openly accusing the parliamentary party of 'incompetence', 'betrayal' and 'arrogance'.[46] As the Tories come to terms with their loss of power, it seems likely that there will be some long and fractious debates about the future of their organisation.

Notes

1   *Sunday Telegraph*, 24 May 1997; *Guardian*, 28 May 1997.
2   Cited in P. Whiteley, P. Seyd and J. Richardson, *True Blues* (Oxford, Oxford University Press, 1994), p. 39.
3   Charter Movement, *A Charter to Set the Party Free* (Beckenham, Charter Group, 1988).
4   R. Kelly, 'Choosing Tory Leaders', *Politics Review*, September 1996.
5   Conversation with R. Kelly, 7 October 1986.
6   R. T. McKenzie, *British Political Parties* (London, Heinemann, 1955).
7   R. Rose, *The Problem of Party Government* (London, Pelican, 1976), p. 154.
8   *Charter News*, September 1989.
9   H. J. Laski, *Parliamentary Government in England* (London, Allen and Unwin, 1938), p. 71.
10 D. Butler and D. Kavanagh, *The British General Election of 1992* (London, Macmillan, 1992), pp. 92–3.
11 V. Bogdanor, 'The Selection of the Party Leader', in A. Seldon and S. Ball (eds), *Conservative Century* (Oxford, Oxford University Press, 1994).
12 R. Shepherd, *The Power Brokers* (London, Hutchinson, 1991), ch. 2.
13 P. Norton, 'The Pattern of Backbench Dissent', in M. Burch and M. Moran (eds), *British Politics: A Reader* (Manchester, Manchester University Press, 1987), pp. 246–62.
14 *Guardian*, 6 July 1995.
15 R. Kelly, 'The Left, the Right and the Whipless: Conservative Divisions Since 1992', *Talking Politics*, autumn 1995.
16 Kelly, 'Choosing Tory Leaders'.

17 M. Burch and M. Moran, 'Who Are the New Tories?', *New Society*, 11 October 1984.
18 B. Criddle, 'Members of Parliament', in Seldon and Ball, *Conservative Century*, p. 161.
19 Burch and Moran, 'Who Are the New Tories?'.
20 D. Cannadine, 'John Major: Just an Undertaker on Overtime', *Spectator*, 16 April 1994.
21 P. Norton, 'The Parliamentary Party', in Seldon and Ball, *Conservative Century*, p. 112.
22 Norton, 'The Parliamentary Party', p. 119.
23 Norton, 'The Parliamentary Party', p. 128.
24 S. Ball, 'Local Conservatism and the Evolution of the Party Organization', in Seldon and Ball, *Conservative Century*, p. 263.
25 Whiteley, Seyd and Richardson, *True Blues*, pp. 171, 173; Conservative Party Conference Handbook, 1994.
26 *Daily Telegraph*, 25 June 1997.
27 *National Union of Conservative and Unionist Associations: Model Rules 1993*, p. 12.
28 R. Kelly, 'The Whip Hand Tory Rebels Could Hold', *Parliamentary Brief*, February 1995.
29 P. Seyd and P. Whiteley, *Labour's Grass Roots* (Oxford, Clarendon, 1992); Whiteley, Seyd and Richardson, *True Blues*.
30 Seyd and Whiteley, *Labour's Grass Roots*, p. 199.
31 Whiteley, Seyd and Richardson, *True Blues*, pp. 43, 45, 68.
32 D. Denver and G. Hands, 'Constituency Campaigning', *Parliamentary Affairs*, 1992, pp. 528–44.
33 P. Kellner, *Observer*, 3 May 1997.
34 P. Norton and A. Aughey, *Conservatism* (London, Temple Smith, 1981), p. 217.
35 S. Ball, 'The National and Regional Party Structure', in Seldon and Ball, *Conservative Century*, p. 175.
36 R. Kelly, *Conservative Party Conferences* (Manchester, Manchester University Press, 1989), p. ix.
37 R. Kelly, 'The Party Conferences', in Seldon and Ball, *Conservative Century*.
38 Kelly, *Conservative Party Conferences*.
39 Ball, 'The National and Regional Party Structure', p. 179.
40 *Charter News*, 1987–9.
41 *Charter News*, 1993, issues 32–3.
42 R. Kelly, 'Power in the Tory Party', *Politics Review*, April 1995.
43 R. Kelly, 'The Centralising of the Local Tory', *Parliamentary Brief*, May 1995.
44 Conference Handbook, 1995, pp. 132–9.
45 M. Trend, *Spectator*, 28 February 1987.
46 *Daily Telegraph*, 9 October 1997.

5

The Labour party: theory and practice

Labour has often been described as a 'broad church', in the sense that its ideological boundaries are wide. Bealey's 'peasant's stockpot' metaphor for the ideas of a political party, then, is certainly applicable to Labour.[1] Indeed, this is hardly surprising given that, since the decline of the Liberals in the 1920s, Labour has been the major party on the centre-left of British politics and a number of impressive volumes have sought to document the variety of ideas that have been put forward within the confines of the party.[2] Our purpose, however, is more limited. In a book of this size it is necessary to focus on the ideas that have had the biggest impact on the party's development.

For much of the party's history, it is possible to identify what may be described as a mainstream ideology which dominated Labour's theory and practice. From time to time, after the 1931 and 1979 election defeats in particular, ideas associated with the left of the party became more prominent, but this has always proved to be only a passing deviation from the norm. The left's defeat after the 1983 election debacle was swift and decisive. Subsequent developments, however, are less clear. For some commentators, Labour's 'modernisation' since that defeat has resulted in a return to the mainstream ideology. For others, the overwhelming priority given to restoring Labour as a governing party has necessitated the abandonment of these ideas and an accommodation to the political agenda cultivated by Conservative governments since 1979.

Labour party socialism

Before considering its origins and the challenges it has faced during the party's history, it is worthwhile sketching out the major characteristics of Labour's dominant ideology, which we will refer to as Labour party socialism. It might be argued that a more appropriate term for this ideology is social democracy. The problem here, though, is that in the early part of the present century, the label social democracy had Marxist connotations.

Thus, the Social Democratic Federation in Britain – which for a short time was affiliated to the infant Labour party – was a Marxist group and the very fact that it felt unable to remain within the party illustrated its ideological incompatibility.[3] It was only in the post-war period that the label social democrat began to be regularly applied to certain (moderate) individuals and factions within the Labour party to denote their acceptance of the mixed economy created by the 1945 Labour government and to distinguish them from those who sought a further socialist transformation. In practice, it has been the social democrats who have usually dominated the party. It is doubtful, though – for reasons explored below – whether such a distinction can be profitably applied in the inter-war years. Furthermore, many of those in the post-1945 Labour party who would not have described themselves as social democrats would accept at least some of the characteristic features of what we have described as Labour party socialism.

So, what are these characteristics? First, Labour's theory and practice have been fashioned around a belief in the primacy of parliamentary action. Mainstream Labour socialism regards legislative enactments as the only means of achieving its aims. Extra-parliamentary action is considered to be both illegitimate and unnecessary. A corollary of this is a belief in the neutrality of the state. The state is not, as for Marxists, the vehicle of an economically dominant class but is infinitely malleable, to be used effectively by any government with a majority of MPs in the Commons.

Secondly, Labour socialism is a classless doctrine. The existence of classes is recognised, as is the point that the working class stands to gain most from socialism. Socialism, however, is not a doctrine aimed at one particular class or section of society and does not, as Marxists would claim, involve a class war, the result of which would be the victory of the working class. Rather, changes in a socialist direction will come about when people from all sections of society come to see the validity of the arguments put forward.

Thirdly, Labour socialists have regarded public ownership in particular and collectivist state action in general as the main means to achieve their ends. The early Labour socialists, exemplified by Ramsay MacDonald – the first Labour Prime Minister – consistently stated that their long-term objective was the creation, albeit gradual, of a socialist society in the sense of the emasculation of private ownership of the economy. Most post-1945 Labour socialists, on the other hand, have adopted the less visionary aim of the effective and just management of the mixed economy. This was to be achieved by the use of Keynesian demand management techniques designed to maintain full employment coupled with a system of progressive taxation, the proceeds of which would sustain a comprehensive welfare state. This latter approach can, as we indicated, be more profitably described as social democratic in tone. In practice, however, the distinction between the two really became apparent only after the achievements of the 1945 Labour government.

The impact of the trade unions

No adequate account of Labour's ideology can ignore the impact of the trade unions. It was the desire for independent labour representation in the latter part of the nineteenth century that led to the creation, in 1900, of the Labour Representation Committee, which was renamed the Labour party after the 1906 general election. Admittedly, a number of socialist societies – the Fabians, the Independent Labour party (ILP) and the Social Democratic Federation – were also involved. It was the finance and workforce of the trade unions, however, which were vital in the party's development and, although the trade union influence on the party has declined over the past decade or so, Labour continues to have a considerable organisational reliance on them.

Given the role of the trade unions, it is important that we tackle immediately their impact on Labour's ideological development. The established orthodoxy among commentators seems to be that the trade unions have generally had a moderating influence on the Labour party. Bealey, for instance, concludes that for the most part the effect of the trade unions has been 'highly practical and immediate'. Similarly, Foote regards the aim of desiring a better reward for workers within a capitalist society as the 'Labourist' boundaries of the party's political thought. For any ideological faction to have any success within the party, he argues, it must 'adapt itself to the Labourism of the trade unions'. Ingle is equally adamant that the trade unions moved 'Labour decisively away from socialism, making it very much a trade union party'. Finally, McKibbin in his study of Labour's development up to 1924, suggests that the party's adoption in 1918 of a socialist commitment was unimportant because the trade unions' organisational dominance ensured it would never be put into effect.[4]

It can be seen that these authors ascribe to the unions a particular ideological contribution. For want of a better word, this may be defined as labourism. Labourism refers to the theory, insofar as it exists, and practice of the protection and elevation of working-class living standards. Thus, it is concerned with the sectional interests of the working class within the existing framework of society rather than with attempts to change that society fundamentally. As Peter Gay has written:

> A trade union leader, if he wishes to stay in power, must produce immediate and tangible results; higher wages, shorter hours, better working conditions. He knows that man cannot live on hope alone nor can present hunger be satisfied by thoughts of the happiness of future generations. He knows too that short run gains are best achieved by working within the existing social framework.[5]

Before 1918, certainly, the party was little more than a pressure group for the trade union movement. Thus, the main purpose of the parliamentary

Labour party (PLP) was not to form a government but to put pressure on the government of the day to adopt legislation in the interests of organised labour. After 1918, however, Labour was transformed – partly, at least, because of the impact of the Representation of the People Act, which massively increased the number of working-class voters – into a national party of government with a constitution emphasising socialism as its objective.

Clearly, there is a conflict between the labourism of the trade unions and the Labour socialism we identified above. First, labourism lacked the vision of early Labour socialism. The former seeks only the improvement of working-class living standards. The latter, at least in its early days, advocated the creation of nothing less than a new kind of society. R. H. Tawney, a leading Labour socialist thinker in the inter-war years, put the difference nicely when he pointed out that the ultimate aim of socialists was not simply a society 'in which money and economic power will be somewhat differently distributed' but one 'in which money and economic power will no longer be the criterion of achievement'.[6] Secondly, and more importantly in practice, labourism asserts the interests of one section or class of society. This is clearly at odds with the Labour socialist denial of the value of a class-specific doctrine and the desire of all Labour governments to govern in the 'national' interest.

The conflict between labourism and Labour socialism has manifested itself on numerous occasions in the party's history. In the 1920s, for instance, the first Labour government's defence of the 'national' interest when refusing to support the striking transport workers in 1924, and the leadership's lukewarm support for the general strike in 1926, were both illustrations of the conflict.[7] In the modern period, the Labour government's unsuccessful attempt to reform the trade unions in 1969 and the imposition of pay norms in the late 1970s were both sources of conflict, as was the Kinnock leadership's lukewarm response to the miners' strike in 1984, the latter providing a classic case study of the traditional Labour socialist view that the party should not condone industrial action conducted by one section of society to the detriment of society as a whole. That is not to say, of course, that the justice of the particular group of workers taking industrial action cannot be proclaimed – only that the methods utilised to correct this injustice are unfortunate, a last resort requiring speedy resolution.

The response of Labour governments to the activities of trade unions, of course, has been inspired as much by electoral considerations as a principled stance. This is not, on the other hand, to say that Labour leaders have not had a choice. They have, and on most occasions they have chosen to sacrifice the interests of particular sets of workers, or even the trade union movement as a whole, in order to uphold what they have seen as the national interest. As a consequence, there have often been bitter recriminations within the party, usually fought out at the Labour conference and, in the case of the white paper on industrial relations introduced in 1969, *In Place of Strife*, the Labour government was forced – owing to pressure from within the PLP and even in the cabinet, as well as the bulk of the extra-parliamentary party – to back down.

Clearly, then, we cannot ignore labourism as an ideological force within the Labour party. Its importance, however, should not be exaggerated. First, as Minkin has observed in his colossal study of party–union links, trade unions have traditionally recognised the 'formal boundaries' between the political and the industrial wings of the labour movement and have recognised that it is not their role to seek to dominate the former, particularly in policy areas in which they do not have any direct interest.[8] A related point is that labourism does not provide a programme for government. Before 1918, the PLP could simply act as a mouthpiece for the trade union movement because it was not in a position to take on the reins of government. After 1918, when Labour was seeking to replace the Liberals as one of the two main parties, the party needed a programme dealing with a wide variety of issues and appealing to a wider audience than the organised working class. This was recognised by Arthur Henderson, the party's secretary and a key figure in the reorganisation after 1918, when he wrote that Labour's appeal up to 1918 had been limited because:

> it was regarded as the party of the manual wage-earners. Its programme
> was assumed to reflect the views of trade unionists not as citizens with a
> common interest in good government, but as workers seeking remedies for
> a series of material grievances touching hours of labour, rates of wages,
> conditions of employment.[9]

Thus, after 1918, the trade unions were forced to rely on the Labour socialists to formulate a general programme which would attract wide enough support for the party to win elections. The demands of trade unionists constituted a part, but only a part, of that programme.

Secondly, at certain times in the party's history, the trade unions have been forced to depend on the political leadership of the Labour socialists because their bargaining power in the industrial sphere, through recession and/or legislation, has been severely limited. This happened in the 1920s after the exhausting failure of the general strike in 1926 and the Conservative government's draconian trade union legislation enacted in the following year (see chapter 6). It also occurred in the period of Conservative governments between 1979 and 1997 for the same reasons. Indeed, Labour leaders since 1983 have been able to secure the loyalty of the bulk of trade union leaders precisely because the union movement has needed a friendly government to legislate in its interests. With Labour now back in power, a clash between the political and industrial wings of the labour movement is unavoidable, although it is likely, in a very changed environment, to be less severe than past conflicts.

The final point to make here is that although we have identified one facet of the ideological make-up of the trade unions, it would be too simplistic to ascribe to them an homogenous labourism which has been universally hostile to Labour's socialism. This would be to underestimate the difficulty of locating the unions within Labour's overall theory and practice.[10] Some trade unionists have regarded themselves as socialists with a vision or a goal of what society should look like which goes way beyond the limited aims of labourism and indeed of the social democracy of Labour's post-war parliamentary leadership. For example, as we shall see in chapter 6, Labour's move to the left in the 1970s and early 1980s came about at least partly because the major unions had elected a more left-wing leadership, who had become hostile to the moderation of the party's parliamentary leadership in the 1960s and 1970s. In the 1950s, on the other hand, the key leading union leaders, far from representing an ideological and political threat, were fully behind Hugh Gaitskell's social democratic leadership of the party.

The inter-war years

Labour socialism was established as the party's mainstream ideology in the 1920s. Labour's 1918 constitution had two vital provisions. First, there was the opening up of the party to individual members in local constituencies to supplement the existing affiliated membership. This had the effect of reducing the dominance of the trade unions, thus making Labour look more like a national political party capable of governing rather than merely a pressure group. Secondly, there was the adoption of a socialist objective (clause 4, part V of the party's constitution). This committed the party for the first time to:

> secure for the producers by hand and by brain the full fruits of their industry, and the most equitable distribution thereof that may be possible, upon the basis of the common ownership of the means of production and the best obtainable system of popular administration and control of each industry and service.

Two statements of aims were also published in the inter-war period, *Labour and the New Social Order* in 1918 and *Labour and the Nation* in 1927. Both remain classic examples of Labour socialism, committing the party to the eventual creation of a socialist society through nationalisation in addition to various reforms to improve the lot of the working class until that change could be effected. Both programmes were to be carried into completion 'by peaceful means, without disorder or confusion, with the consent of the majority of the electors and by the use of the ordinary machinery of democratic government'.[11]

Central to the adoption by Labour of these aims were the activities of three individuals. First, Sidney Webb, the leading Fabian thinker, was instrumental in drawing up *Labour and the New Social Order*. Indeed, much of what we have described as Labour socialism derives from the gradual, evolutionary socialism advocated by the Fabian Society. Secondly, Arthur Henderson, as previously mentioned, played a key role in Labour's re-organisation after 1918. He saw that it was vital for Labour to become a national party capable of legislating in the interests of all classes. Finally, and most importantly, there was Ramsay MacDonald. Dominating the party as Labour leader from 1922 until 1931, he did most to popularise Labour socialism both by his actions and in a series of books written immediately before and after the First World War.[12]

Labour socialism was seen in action during the 1920s. We have observed it in the leadership's response to the trade unions. It was also evident in the party's continual refusal to allow the Communist party of Great Britain to affiliate and the expulsion of known communists within the Labour party. The ideological incompatibility between communism and Labour socialism was noted in a letter sent out by Labour's NEC to all affiliated societies in 1924:

> The Labour Party seeks to achieve the Socialist Commonwealth by means of Parliamentary democracy. The Communist Party seeks to achieve the 'Dictatorship of the Proletariat' by armed revolution. The Labour Party realises that this country possesses almost a wholly enfranchised adult population, and a Parliament and system of government that will respond to the direction of the working people, so soon as they express intelligent desire for change through the ballot box.[13]

The two Labour governments in the 1920s achieved very little in the way of carrying out their programme. In 1924, MacDonald was clearly concerned above all to show how moderate and respectable Labour was in order not to frighten off the voters. Nevertheless, there were other excuses. Both Labour governments were minorities, so they did not have a mandate to carry out their full programme. In addition, during the second period of office, between 1929 and 1931, the government was unable to cope with a devastating economic crisis. Arguably, this failure was rooted in the party's ideology. Labour socialism in the inter-war years – before the party absorbed Keynesian economics – largely consisted of an ethical vision of a new social order. Consequently, it had little idea how the transition was to be achieved in practice and even less how to handle a capitalist economy in crisis.[14]

Of course, the Labour socialism of MacDonald and others did face opposition within the party. We have already seen the challenge presented by the industrial militancy of the trade unions. Another came from the left of the party, centring on the ILP, a socialist society affiliated to the party. The ILP, originally dominated by MacDonald loyalists, came to be the focus of opposition to Labour's gradualist socialism. Led by the fiery Clydesider James Maxton, the ILP mounted a campaign for 'Socialism in our Time', which sought a parliamentary road to socialism but one which would be achieved rapidly. The campaign had little impact on Labour's development, however, and the ILP disaffiliated from the party after the resignation of MacDonald's government, due to a split over a proposal to cut unemployment benefit, and the Prime Minister's decision to continue in office as head of a national government.[15]

A more serious challenge to Labour socialism came after the events of 1931 when a number of key thinkers began to question the validity of a cautious parliamentary approach. One kind of analysis, presented by Stafford Cripps (a Labour minister) and Tawney, concentrated on the need for a future Labour government to act quickly to control the power of capital. They remained committed, however, to a parliamentary approach.[16] The second kind, presented by G. D. H. Cole and Harold Laski (both academics and Labour activists) adopted an uncompromising Marxist analysis which involved the – for them – pessimistic conclusion that socialism was not obtainable by constitutional means.[17]

Despite the increased influence of Marxism among British socialists in the 1930s, the decade was marked by the refinement of Labour socialism rather than its abandonment. Crucial here was the absorption of Keynesian economic management techniques and the general idea of planning into mainstream Labour socialism.[18] The party also settled upon the public corporation model of nationalisation, popularised by Herbert Morrison, a senior member of Attlee's post-war government and, incidentally, Peter Mandelson's grandfather. Under this model, industries were to be run by a board of experts replacing the earlier participatory ideals of public ownership in British socialist thought exemplified by Cole's guild socialism.[19] These refinements were included within the two Labour programmes published in the period, *For Socialism and Peace* in 1934 and *Labour's Immediate Programme* in 1937.

Revisionism versus fundamentalism

The Labour government elected in 1945 carried out much of the programme adopted in 1918 and refined in the 1930s. With the consent of the people, manifested in a huge parliamentary majority, Labour nationalised a whole range of industries, from coal to road haulage, and took it upon themselves to provide and maintain full employment through the use of demand management techniques derived from Keynes. In addition, through the creation of the welfare state, a safety net was provided, below which no one was to fall. This was to provide the basis for the social democratic consensus which dominated British politics for the next twenty-five years. After the fall of the Labour government in 1951, however, an ideological battle broke out within the party. Put very simply, on the one side were the revisionists, led by Hugh Gaitskell and Tony Crosland, and on the other were the fundamentalists, whose main champion, at least for the first part of the 1950s, was Aneurin Bevan.

The ideological divisions were provoked by the need for Labour to come off the fence. Before the Second World War, Labour socialism was sufficiently vague to keep the party relatively ideologically united. More specifically, the gradualist socialism, propagated most of all by MacDonald, had the effect of keeping those who regarded Labour's true purpose to be the creation of a socialist society active within the party while not frightening off those who had less ambitious aims. Thus, for the latter group, socialism was so far off as not to be worth worrying about, while for the former socialism was still very much on the agenda.

This ideological glue was not available for Labour after 1951. MacDonald, Snowden and other Labour leaders in the 1920s could be described as social democrats in the sense that they would probably have accepted the mixed economy and the welfare state as Labour's ultimate goal. Certainly, their actions, as opposed to their writings, suggest this. Because they were not put to the test of implementing their preferred programme in the inter-war years, however, they avoided the inevitable debate about Labour's future direction. After 1951, such a debate was unavoidable because the labels socialism and social democracy began to have great importance within the Labour party.

The main theoretical exponent of revisionism was Tony Crosland.[20] He argued that, in Britain, through the action of the post-war governments, Labour and Conservative, capitalism had been 'reformed and modified almost out of existence'.[21] State management ensured that the economy worked effectively, guaranteeing a high level of economic growth and employment, thereby proving Marxist predictions of the collapse of capitalism unfounded. In addition, the Marxist model of two classes – the bourgeoisie and the proletariat – with diametrically opposed interests and in constant conflict, failed to take into account the fact that financial ownership of the private sector was now increasingly separate from its day-to-day control, which tended to be in the hands of a class of salaried managers with their own set of goals and motives. Crucially, too, the welfare state was in position to provide free health care and education as well as various social benefits for those in need of help. Yes, Crosland argued, the main mechanism of the economy was still the market and the profit motive, but this was a necessary device in any society. The key difference since the war was that part of this profit was taken and used by the state in the interests of all.[22]

For Crosland, then, further public ownership of the economy was irrelevant to the achievement of the basic socialist goal of equality. Instead, Crosland suggested, Labour's goal of further nationalisation should be abandoned and the mixed economy/welfare state accepted as the permanent social arrangement within which the party should work. Labour should then turn its attention to removing the remaining inequalities in society through a programme of social reforms, including the introduction of comprehensive education and reform of the tax system.

Crosland had powerful support for his views within the party's leadership. Above all, it was Gaitskell – Labour leader after Attlee's retirement in 1955 – who fought for revisionism. Thus, he sought (unsuccessfully) to remove clause 4 (which, it will be remembered, indicated that Labour's main means to the socialist end was to be public ownership) from the party's constitution at the 1959 conference.[23] Despite this failure, the party's policy documents at this time (including the 1959 manifesto) were fully in line with the revisionist prognosis, and Labour governments in the 1960s, with Crosland as a member, were essentially committed to the revisionist analysis, in that they aimed to institute greater planning of the mixed economy rather than any significant change in the mixture (the nationalisation, or renationalisation, of iron and steel being the only such measure carried out between 1964 and 1970).

Crosland's analysis, and its attractiveness to most of Labour's parliamentary leadership, was very much a product of the political and economic environment of the 1950s. During this decade, the British economy was booming and in these circumstances it was easy to see how it could be thought that the depression and mass unemployment of the 1930s were a thing of the past. In addition, the three consecutive Conservative election victories in the 1950s led to claims that, because of the growing prosperity of the working class, Labour would never win an election again unless it significantly modified its approach and image.[24]

This revisionist approach was challenged from the left of the party. During the 1945–51 Labour governments, the left's voice was muted. There was some disquiet at the government's moderation – the generous compensation given to the former owners of nationalised industries, for instance, and the failure to take into public ownership more of the profitable parts of the private sector – and the Keep Left group of Labour MPs was formed in 1947 to urge the government to take bolder measures. Divisions were mainly concerned, though, with foreign and defence policy, with dissent provoked by the strong anti-Soviet line of the Foreign Office under Ernest Bevin's ministerial leadership.[25] The largest conflict, linking together external and domestic policy, occurred in 1951, when financing the Korean war necessitated the introduction of charges in the National Health Service. The subsequent resignation of three ministers – Bevan (who, as Minister of Health, had been responsible for piloting the National Health Service Bill through parliament), Harold Wilson and John Freeman – was to provide the impetus for left-wing opposition to Labour's leadership when the party lost the 1951 election.

During the 1950s, internal wrangling became a feature of Labour party politics. Defence again, and particularly the Labour leadership's support for an independent British nuclear weapons system, was a key source of division.[26] In 1955, Bevan was expelled from the PLP for mounting a Commons attack on Attlee's pro-nuclear sympathies and, with the growing support for the Campaign for Nuclear Disarmament (itself formed in 1958) within the party, the 1960 conference voted for a unilateralist resolution, thereby inflicting a rare defeat on the parliamentary leadership (see chapter 6). By this time, though, Bevan himself had patched up his differences with the leadership and, as shadow Foreign Secretary, he instituted a remarkable about-turn by imploring delegates at the 1957 conference to accept multilateral nuclear disarmament as Labour's goal.[27]

In domestic policy, the left, with very little success, opposed the revisionists' claim that nationalisation was no longer relevant. Bevan's *In Place of Fear*, published in 1952, became the main text of the fundamentalists. In it, he argued that Labour had not transformed capitalism. Indeed, the basic class and power structure in Britain had hardly been touched. Consequently, it was necessary for further nationalisation in order to change the balance between the public and private sectors. Bevan's analysis was also significant in the sense that its class-based approach differed from the mainstream Labour socialism we have described. The aim of Labour should be – as, for Bevan, it always had been – the transformation of society in the interests of the working class. This could be achieved only by an attack on the class who owned private property.[28] Bevan, though, shied away from criticising the neutrality of the state. Universal suffrage had provided the potential for the conflict between classes to be fought out in parliament. It was Labour's job to make sure that parliament performed this function.[29]

By the early 1960s, however, the debate between the revisionists and the fundamentalists was overtaken by events. Of crucial importance was Harold Wilson's arrival as leader after the shock of Gaitskell's early death in 1963. Wilson was able to unite the party for three main reasons. First, by the early 1960s, the Conservative government was running into difficulties, not least because of the state of the economy, and Labour began to pull ahead in the opinion polls. The prospect of winning after so long in the wilderness had a disciplining effect and all sections of the party rallied around the new leader. Secondly, Wilson was in a good position to secure unity. He was respected by all sections of the party. His gritty, no-nonsense, northern image was attractive to a working-class party and, in addition, he was regarded as 'one of us' by the left, who had not forgotten his resignation, with Bevan, in 1951. Finally, Wilson was able to transcend the ideological dispute in the party by emphasising the need for Labour to modernise the economy. Not only was this a skilful way of bypassing the divisions within the party – modernisation was a neutral term which did not involve coming down on the side of the fundamentalists or the revisionists – it was also an ideal weapon with which to attack the Conservatives. Thus, the old aristocratic Tories were to be swept away as Labour portrayed itself as the only party able to capitalise on the economic benefits which would derive from, in Wilson's words at the 1963 Labour conference, the 'white heat of the technological revolution'.

The Labour governments of 1964–70

For much of the period between 1964 and 1970, the left – with what seems in retrospect as hopelessly misplaced optimism – was willing to give Wilson the benefit of the doubt until it became clear that his pragmatism was not furthering the socialist cause, as they saw it, one bit. The Labour governments of the 1960s were clearly social democratic in tone, concerned with the management of the mixed economy rather than with any attempts to transform that system. For the fundamentalists, of course, this was a betrayal of the party's true purpose. For the revisionists, many of whom held governmental office in the 1960s and 1970s, this mixed economy was at least no longer a purely capitalist one. This clash was inevitable, as we have seen, once Labour's basic post-war programme had been implemented. Whereas in the 1950s the debate was merely theoretical, from the 1960s onwards it was to go to the heart of what Labour governments actually did. Wilson was the first Labour Prime Minister to face this problem. In reality he was no more or less moderate than, say, MacDonald had been in the 1920s. He was forced, however, to come off the fence and declare himself.

The cause of the social democrats was not helped by the fact that Wilson's governments were in their own terms largely a failure. True, some of the revisionist themes were heeded. Welfare benefits rose, particularly for those in the direst need, as did the number of houses built in the public and private sectors. In addition, the government began to create a system of comprehensive education, a key Croslandite proposal.[30] Nevertheless, the attempt to carry through Britain's first 'National Economic Plan', the flagship of the administration, was a flop and general economic decline undermined the revisionist claim that socialism should now be concerned with the more effective redistribution of abundant resources.

It all started well enough. The government created a Department of Economic Affairs – with equal status to the Treasury – to develop and co-ordinate the Plan, and a National Prices and Incomes Board. By 1966, however, following a balance-of-payments crisis, Labour was forced to abandon the planned growth in the economy and introduce severe cuts in public spending. Despite the confidence boost of the general election victory in 1966, things did not get any easier. The following year, the recurring problem of Britain's balance of trade forced the government to devalue sterling and initiate another round of spending cuts. In addition, the growth of strikes (particularly unofficial ones) provoked the government into introducing a white paper aimed at reducing the power of the unions in order to curb wage rises. The ignominy of having to drop the proposals owing to pressure from within the party seemed the final nail in the coffin of an exhausted government.

The Labour governments of 1974–9 and the challenge of the left

After the failures of the Wilson governments in the 1960s, the left began to flex its muscles and engage in some serious thinking about Labour's objectives and the strategies which would bring them about. During the 1970s, a number of intellectuals – such as Michael Barratt Brown, Ken Coates and Stuart Holland – produced a series of articles and books seeking to articulate a new approach.[31] Central to the fundamentalists' challenge to the social democratic leadership was their divergent economic policy, which became known as the alternative economic strategy.[32]

Some of the features of the left's new programme were familiar. The demand for class-based action and its willingness to support extra-parliamentary activity were still the essential features which distinguished the left from the Labour socialist leadership. In addition, the left regarded itself as the heir of Labour's 'true' purpose, the transformation of capitalism. Thus, the goal was to create full employment and economic growth through increased state intervention and planning in the form of the creation of a national enterprise board (to raise the rate of investment in manufacturing industry) and the nationalisation of the clearing banks together with many of the most profitable manufacturing companies. In addition, a Keynesian reflationary policy was advocated with a permanent prices and incomes policy to combat inflationary pressures.

There were also innovations in this strategy, as the old fundamentalist left, to some extent, had been transcended. First, the fundamentalism of the 1950s had been tinged, from outside the party, with the ideas of the New Left. This New Left was created in the late 1950s by a number of intellectuals who, disillusioned by the excesses of Stalin, left the Communist party in 1956.[33] The New Left emphasised that socialism was about power relationships in society as much as it was about economic equality. Thus, a top-heavy, suffocating centralism was not conducive to improving quality of life, whether it occurred in a socialist or a capitalist society or, more to the point, whether it occurred in a Morrisonian public corporation or a multi-national company. As a consequence of this analysis, a decentralised, participatory socialism was advocated and long-forgotten issues such as industrial democracy and workers' control were rediscovered. Indeed, many of the arguments used were remarkably similar to those of the guild socialists who, earlier in the century, had attacked the Fabians for their vision of a socialist society run by state technocrats.[34]

Secondly, and crucially, the new strategy recognised the importance of external constraints on a Labour government. If Labour was to be able to pursue the radical domestic policy intended – and not be directed off course by foreign capitalist interests which would seek to impose their will on a Labour government – it would have, as far as it was possible, to cut its ties with the world economy. This would necessitate controls on imports (through quotas) and the export of capital, together with Britain's withdrawal from the European Community.[35] Clearly, this strategy was based upon the experience of the Labour governments in the 1960s, which were forced to deflate the economy and eventually devalue sterling because of persistent balance-of-payments difficulties. By the end of the 1970s, the left's analysis provoked even more discussion given the influence of the International Monetary Fund on the Labour government's economic policy (see below).

Perhaps the most significant feature of this period was that Tony Benn (the man who was, by the end of the 1970s, to become the unchallenged leader of the left, following in the footsteps of James Maxton in the 1920s and Aneurin Bevan in the 1950s) was, in the early 1970s, beginning to emerge as the political leader of the left's attack on the social democratic leadership. Peter Shore, a leading Labour politician in the 1970s, has described Benn as probably the most important single figure in the history of the Labour party. There is a good deal to be said for this. Not only was he, in the 1970s and early 1980s, an inspirational orator and the 'darling' of the party's rank and file, he also had the key advantage of being, an initially uncritical, member of the Labour governments led by Wilson and Callaghan. He could therefore speak with authority, as an 'insider', about their failings and the need for Labour, as he saw it, to adopt a more left-wing standpoint.[36] We should not, however, exaggerate Benn's role. By the end of the 1970s he had become the figurehead of the Labour left but, as Patrick Seyd rightly points out, he was not the primary 'source of Labour Left ideas and neither did he provide the organisational drive for Labour Left campaigns'. In addition, his middle-class social origins and his participation in successive social democratic Labour governments provoked some hostility on the left.[37]

Benn, although a fundamentalist in his support for class-based activity and his refusal to condemn extra-parliamentary action, was also influenced by the New Left emphasis on democracy. Thus, he rejected the public corporation model of social ownership in favour of industrial democracy, supporting the work-in at the Upper Clyde shipbuilders' in 1971 and encouraging the development of workers' co-operatives as Industry Secretary between 1974 and 1975. His characteristic concern, though, has been with the democratisation of the British constitution itself. Only a system which was truly open and democratic could, he argued, be fully accountable to the electors. To this end, he has proposed a whole series of measures, from a Freedom of Information Act to the ending of the royal prerogative and the abolition of the House of Lords. His attacks on nuclear weapons, Britain's membership of the European Community and the influence of international capital are based on the same grounds. All three, for Benn, are undermining parliamentary sovereignty and the right of British people to participate in decisions which greatly affect them.[38]

As the 1970s progressed, and Britain's economic situation worsened, the Labour party began to move leftwards. Crucial here was the adoption at the 1973 conference of *Labour's Programme*, which marked a decisive shift to the left. Among other things, it proposed the creation of a national enterprise board to purchase controlling interests in twenty-five leading firms (a proposal which was only narrowly accepted by Labour's NEC), a major redistribution of wealth, the institution of planning agreements, industrial democracy and controls on the movement of capital. This programme was confirmed and built upon by other documents during the 1970s. The party's manifesto for the February 1974 general election was a watered down version of the policy programmes approved by conference (not surprisingly, given the parliamentary leadership's greater control over the manifesto content and Wilson's antipathy to much of the left's programme). Nevertheless – with promises to extend nationalisation in areas such as shipbuilding and road haulage, an expansion of welfare provisions, steeply progressive income tax proposals and the introduction of a wealth tax – as David Howell points out, its 'tone and the contents were more radical than anything produced by the party since 1945'.[39]

The opportunity to implement this programme came with Labour's return to government in 1974. Initially, there was relatively little for the left to complain about. Wilson appointed Benn and another well known left-wing MP, Michael Foot, to two important posts – Industry and Employment – which offered some prospect of the left's programme being translated into action. In addition, there was a generous settlement with the miners, legislation was introduced improving the legal status of trade unions and the economy was expanded through deficit financing, thus enabling the government to keep its side of the bargain in the 'social contract' with the unions. Ultimately, though, the hopes of the left, and indeed the party in general, were to be sorely disappointed.

Despite the appointment of Benn and Foot, the centre-right of the party held the senior posts in the governments and Wilson, Callaghan (who became Prime Minister in 1976) and Healey (who was to remain as Chancellor throughout the period 1974–9) regarded much of the left's programme as unacceptable. In particular, the National Enterprise Board created by the Industry Act 1975 was a pale reflection of the socialist 'battering ram' envisaged by the left. Deprived of the necessary funds and bereft of its power to institute compulsory planning agreements, its major function was to bale out firms in financial trouble.[40] Benn fought his corner at the Department of Industry, seeking to prevent the downgrading of the National Enterprise Board and encouraging workers' co-operatives, but he was gradually isolated as his departmental officials sought to obstruct him, probably on Wilson's orders. After the defeat of the anti-marketeers in the 1975 referendum, Wilson took the opportunity to demote Benn to the Department of Energy, thus effectively ending his influence within the government.[41]

As we explained in chapter 1, even the Labour government's commitment to Keynesian social democracy was, by the end of their period in office, severely in doubt. To be fair to the government, the long-term weaknesses of the British economy had, by the middle of the 1970s, led to the phenomenon of 'stagflation' – both rising unemployment and rising inflation – provoking an agonising choice. The massive deflation adopted, in addition, was to a large degree necessitated by the conditions of the loan from the International Monetary Fund, required as a result of a serious run on the pound in 1976. Nevertheless, there was a left group in the cabinet – including Benn, Foot, Albert Booth and Stan Orme – who (together with the more cautious Peter Shore) unsuccessfully sought the adoption of an alternative strategy, based upon reflation and import controls.[42]

As it was, monetary discipline precipitated a growth in unemployment while the government reneged on its part of the 'social contract', imposing lower ceilings on wage rises despite public spending cuts and still high levels of inflation. The government stumbled on through 1977–8, deprived now of an overall majority and dependent upon the smaller parties, until the outbreak of a succession of strikes among low-paid workers in the 'winter of discontent' put paid to hopes of a recovery in its fortunes. After losing a vote of no confidence in the Commons, Labour was defeated in the May 1979 election by the Conservatives under the radical leadership of Margaret Thatcher. The time was ripe now for the left to mount its most successful challenge to the prevailing social democracy within the party.

The rise and fall of the left, 1979–83

By ignoring much of the left's programme between 1974 and 1979, the parliamentary leadership had demonstrated clearly that the party's constitution insulated it from the decisions taken at Labour conferences. The final straw came when Callaghan supposedly used his position to determine the (moderate) nature of Labour's 1979 election manifesto. Thus, after the election defeat in 1979, the left (now firmly in control of the extra-parliamentary party) sought to change Labour's constitution in order to make the leadership more accountable to the party outside parliament. The causes and nature of these changes are considered in more detail in chapter 6. For now, it should be noted briefly that the campaign to involve the extra-parliamentary party in the election of the leader and deputy leader and to give local activists greater powers to remove sitting Labour MPs succeeded because the left secured enough support from the trade unions at conference. This was partly because there were more left-wingers in key union positions. More important, perhaps, was the labourist demand from trade unions in general that any future Labour government be under their control, thereby preventing any repeat of, what they saw as, the attacks on the organised labour movement between 1974 and 1979.

By the early 1980s – with the left in the ascendant – the social democrats, associated with the failed policies of the Wilson and Callaghan governments, were on the defensive. After Callaghan had stood down, Michael Foot – the most left-wing Labour leader since the war, although no friend of Benn – was elected. Foot's election and the conference's confirmation of the constitutional reforms (discussed in chapter 6) were the final impetus for a number of key social democrats who left in 1981 to set up their own party (see chapter 7). The way was left clear for Benn to utilise the new constitutional provisions. He duly challenged Denis Healey for the deputy leadership at the 1981 conference and, in a nail-biting climax, was narrowly defeated.

Despite this setback for the left, the party went into the 1983 election with a manifesto which at last reflected the left's dominance over conference policy making. A considerable extension of state intervention in the economy was coupled with other proposals – such as withdrawal from the European Community, unilateral nuclear disarmament and abolition of the House of Lords – which had long been on the left's agenda. Labour's resounding defeat – which was at least partly to do with the tone of the manifesto – was the beginning of the end for the most successful challenge to the party's dominant ideology ever mounted by the left.

Foot stepped down as leader immediately after the 1983 election and was replaced by the so-called 'dream ticket' of Neil Kinnock and Roy Hattersley. From this point on, the influence of the left substantially declined. The left's claim that its ideas would be electorally popular if only they were given prominence within the party was severely dented by the 1983 defeat. Neil Kinnock, and subsequent Labour leaders, have made a good deal of the truism that principles are of little use without the power to put them into effect, and for the trade unions in particular a Labour government legislating in its interests was becoming, by the mid-1980s, an ever-growing priority. The rise of a new generation of moderate trade union leaders such as Bill Jordan, Gavin Laird and John Edmonds, and the virtual eclipse of union left-wingers such as Arthur Scargill, undoubtedly helped Kinnock's cause, as did the emergence of a new breed of talented Labour parliamentary moderates such as John Cunningham, Tony Blair, Gordon Brown and Robin Cook.

In retrospect, though, it is clear that the influence of the left had already begun to decline before the 1983 election, as witnessed by the failure of five left-wingers to secure re-election to the party's NEC in 1981.[43] Further, the left's growing influence within the extra-parliamentary party cannot entirely explain why Foot was elected as leader or why the party went into the 1983 election with a left-wing manifesto without, apparently, much objection from leading moderates. Shaw, for one, sees the adoption of the manifesto as a 'calculated move' by opponents in the parliamentary leadership. Thus, their view had become that 'If the party was going to capsize it might as well sink to the ocean bed with a red flag tied to its mast'.[44]

Whether or not this was the intention of some, Labour's defeat certainly had the desired effect. By the mid-1980s, the Bennites were isolated in the Commons as a realignment of the left saw the bulk of the old Tribune group of Labour MPs gravitating towards the Kinnock camp. In addition, Benn's demise as a champion of Labour activists in the country was assured when, in the autumn of 1988, he polled little over 10 per cent of the vote in his attempt to unseat Kinnock as leader (see chapter 6).

The politics of 'catch up'?

That Labour has been ideologically transformed since the 1983 defeat is irrefutable, but there has been some debate about the exact nature of this transformation. On the one side are those who suggest that Labour has reverted to the revisionist social democracy associated with Crosland and characteristic of post-war Labour governments.[45] On the other are those who hold that Labour has accommodated itself to, or caught up with, the political agenda associated with the Thatcher governments, 'in much the same way that the Conservative governments of the fifties accepted the parameters of the Attlee Settlement'.[46] The latter camp is occupied mainly by left-wing critics of Labour's ideological development. They recognise that for much of its history the party's ruling ideology has been a moderate, non-fundamentalist form of social democracy, but what they are claiming now is that the party has abandoned even this in its desperate urge to win back lost votes. 'New Labour', according to this view, has adopted, in Shaw's words, a 'post-revisionist' outlook.[47]

Assessing these diametrically opposed interpretations of Labour's ideological development is difficult. To a certain extent, of course, the answer given will depend upon the frame of reference adopted. The dichotomy between past and present is much reduced, for instance, if we compare the approach of 'New Labour' with the practice of past Labour administrations rather than past policy documents and conference decisions. Herbert Morrison's much-quoted aside that socialism 'is what Labour Governments do' has always had an element of truth in it, only now, as one front-bencher sarcastically remarked, socialism 'is what Mr Mandelson says it is'![48] A further point is that it may well be profitable to distinguish between Labour's ideological development under Kinnock's leadership and the, arguably, more right-wing drift that has taken place under Tony Blair.

By the 1987 election, the party's ideological transformation was only partly complete. Gone from the 1987 election manifesto were the left-wing demands for withdrawal from the European Community, abolition of the second chamber and a major extension of public ownership. Even the party's defence policy was weakened. Unilateral nuclear disarmament remained but Labour was committed to an increase in spending on conventional defence within the North Atlantic Treaty Organisation. The really significant transformation came after the party's third successive electoral set-back, when Kinnock's organisational and ideological hold on the party tightened.

Almost immediately, the party undertook a major examination of its policies. Seven policy groups were set up with a brief to consult widely (itself an illustration of Labour's greater willingness to compromise principles in order to win votes) before drawing up a report to be discussed by the NEC and the conference. This two-year policy review culminated in the publication, in May 1989, of a 70,000-word document *Meet the Challenge, Make the Change*.[49] This report was primarily a set of policies rather than a restatement of basic principles but, together with a revised, slimmer 'son of the policy review', called *Looking to the Future* published in May 1990, and a document called *Aims and Values* (written primarily by Kinnock and Hattersley and the first official statement of socialist values since clause 4 was incorporated into Labour's constitution in 1918), it provided the best guide available to the future course a Labour government was likely to take and, indeed, it formed the basis of Labour's 1992 election manifesto.

As a result of the policy review process and the subsequent ideological development of the party under Smith and Blair, there is no doubt that Labour has accommodated a significant portion of the Thatcher agenda. In particular, there has been, for the first time in the party's history, an official and explicit acceptance of the market as a mechanism which provides a 'generally satisfactory' method for allocating most goods and services.[50] As a corollary, the Conservative trade union reforms, designed to prevent union muscle from distorting the market, were largely accepted.

Public ownership, too, has gradually been abandoned. In the policy review, state ownership was replaced by a vague commitment to 'social ownership'. Gone were the 'shopping lists' of nationalisation intentions prevalent in Labour documents during the 1970s and early 1980s. Indeed, even the public utilities privatised by the Conservatives were to be returned to public ownership only if 'circumstances' allowed.[51] In *Looking to the Future*, references to social ownership were dropped completely and only the water industry was to be taken back into public ownership, and in the 1992 manifesto public ownership was diluted to public control. As Eric Shaw remarks, 'for the first time in its history, Labour ceased [in 1992] to regard any modification to property relationships as a significant object of political endeavour'.[52]

This shift away from state ownership gathered pace after Blair's accession to the leadership. In policy terms, this is confirmed by Labour's 1997 manifesto, in which reference to the public control of the water industry is replaced by a commitment to 'pursue tough, efficient regulation' of the utilities which is 'fair both to consumers and to shareholders'.[53] In symbolic terms, Blair was able to achieve what Gaitskell had been unable to and reform clause 4 of the party's constitution. Replacing the commitment to the 'common ownership of the means of production' is a passage, agreed (by 65.2 per cent to 34.8 per cent) at a special party conference on 29 April 1995, which pledges the party:

> to work for a dynamic economy, serving the public interest, in which the enterprise of the market and the rigour of competition are joined with the forces of partnership and co-operation ... with a thriving private sector and high quality public services.[54]

It is true, of course, that governments can intervene in the workings of the economy to significant effect without actually taking on the burden of ownership. In the late 1980s, a debate ensued within the party between advocates of the 'enabling' state on the one hand and advocates of the 'developmental' state on the other.[55] The former, including Kinnock and much of the party leadership, saw a limited role for the state, which would merely facilitate the market to work more effectively by intervening, for instance, to ensure an adequately trained workforce. The latter, including most notably Bryan Gould, who, until 1989, was the party's shadow Industry Secretary, were much more critical of the market's ability to ensure long-term stability, protect the environment and provide a decent standard of living for those at the bottom of the economic pile. As a consequence of the market's limitations, the developmentalists advocated major state intervention to regulate the City and provide industrial investment, a project which, Gould thought, was incompatible with European Monetary Union.[56]

As in most other areas of policy, Kinnock got his way. Gould was replaced as shadow Industry Secretary by Gordon Brown and, becoming increasingly disillusioned with Labour's direction, left active politics to take up an academic post in New Zealand, although not before challenging John Smith for the leadership after Kinnock's resignation in 1992. Apart from a brief flirtation in the 1960s, Labour has never advocated the major state intervention recommended by the developmentalists and the latest failure, therefore, cannot be regarded as an abandonment of a previous objective. More significant here is Labour's rejection of Keynesian demand management in favour of a 'supply side' socialism which aims to create a 'monetary framework which will provide long-term exchange rate and interest rate stability'.[57]

By accepting the new economic orthodoxy, as Gordon Brown as Chancellor has clearly done, Labour has abandoned one of the key tenets of the post-war settlement – that it is government's role to ensure full employment. As a result, committed to low taxation and a cautious attitude to public spending, it might be argued that Labour has also abandoned any idea of trying to create a more equal society. At the very least, the radical egalitarianism of Croslandite revisionism has been diluted. Labour's shift under Blair was starkly revealed when even Roy Hattersley, not previously regarded as someone on the left of the party, declared that he was no longer loyal to Labour because its programme 'confirm[s] that the hope of equality has been abandoned'.[58]

A return to revisionism?

In response to the arguments above, which suggest that Labour has rejected what had previously been central to its ideological character, a number of points can be made. We can exaggerate the radicalism of Labour's past theory and practice. All Labour governments in practice, for instance, have accepted the pivotal role played by a competitive market and such an acceptance is entirely consistent with Crosland's revisionist social democracy, the central theme of which was the irrelevance of further public ownership.[59] Moreover, Keynesianism was abandoned not just by the present leadership but by the Labour governments led by Wilson and Callaghan in the 1970s.

Arguably a more important reference point is the extent to which there is still an element of collectivism in Labour's ideological baggage which can be distinguished from the individualism characteristic of Thatcherism. During Kinnock's period as leader, this was certainly the case. In the various policy documents produced, state intervention was justified on the grounds that the market 'restricts individual choice to individual resources', thereby denying vital provisions to many.[60] This emphasis on 'real' choice was the means by which socialism was to be reconciled with individual liberty. Thus, in the *Aims and Values* document (itself echoing the major theme in Roy Hattersley's book *Choose Freedom*) it was argued that individual liberty can be maximised only through the redistribution of power and wealth, since 'unless we have the power to choose, the right to choose has no value'.[61] Thatcherism was to be condemned, then, not for its espousal of individual choice, but for its failure to use the state to make that choice a reality for many people.

It might be argued, of course, that the revised policies deriving from the policy review would not, in practice, produce the desired objective of making choice a reality for many people. Nevertheless, Labour, at least under Kinnock, did see an active role for the state. The 1992 manifesto, for instance, advocated moderate tax increases, specific welfare commitments, and additional resources for education and the National Health Service.[62] As Martin Smith remarks, then:

> Labour's continued belief in a regulated market economy as a mechanism for increasing equality and social justice is more distinct from Thatcherite Conservatism than Harold Wilson's social democracy was from Edward Heath's Conservatism.[63]

Kinnock was originally a left-wing radical and, although he shifted to the right as leader, he was always more steeped in the ideological and organisational traditions of the Labour party than Blair. Under the latter's leadership, however, it might be suggested that Labour's commitment to collectivism is more questionable. It is certainly true that Blair's completion of the party's modernisation has been based on the belief, confirmed for many by Labour's experience in the 1992 election, that the old collectivist image is irrelevant to a new individualistic age. On the other hand, Blair was strongly influenced by the communitarian ideas of the Scottish philosopher John MacMurray and his individualism is tinged with themes which have an echo in an ethical socialist tradition dating back to the nineteenth century. Like many Labour socialists before him, therefore, Blair has decried the fragmented and acquisitive society created, at least partly, by Thatcherite individualism, and seeks to replace it with a greater sense of community, since only in a cohesive society can individuals flourish. This emphasis on community is recorded in the first part of the new clause 4, written principally by Blair, which states that the Labour party:

> believes that by the strength of our common endeavour we achieve more than we achieve alone, so as to create for each of us the means to realise our true potential and for all of us a community in which power, wealth and opportunity are in the hands of the many not the few, where the rights we enjoy reflect the duties we owe, and where we live together, freely, in a spirit of solidarity, tolerance and respect.[64]

This emphasis on community, belonging and social cohesion provides the skeletal outline for what might be regarded as a post-statist form of socialism. It provides the intellectual baggage, for instance, for Blair's – apparently brief – flirtation with the idea of a 'stakeholder' society. The unifying idea here is the idea of inclusion, the individual as a member or citizen of society, rather than as a subject. Applied to the workplace, it involves treating employees as partners through, for instance, the ownership of shares and participation in decision making, rather than as mere factors of production.[65] Likewise, New Labour's substantial interest in maintaining standards in public life and in altering the way British people are governed is predicated on the need to foster greater social cohesion through encouraging participation in a political system which is more accountable to the people it is meant to serve.

However commendable, this ethical dimension to Blair's political approach is not, by itself, necessarily consistent with any meaningful definition of socialism. Traditional ethical socialists, such as R. H. Tawney, for instance, stressed, unlike Blair, the incompatibility between 'the ideals of community, solidarity, mutual obligation and social responsibility, on the one hand, and the acquisitive and materialistic values of the market, on the other',[66] and this is precisely why they, unlike Blair, rejected the market in favour of public control of the economy.

Conclusion

What is surprising in an examination of the theory and practice of socialism in the Labour party is not the variety, but the similarity of the ideas which have informed Labour's practice. Thus, the basic programme of the party written in 1918, and developed during the 1930s and early 1940s, was largely implemented between 1945 and 1951 and remained a central plank of both major parties in the twenty or so years of consensus that followed. For the left, which has very rarely come close to challenging this mainstream doctrine, this is a damning indictment of Labour's failure to transform fundamentally the capitalist system. For many others, it is a confirmation of Labour's central role in creating a more humane and civilised society.

In 1979, this consensus was abandoned, at least in part, by the Thatcher government and by a Labour party increasingly dominated by the left. After Labour's defeat in 1983, Neil Kinnock and his successors have moved the party back to the political mainstream. As we saw, there has been a debate about the extent to which they have abandoned Labour's traditional ideas and values in the process. There is no doubt that concessions have been made to the Thatcherite project, but at the heart of the policy review was a collectivism which was anathema to Thatcherism, although less so to the Major brand of Conservatism. The fact that the Conservatives felt they had to dispose of the services of

Thatcher, in the context of a large Labour lead in the opinion polls, suggests the enduring popularity of many themes in Labour's revised social democracy.

Debates over the exact nature of Labour's ideological character tend to disguise a perennial problem. This has been the party's inability to translate its values into effective public policy. For a while in the post-war period, it appeared the party had found an effective vehicle but the economic and political crises of the 1970s, coupled with profound social and economic change, have severely dented the moderate left's confidence. Blair's answer has been to reject much of Labour's public policy inheritance while claiming that the party's values – of social justice, equality and community – can be secured through the promotion of a dynamic market economy encouraged and cajoled by an enabling state which will continue to control those areas of life – education, health and so forth – where the market palpably fails. The extra resources provided for health and education and the introduction of measures to deal with youth unemployment in the new Labour government's first budget are signs of Labour's continual commitment to collectivist solutions. Given the one-off nature of the windfall tax, the determination to balance the books, and the reluctance to increase tax further, however, it is doubtful whether Labour has the necessary instruments to create a more cohesive society.

Notes

1   F. Bealey (ed.), *The Social and Political Thought of the British Labour Party* (London, Weidnenfeld and Nicolson, 1970), p. 1.

2   See G. D. H. Cole, *History of Socialist Thought*, five volumes (London, Macmillan, 1953–60); M. Beer, *History of British Socialism*, two volumes (London, Allen and Unwin, 1921); G. Foote, *Labour Party's Political Thought* (London, Croom Helm, 1985).

3   H. Pelling, *A Short History of the Labour Party*, 4th edn (London, Macmillan, 1972), pp. 9–10.

4   Bealey, *Social and Political Thought*, p. 6; Foote, *Labour Party's Political Thought*, pp. 1–6; S. Ingle, *The British Party System* (Oxford, Blackwell, 1987), pp. 136–7; R. McKibbin, *The Evolution of the Labour Party 1910–1924* (Oxford, Clarendon Press, 1974).

5   P. Gay, *The Dilemma of Democratic Socialism* (New York, Columbia University Press, 1962), p. 130.

6   Quoted in R. Terrill, *R. H. Tawney and his Times* (London, Andre Deutsch, 1973), p. 188.

7   See H. A. Clegg, *A History of British Trade Unions Since 1899, Volume II, 1911–33* (Oxford, Clarendon Press, 1985), pp. 370–3.

8   L. Minkin, *The Contentious Alliance* (Edinburgh, Edinburgh University Press, 1992), pp. 456–61. Note here too that it is incorrect to characterise labourism as having a moderating influence since it allowed for militant and bitter industrial action, if only for limited ends.

9   A. Henderson, *The Aims of Labour* (London, Labour Party, 1918), p. 22.

Henderson was later to hold senior positions in both inter-war Labour governments and he became leader for a brief period in 1931.

10   The ideological variety of trade unionism is admirably documented in Minkin, *Contentious Alliance*.

11   *Labour and the Nation* (London, Labour Party, 1927), p. 13.

12   See B. Barker, *Ramsay MacDonald's Political Writings* (London, Allen Lane, 1972).

13   *NEC Minutes*, 24 September 1924.

14   See R. Skidelsky, *Politicians and the Slump* (London, Macmillan, 1967).

15   See R. E. Dowse, *Left in the Centre* (London, Longman, 1966).

16   S. Cripps, *Can Socialism Come by Constitutional Means?* (London, New Statesman, 1933); R. H. Tawney, 'The Choice Before the Labour Party', *Political Quarterly*, July–September 1932.

17   G. D. H. Cole, *What is this Socialism?* (London, Clarion Press, 1933); H. Laski, *The State in Theory and Practice* (London, Allen and Unwin, 1935).

18   See R. Samuel, 'The Cult of Planning', *New Socialist*, January 1986, pp. 25–9.

19   See A. W. Wright, *G. D. H. Cole and Socialist Democracy* (Oxford, Clarendon Press, 1979).

20   See C. A. R. Crosland, 'The Transition from Capitalism', in R. H. S. Crossman (ed.), *New Fabian Essays* (London, Turnstile Press, 1953); C. A. R. Crosland, *The Future of Socialism* (London, Cape, 1956).

21   Quoted in A. W. Wright (ed.), *British Socialism* (London, Longman, 1983), p. 19.

22   Crosland, *Future of Socialism*, p. 35.

23   See S. Haseler, *The Gaitskellites* (London, Macmillan, 1969).

24   See M. Abrams, R. Rose and R. Hinden, *Must Labour Lose?* (London, Penguin, 1960).

25   A. Ball, *British Political Parties* (Basingstoke, Macmillan, 1987), pp. 163–4.

26   Ball, *British Political Parties*, pp. 167–8.

27   See M. Foot, *Aneurin Bevan. Volume II, 1945–1960* (London, MacGibbon and Kee, 1973).

28   Foote, *Labour Party's Political Thought*, pp. 272–4.

29   Foote, *Labour Party's Political Thought*, pp. 274–7.

30   Ingle, *British Party System*, p. 110.

31   See M. Barratt Brown, *From Labourism to Socialism* (Nottingham, Spokesman Books, 1972); K. Coates and T. Topham, *The New Unionism* (London, Owen, 1972); S. Holland, *The Socialist Challenge* (London, Quartet, 1974). For an excellent summary of left ideas in this period see Foote, *Labour Party's Political Thought*, chs 13 and 14.

32   P. Seyd, *The Rise and Fall of the Labour Left* (Basingstoke, Macmillan, 1987), pp. 21–9; see also A. Gamble, *Britain in Decline* (London, St Martin's Press, 1990), pp. 157–79, for a summary of the alternative economic strategy. The most important statements of it are Holland, *Socialist Challenge*, and Cambridge Political Economy Group, *Britain's Economic Crisis* (Nottingham, Spokesman Books, 1975).

33   E. P. Thompson and Raymond Williams are the best-known figures. In 1960, a journal called *New Left Review* was created as an arena for New Left ideas.

34   See Wright, *G. D. H. Cole*, pp. 50–71.

35   Gamble, *Britain in Decline*, pp. 157–61, 174–9.

36   Quoted in P. Whitehead, *The Writing on the Wall* (London, Michael Joseph, 1985), p. 356.

37   Seyd, *Rise and Fall*, pp. 95–9.

38　See T. Benn, *Arguments for Socialism* (London, Cape, 1980); *Arguments for Democracy* (London, Cape, 1981); *Parliament, People and Power* (London, Cape, 1982).

39　D. Howell, *British Social Democracy* (London, Croom Helm, 1980), p. 291.

40　See J. Dearlove and P. Saunders, *Introduction to British Politics* (Cambridge, Polity, 1984), pp. 276–86.

41　Whitehead, *Writing on the Wall*, pp. 140–7.

42　Whitehead, *Writing on the Wall*, pp. 194–201.

43　A. Thorpe, *A History of the British Labour Party* (Basingstoke, Macmillan, 1997), p. 209.

44　E. Shaw, *The Labour Party Since 1945* (Oxford, Blackwell, 1996), p. 167.

45　See M. J. Smith, 'The Labour Party in Opposition', in M. Smith and J. Spear (eds), *The Changing Labour Party* (London, Routledge, 1992); M. J. Smith, 'Understanding the "Politics of Catch-Up": The Modernization of the Labour Party', *Political Studies*, December 1994; C. Hughes and P. Wintour, *Labour Rebuilt: The New Model Party* (London, Fourth Estate, 1990); P. Seyd, 'Labour: The Great Transformation', in A. King (ed.), *Britain at the Polls 1992* (New Jersey, Chatham House, 1993), pp. 70–3; D. Butler and D. Kavanagh, 'Labour: Seeking Electability', in *The British General Election of 1992* (London, Macmillan, 1992), pp. 43–66; D. Marquand, *The Progressive Dilemma: From Lloyd George to Kinnock* (London, Heinemann, 1991).

46　C. Hay, 'Labour's Thatcherite Revisionism: Playing the "Politics of Catch Up"', *Political Studies*, December 1994. See also G. Elliot, *Labour and the English Genius: The Strange Death of Labour England?* (London, Verso, 1993); R. Heffernan and M. Marqusee, *Defeat from the Jaws of Victory* (London, Verso, 1992); P. Jenkins, *The Thatcher Revolution: The Post-Socialist Era* (London, Pan, 1988).

47　Shaw, *The Labour Party Since 1979: Crisis and Transformation* (London, Routledge, 1994), p. x.

48　Quoted in K. Jefferys, *The Labour Party Since 1945* (Basingstoke, Macmillan, 1993), p. 128.

49　See R. Garner, 'Modernisation and the Policy Review: The Labour Party since the 1987 Election', *Talking Politics*, summer 1989, pp. 101–4.

50　*Labour Party News*, June 1988, pp. 24–5.

51　*Meet the Challenge, Make the Change* (London, Labour Party, 1989), p. 15.

52　Shaw, *Labour Party Since 1979*, pp. 87–8.

53　*New Labour Because Britain Deserves Better* (Labour party manifesto) (London, 1997), pp. 15–16.

54　Quoted in Shaw, *Labour Party Since 1945*, p. 199. See also T. Jones, *Remaking the Labour Party: From Gaitskell to Blair* (London, Routledge, 1996), pp. 139–48.

55　See Shaw, *Labour Party Since 1979*, pp. 89–94.

56　Academic support for a developmental state is provided, most notably, by D. Marquand, *The Unprincipled Society: New Demands and Old Politics* (London, Fontana, 1988).

57　*Looking to the Future* (London, Labour party, 1990), p. 7.

58　R. Hattersley, 'Why I'm No Longer Loyal to Labour', *Guardian*, 26 July 1997.

59　Smith, 'Modernization of the Labour Party', p. 709.

60　*Meet the Challenge, Make the Change*, p. 41.

61　*Labour Party News*, June 1988, p. 25; R. Hattersley, *Choose Freedom: The Future for Democratic Socialism* (London, Penguin, 1987).

62　See B. Coxall and L. Robins, *Contemporary British Politics*, 2nd edn (Basingstoke, Macmillan, 1994), pp. 234–6.

63 Smith, 'Modernization of the Labour Party', p. 710.
64 Quoted in Jones, *Remaking the Labour Party*, p. 144. See also, T. Blair, *Socialism* (London, Fabian Society, 1994).
65 See W. Hutton, 'Stake that Claim', *Guardian*, 9 January 1996.
66 Jones, *Remaking the Labour Party*, p. 138.

6

The Labour party:
organisation, membership and authority

This chapter has two main functions. The first is to describe the various elements that together make up the modern Labour party. The second is to consider the relationship between these elements in order to examine the distribution of power in the party. Both these tasks have become more difficult in recent years. Since 1979, organisational reform has been a continual theme in Labour party politics, inextricably linked with ideological conflict and the party's poor electoral performance up to 1997. Between 1979 and 1981, in a climate of internal turmoil, the left secured reforms which altered the balance of power in the party towards the left-inclined extra-parliamentary elements. Since the 1983 election defeat, further reforms – this time initiated from the top down by an increasingly centralised authority structure under the control of the leader – were designed to move Labour back to the ideological mainstream and make the party electable. As a result, Labour's organisational structure looks very different now from when the party left office in 1979.

A unique organisation

Labour is unique among the major British parties, since it is the only one that originated outside parliament. Both the Conservatives and the Liberals originated as groupings within parliament, grafting on extra-parliamentary organisations when, from 1867, it was increasingly necessary to attract the votes of the newly enfranchised. The Labour party, on the other hand, was created owing to pressure from below. In particular, it was created in order to secure representation in parliament for the trade unions. Before this, trade unions had relied mainly upon the Liberal party to put forward legislation in their interests. Indeed, trade union officials were often chosen as parliamentary candidates by local Liberal parties, which were well aware of the growing need to appeal to working-class voters. For a variety of reasons (not least the fact that the Conservatives had dominated electoral politics since the mid-1880s), as the nineteenth century drew to a close, this arrangement was no longer regarded as satisfactory by many unions.[1] In 1900, because of the growing demand for independent labour representation, a number of unions – together with a small number of socialist societies – formed the Labour Representation Committee, which, after winning twenty-nine seats in the 1906 election, was renamed the Labour party.

The role of the trade unions is the key to understanding the nature of the party. Before 1918, Labour existed as a parliamentary mouthpiece for the unions and, since it was possible to join only through one of its affiliated unions (or socialist societies), the party was a loose confederation of autonomous organisations. The new constitution drawn up in 1918 created a system of party branches and direct party membership under the control of the NEC, but this structure co-existed with, rather than replaced, the affiliated trade unions, and some local Labour parties remained little more than trade union branches.[2] In reality, the massive financial contribution of the unions has always ensured that they have maintained a privileged position within the party, although, as we shall see, less so now than in the past.

Constituency Labour parties

Most parliamentary constituencies in Britain have a CLP. As with the Conservatives, to become an individual member of the Labour party it is necessary to become a member of one of the local parties. Since January 1989, as part of the campaign to increase Labour's membership, it has been possible to join the party nationally. The party's headquarters (which now keeps a computer record of members) provide applicants with provisional membership which becomes permanent if the relevant local party raises no objections within eight weeks.[3] Each CLP contains a number of ward parties, which elect delegates to the ruling body of the CLP – the general committee – which, in turn, elects an executive committee to deal with the day-to-day running of the party.

In common with other parties, Labour has experienced a decline in membership during the last thirty years or so. The extent of this decline is difficult to gauge because over the years different methods have been used to calculate the numbers. Before the new national computerised system, the figures were based upon the affiliation fees paid by each CLP, but these did not provide an accurate measure because each party has to affiliate a minimum number of members. Between 1963 and 1980, this figure was 1,000, giving a minimum number of around 600,000 members in total. Many parties, however, did not have anywhere near the minimum figure of 1,000.[4] From 1980, the minimum affiliation fell to 200, so it was possible to provide a more realistic guide. Thus, in April 1988, the membership was calculated at 288,829, a fall of 8,500 (2.9 per cent) on the previous year, and a further fall to around 265,000 was recorded between 1988 and 1989.[5] The membership drive begun in 1989 was initially a flop, with membership falling to 256,000 in 1993, but the numbers increased, no doubt partly as a result of Blair's accession to the leadership and the probability of a Labour government, to 310,400 in 1994 and 400,000 three years later.[6] Despite the increase, this was far from being the mass party that the party leadership in general, and Blair in particular, has advocated.

In addition to individual members, each CLP replicates the party's national structure by having an additional type of membership, of those belonging to various autonomous organisations which affiliate to the local party. These could be socialist societies like the local branch of the Fabians or the Co-operative Society, but the affiliated membership at the local level is dominated by members of union branches situated within the boundaries covered by the CLP. Branches are entitled to send delegates to the general committee and, depending upon the particular area, can dominate the proceedings, not least because union affiliation brings badly needed cash into the local party coffers.

The evidence suggests that the decline in individual membership is due, in large part, to the decline of working-class participation in Labour party politics – itself a product of social changes which have reduced the number of manual workers and fragmented working-class communities (see chapter 10). As a consequence, the public sector middle class – those such as teachers, lecturers, health service and local government employees (what Peter Jenkins referred to as the 'lumpenpolytechnics') – now play a much more important role in the activist strand of CLPs.[7] This was confirmed by the largest ever survey of Labour's membership, undertaken by Patrick Seyd and Paul Whiteley in 1990, which revealed that only 22 per cent of the party's individual membership is working class while 56 per cent of party members are in the 'salariat' (teachers, lecturers, social workers, etc.).[8] Two consequences follow from all of this. First, the membership decline in the late 1960s left some inner-city CLPs (those in Liverpool being the most notable examples) moribund and ripe for take-over by committed hard-left activists associated with revolutionary organisations such as the Militant Tendency.[9] Secondly, as Eric Shaw points out, middle-class activists joining in the 1970s 'tended to be radical in outlook and imbued with a participatory ethos' and thus less likely to be deferential to the party's leadership.[10]

The CLPs have a number of important functions. They are electoral machines concerned with trying to get Labour candidates elected to local councils and the Commons. This involves making sure that potential supporters are registered to vote, canvassing support during the campaign and making sure that previously identified supporters turn out on polling day. The importance of this function is often underestimated, the accepted wisdom being that the national – media-oriented – campaign is all that matters. Whiteley and Seyd have shown, however, that in the 1992 election there was a correlation between the number of Labour members and their level of local political activity, on the one hand, and the Labour vote, on the other. More specifically, the research reveals that Labour's grass roots had become 'de-energized' and the resulting decline in political activity decisively influenced the outcome in a number of key marginals, thereby preventing Labour from depriving the Conservatives of an overall majority.[11]

For the work that party activists put in, it is not unreasonable for them to expect some influence within the Labour party. According to John Prescott, however, the NEC's attempts to deny this influence in recent years (see below) offers a clear reason for Labour's inability to build a mass membership. There have been recent organisational changes designed to enhance the importance of CLP members. All individual, as opposed to affiliated, party members are now balloted to decide which candidates should be supported in the electoral college for the election of the leader and deputy leader, who should be the conference delegates from each CLP (although general committees still decide the stance the delegates take at conference) and (since 1991) which candidates should be supported in the elections for the constituency section of the NEC. In addition, recent changes to decrease the trade union vote at conference provide individual party members with more influence over national policy making (see below).

The most important power in the hands of CLPs is the selection and reselection of parliamentary candidates. This is a key function in the British political system, because – since most seats are 'safe' for one or other of the two major parties – the selection of a parliamentary candidate is, in effect, to choose the MP. It is not surprising, then, that a great deal of the internal organisational debates within the Labour party have focused on the role of CLPs in candidate selection and the extent to which they should have the autonomy to determine the nature of the PLP (see box 6.1, p. 130).

The CLPs, however, do not have a free hand in the selection of candidates. First, candidates must be nominated by an affiliated branch of the local party – a union, socialist society or ward branch – and the general committee must add to the short-list those with a quarter of the nominations. In addition, the short-list must contain at least five candidates (if five or more candidates applied) and, if a reselection contest, the sitting MP must be nominated. Furthermore, since 1988, it has been compulsory for at least one woman to be placed on a short-list and from 1993, in a more sustained attempt to increase female representation in the House of Commons, the party decided that all-women short-lists should be compulsory in half of the winnable seats without a sitting Labour MP. Many in the party were hostile to this proposal and Blair himself regarded its use as a one-off strategy, to be dropped after the election. The conflict this might have generated was prevented when, in 1996, after a case was brought by two male candidates precluded from standing for selection, an industrial tribunal ruled that such short-lists breached the 1975 Sex Discrimination Act and no further women-only short-lists were drawn up. By this time, however, no less than thirty-five female candidates had been selected under the procedure and this was a pivotal reason behind a record number of female Labour MPs (101) being elected in the 1997 election.[12]

In theory, the NEC, as the party's ruling body, has the power to intervene in the selection procedure. In practice, its willingness to do so has varied in different periods of the party's history. Under Kinnock's leadership, an interventionist approach was adopted. Thus, the NEC was willing to veto candidates chosen by CLPs, as it did in Lewisham and Nottingham East, before the 1987 election. In addition, after Labour's heavy defeat at the hands of SNP at the Govan by-election in 1988 and the selection of hard-left candidates (as at the Bermondsey and Greenwich by-elections in 1983 and 1987, respectively), the NEC decided to take more control over the selection of by-election candidates. Thus, it has become normal practice for the NEC to liaise with CLPs in drawing up short-lists in addition to imposing candidates when thought necessary, as in the case of Kate Hoey in Vauxhall (1989) and Sylvia Heal in Mid-Staffordshire (1990) – both of whom won impressive victories.[13] However, the imposition of a 'Blairite' candidate in the Uxbridge by-election in July 1997, which resulted in the discarding of the local candidate who had narrowly failed to win the seat for Labour at the 1997 general election, was seen by many as the major reason for Labour's failure to win the seat. As a result, it is possible the procedure may be amended.

In recent years there have been changes to the electorate entitled to vote in the final choice of candidate (see box 6.1) and this issue has provoked the most sustained conflict between the trade unions and the party modernisers. Before 1989, it was the delegates on the general committee who would make the final choice. Then, at the 1987 conference, it was decided to introduce – from January 1989 – an electoral college, whereby at least 60 per cent of the vote was allocated to individual members of the CLP and a maximum of 40 per cent to affiliated organisations. It quickly became apparent, however, that the electoral college was too cumbersome and the 1990 Labour conference voted to change the system for the next round of selections after the 1992 election.

Both Kinnock and – after 1992 – John Smith favoured the introduction of an OMOV system, but ending the union's influence in the selection of candidates was clearly a contentious move. As a result, initial attempts at reform were compromises which threatened to complicate the system even further. In 1991, for instance, the NEC decided upon a replacement (approved by that year's conference) which introduced OMOV for individual party

Box 6.1. Selecting Labour candidates: procedures since 1993

(1) NEC determines 'freeze date' by which time all members and affiliated bodies must be registered.[a] CLP executive committee determines precise selection timetable.

(2) Regional office distributes national approved list of candidates to all nominating bodies.[b]

(3) Nominations are made by nominating bodies.[c]

(4) CLP general committee constructs short-list on basis of nominations.[d]

(5) Selection meeting and OMOV ballot.[e]

(6) Successful candidate seeks NEC endorsement.

[a]No one whose membership began less than twelve months before the freeze date may participate in the ballot.
[b]Nominating bodies are all those entitled to send delegates to the general committee of the CLP – ward and branch parties, affiliated trade unions and socialist societies, plus the CLP executive committee; each is entitled to one nomination. The approved list is a merger of the old A, B, C and W lists, which embraced trade union, CLP, affiliated society and women's section candidates, respectively. According to Maureen O'Mara (spokesperson at Labour headquarters) the list is '273 pages long, laid out in a singularly unattractive way and seldom read carefully by CLP officials' (conversation with Kelly, 13 December 1995).
[c](i) There is no compulsion to nominate only candidates from the list – and most nominees are not on it – but inclusion does show that a candidate has been vetted by the NEC and reduces the chance of friction between local and national organisers in the final stage of proceedings (see point 6, above).
(ii) Nominees must have been members of the party for at least two years and must undertake to accept the standing orders of the parliamentary party.
[d](i) Until 1993, short-listing was done by the executive committee. As its membership is only twenty to twenty-five, compared with the general committee's forty to a hundred, this could be seen as another example of 'democratising' the selection process.
(ii) If the CLP is represented by a Labour MP, he or she must be included on the short-list. If the MP is nominated by two-thirds of nominating bodies, he or she shall be automatically reselected; provided he or she has at least one nomination, the CLP may vote for automatic reselection anyhow.
(iii) Any candidate receiving 25 per cent of nominations (including at least one from a ward or branch party) is automatically short-listed, as is anyone with 50 per cent of nominations from affiliated organisations.
(iv) Where no Labour MP is in contention, at least four candidates must be short-listed.
(v) Those general committees not subject to the all-women ruling must include at least one nominated woman on their short-lists.
[e](i) Entitled to attend are full CLP members of seventy-two months' standing (membership fee 1993: £18) and members of affiliated unions subscribing to the 'levy plus' scheme (membership fee 1993: £3). Postal votes will have been made available by the executive committee at the start of the selection process.
(ii) According to the *Rule Book*, voting is done on a 'single transferable vote' basis, but this is a mistaken description – the system actually employed is that of 'alternative vote'.

Source: *Labour Party Proposed Consolidated Rule Book, 1995*, pp. 19–25.

members but, in addition, proposed that a ballot of individual members should be held before each contest to decide whether affiliated unions should continue to have a vote. If answered in the affirmative, each union member who paid the political levy (see below) would have been entitled to a vote, but this vote should count for only one-third of a full party member's vote.[14]

After the 1992 election, the NEC – under pressure from trade unions – agreed to refer the whole issue to the review committee which was set up to consider, as a whole, Labour's links with the unions. By this time, prospects for the introduction of OMOV had increased as Labour's fourth successive election defeat gave added weight to the party modernisers' claim that Labour should further extricate its electorally unpopular link with the unions. In the event, OMOV was narrowly approved by the 1993 conference (by 47.5 per cent to 44.5 per cent) but only after Smith turned the issue into a confidence vote on his leadership and Prescott had pleaded with the unions to support it. In order to provide some consolation to the unions, a so-called 'levy plus' system was introduced whereby affiliated trade unionists, who already paid the political levy to the party, were encouraged to become full members of their CLPs at a cut-price rate of £3.[15]

In recent years, the issue of the reselection of sitting Labour MPs has been an equally contentious issue. In 1980, a system of 'mandatory reselection' was introduced. Here, those CLPs which had a sitting MP were obliged to initiate a reselection contest at least once during the lifetime of a parliament and, even if no challenger to the incumbent emerged, an affirmative vote was still necessary. This came about partly as a result of the left's campaign to make getting rid of a sitting MP less cumbersome and to end the reliance on the NEC's permission, which was previously required in every case. This is not to say that the deselection of Labour MPs did not take place before the 1980s. On the contrary, conflict between CLPs and right-wing Labour MPs was endemic in the 1970s, with MPs such as Eddie Griffiths (in Sheffield Brightside), Frank Tomney (in Hammersmith North), Dick Taverne (in Lincoln) and Reg Prentice (in Newham North East) all being deselected.[16]

Mandatory reselection was a key reform on the left's agenda in the 1970s and its effect, although not as dramatic as many had feared (or hoped), was significant in moving the PLP to the left (see below). It was hardly surprising, therefore, that under Kinnock's leadership the 'mandatory' principle was effectively abandoned. It was agreed at the 1990 conference that in future a reselection contest would take place only if a ballot of CLP members supported it. Ironically, it is now more difficult to remove a sitting Labour MP than it was before mandatory reselection was introduced, when the power rested with CLP general committees, subject to NEC approval.[17]

The annual conference, the block vote and the trade unions

Labour's conference has traditionally been held annually for a period of five days in the autumn. The conference is where delegates from all sections of the party come together to discuss organisational and policy matters. The key feature is its voting system which, until recently, gave the trade unions a massive predominance. In return, the unions have provided the vast majority of Labour's finances (see chapter 9). Traditionally, votes at conference have been allocated in proportion to the number of members each union affiliated to the party. All members of a union affiliated to the Labour party, unless they 'contract out', pay a political levy and thereby become affiliated members of the party. The number of such members has declined in recent years, from about six million in 1980 to about four million in 1994, but affiliated members still massively outnumber individual members. Of course, this does not mean that affiliated members are Labour activists, or even Labour voters for that matter. In addition, unions do not have to claim their full entitlement of votes and many have failed to do so primarily in order to save money.[18]

Conservative governments have, on two occasions, sought to weaken this link between the unions and the Labour party. In 1927, the Trade Disputes Act replaced 'contracting out' with 'contracting in' and the dramatic fall in Labour's affiliated membership that resulted demonstrated that paying the political levy was not, for many trade union members, a sign of their political commitment to the party. In 1984, the Thatcher government's Trade Union Act stipulated that all trade unions had to ballot their members every ten years in order to confirm a commitment to retaining a political fund. The unions mounted a hugely successful campaign for a 'yes' vote and every union voted by a large majority to retain such a fund.

Party modernisers have argued, with the backing of opinion poll evidence, that trade union influence at conference, and within the party generally, is an electoral liability. Part of the problem has been the highly visible union dominance over the conference. Traditionally, the unions controlled about 90 per cent of the votes. In 1989, for instance, the four biggest unions (Transport and General Workers' Union (TGWU) – 1.25 million block votes; General, Municipal and Boilermakers' Union – 725,000; Amalgamated Union of Engineering Workers (AUEW) – 700,000; National Union of Public Employees (NUPE) – 600,000) accounted for about half the total conference vote and each had more votes than all the CLPs put together. Equally contentious has been the convention that each affiliated organisation, including the CLPs, casts its vote in a block. Under this procedure, no account is taken of minority opinions. If a union executive, for instance, decided by 51 per cent to 49 per cent to vote for a particular motion then all the union's vote was used to back that motion at conference.

The shock of the 1992 election defeat reinforced the case of those seeking to reform the party–union ties. As a result, the NEC appointed a fifteen-strong committee of inquiry (the Trade Union Links Review Group) to address the question. Its interim report, published early in 1993, defended the union's role within the party, while recognising the need for reform. As Lewis Minkin – the chair of the committee and the foremost academic authority on the subject – has pointed out, the trade union link remains vital to the party financially (particularly in the absence of a mass membership and state funding for parties) and also enables Labour to give political expression to the demands of a large section of the workforce. Any denial of this function would, Minkin argues, tear away Labour's roots and deprive it of any real purpose. The fate of the SDP is an apposite reminder to those who would advocate a complete break.[19]

Following the report, a number of reforms were approved at the 1993 conference. First, the decision (originally taken in 1990) to introduce an electoral college system of voting at conference was confirmed. This has the effect of reducing the union (and socialist society) share of the vote to 70 per cent and increasing the CLP share from about 10 per cent to 30 per cent. The original plan was that for every 30,000 increase in the party's individual (or non-affiliated) membership the proportion of the vote going to the CLPs would rise by 1 per cent. Under this plan, the future role of the trade unions at conference would depend upon Labour's ability to attract new members. A doubling of individual membership, for instance, would cut the block vote to 50 per cent.[20] The party's membership by 1995 had increased but certainly not doubled. Despite this, the modernisers' dominant position enabled them to persuade the 1995 conference to reduce the union vote share to 50 per cent anyway.[21]

Secondly, in order to avoid the ridicule that often accompanied the practice of announcing conference decisions in terms of the number of votes cast (usually in the millions), conference votes are now expressed in percentage terms. More importantly, block voting was repealed, with delegations encouraged either to split their vote to reflect the opinions of their levy payers or to allow delegates to vote as individuals. So, for example, the fifty delegates from Unison, now the largest affiliated union, represent 680,000 affiliated members and each delegate casts a vote worth 0.233 per cent of the conference vote.[22]

Of course, there is a difference between encouraging unions to dispense with the block vote and compelling them to do so. Furthermore, the reforms introduced do not take the party much further towards the operation of OMOV at conference and it is highly probable that there would be significant union opposition to such a move. As a result, the modernisers have focused on organisational reforms which will have the effect of devaluing conference as a major player in Labour policy making (discussed below).

The NEC and the party bureaucracy

The NEC is elected by, and is – in theory – the servant of, the annual conference, looking after the affairs of the party and reporting to conference each year. At the time of writing (1997), the NEC consists of twenty-nine members. The leader and deputy are ex-officio members. In addition, there are twelve members elected by trade unions, seven elected by constituency parties, and one place each for the socialist societies and, since 1973, the Young Socialists. Finally, five places are reserved for women, who are elected by the whole conference, as is the party treasurer. The 1990 conference approved a proposal to consider ways in which the proportion of women on the NEC could be increased (to around 40 per cent) and by 1994 this had, at least partly, been acted upon by the decision to reserve two of the seats on the constituency section for women. In the past, because the unions had the vast majority of the votes at conference, they could control eighteen of the seats. Even now, although their influence has been reduced (to 50 per cent of the vote at conference), they have a considerable role in determining the NEC's composition.

The NEC has traditionally been seen as a major source of party policy and an important counterweight to the power of the parliamentary leadership. Trade unions and CLPs do put forward motions to the conference, but the debates have traditionally been structured around NEC proposals, many of which have been developed in NEC committees, most importantly the Home Policy and International Committees. In addition, the NEC, in conjunction with the parliamentary leadership, is responsible for drawing up the party's election manifestos.

Since 1983, however, the policy-making role of the NEC has declined. Kinnock set up a small number of NEC–shadow cabinet joint committees whose activities were co-ordinated by the Policy Co-ordinating Committee, consisting of senior representatives from the shadow cabinet and the NEC. The parliamentarians tended to dominate these committees and thus, for the first time, the Labour front bench was given a constitutional role in the making of policy.[23] The NEC's policy-making authority was further diminished by the policy review process undertaken after the 1987 election, in which policy was developed in specially created policy groups independent of the NEC.

Since the late 1980s, the party has discussed overhauling its policy-making machinery in a way which would devalue the role of both the conference and the NEC. This process began when the 1990 conference approved the creation of the National Policy Forum.[24] The Policy Forum, consisting of 194 members (reduced to about 100 in 1992) elected from all sections of the party, did not meet until 1993 and has not so far had much of an impact on policy making. In the early part of 1997, however, a document outlining further reform, written by the party's general secretary,

Tom Sawyer, was approved by the NEC and, after widespread consultation within the party, was accepted by the conference in the autumn of 1997.

The reform document, called *Party Into Power*, advocates rooting policy making in the Policy Forum and a new Joint Policy Committee chaired by the party leader with members drawn equally from the Labour front bench and the NEC. These reforms will substantially erode the policy-making role of both the NEC and the conference. Instead of discussing every item of policy at conference every year, policy making will operate according to a two-year rolling programme and only two out of the five days of the conference will be allocated to policy debates. Furthermore, instead of deriving from the NEC (which will have a changed composition, giving a greater role to ordinary party members and a lesser role to MPs), policy will emanate from the Joint Policy Committee and the National Policy Forum, both largely under the control of the parliamentary leadership.[25]

In addition to its policy-making role, the NEC has an equally important organisational role. The extent to which it has intervened in the affairs of local parties has, as we saw above, varied. Under Kinnock's direction after 1983, as well as vetoing candidates selected by local parties and imposing candidates on CLPs, the NEC mounted an ultimately effective strategy to rid Labour of the Militant Tendency which, during a more liberal NEC regime in the 1970s, had been allowed to take root in a number of CLPs. The major organisational change that occurred as a direct consequence of the Militant 'experience' was the decision (taken in 1986) to set up the National Constitutional Committee. This body – consisting of eleven members elected by various sections of the party – was set up because Militant was able to persuade the courts that natural justice was not being observed because the NEC was both judge and jury in the moves to expel them. As a result, these two functions were separated, with the new body now adjudicating on cases brought before it by the NEC.[26]

The party outside parliament is run from its south London headquarters in Walworth Road. Unlike the Conservative party – in which the professional bureaucracy is indirectly controlled by the party leader through the appointment of the party chair (see chapter 4) – the NEC, and not the parliamentary leader – at least in theory – supervises the party outside parliament. As a result of Labour's poorly organised election campaign in 1983, Neil Kinnock, after becoming leader, set about persuading the NEC to reorganise the party machine. Larry Whitty replaced Jim Mortimer as general secretary and Peter Mandelson was appointed by the NEC as the party's first Director of Campaigns and Communications (since becoming an MP in 1992, Mandelson has continued to play a hugely important organisational and campaigning role, although his formal position was taken by the television journalist John Underwood, who was succeeded in 1991 by Roy Hattersley's political aide David Hill). Since 1983, as a result, there has been a much greater emphasis on the presentation of the party. In 1986, Mandelson set up the Shadow Communications Agency – consisting of Labour-supporting advertising and marketing experts – which was to play a key role in transforming Labour's image.[27] A sign of the change was the jettisoning of the red flag (the symbol, for many, of hard-line socialism) in favour of the much more 'voter-friendly' red rose. The glossy presentation of the party in the 1987 and 1992 elections and the slick pre-election policy launches (in stark contrast to the early 1980s and indeed, arguably, at any time in Labour's history) demonstrated how far Labour had accepted the requirements of the modern television age.

Predictably, some in the party (not just on the left) were critical of what they dubbed as 'designer socialism', the triumph of style over substance and the tendency to follow, rather than lead, public opinion (a complaint which has some justification given Labour's failure to win in 1987 and 1992 but less so, of course, in 1997). The resignation of John Underwood in 1991 was itself a product of this dispute since, after replacing Mandelson, he wanted to move the presentation of the party from an image-based approach towards a more content-based approach but felt unable to counter the influence of those such as Mandelson and Colin Byrne (Underwood's deputy), who, along with the Shadow Communications Agency, had the ear of Kinnock.[28]

The parliamentary Labour party

The PLP consists of all those who accept the Labour whip in the House of Commons. When in opposition, unlike the Conservative party, Labour MPs elect annually a parliamentary committee, which, together with the deputy leader, the chair of the PLP, the chief whip and a number of peers, is moulded by the leader into the shadow cabinet. Each MP is entitled to as many votes as there are places available (usually between fifteen and twenty) and, as a result of a ruling in 1989, at least four of these votes must be cast for women (if four or more are standing for election). Once in government the leader, following a decision taken in 1980, has been obliged to appoint in the first cabinet those who held shadow cabinet posts, although the leader is not restricted in any later reshuffles. This is a half-way house between the leader's previous free hand as Prime Minister and the demands of those, such as Tony Benn, who have argued that Labour cabinet ministers should all be elected by the PLP.

Factions have traditionally been discouraged in the Labour party but in the 1960s and 1970s they began to proliferate, particularly outside parliament. Within the Commons, the Tribune Group is the oldest surviving faction. Created in 1966 and named after the left-wing journal founded in the 1930s, it was, until the early 1980s, the only home in parliament for left-wing Labour MPs. By the end of the 1970s its membership was eighty-six, 27 per cent of the PLP. It has always been a weak group both numerically and in terms of its organisation. It does not put forward a statement of aims and its members are not instructed to vote in particular ways in the chamber.[29]

After the acrimonious deputy leadership election in 1981 (when the failure of a number of Tribunites, including Kinnock, to vote for Benn led to his narrow defeat by Denis Healey) and the decision to purge the party of Militant, the parliamentary left split. Those supporting Benn and opposed to what they regarded as a 'witch-hunt' of 'good socialists', the so-called 'hard left', formed the Campaign Group in 1982 (which now has a membership of about forty-five) while the majority, who have come to be known as the 'soft left', remained in the Tribune Group. Most of the latter group have tended to support, not always wholeheartedly, the leadership. Up to 1992, there was a desire to 'protect' Kinnock from the clutches of the right of the PLP.[30] Since the election of Blair, loyalty to the leadership has been partly a product of the desire to present a united front to the party's opponents and partly a recognition, accurate as it turned out, that Blair would have government posts to reward loyal supporters. With Labour now back in power, it is possible that factionalism on the left could emerge again, particularly if the government runs into economic difficulties.

Right-wing Labour MPs have tended to be slower to organise and they have not been helped in recent years by the fact that a number of leading members of the Manifesto Group, founded in 1974, defected to the SDP in the early 1980s. Mention should also be made of the Solidarity Group, which was set up in 1981 by 150 Labour MPs who opposed the constitutional changes adopted by the party that year and subsequently backed Healey in the 1981 deputy leadership election.

By the end of the 1980s, the party had (with the exception, perhaps, of the 'hard left', who by then had been marginalised in any case) come to unite behind the leader in the elusive search for electoral success, and factionalism within the PLP had become far less pronounced.

In its early years, Labour's parliamentary party was genuinely working class. It is estimated that in the inter-war years about three-quarters of all Labour MPs were, before entering the Commons, employed in manual working-class occupations, in industries such as mining, textiles and the railways. This changed radically with the 1945 intake, when about half of Labour MPs were middle class. Since then, the proportion of middle-class Labour MPs has increased still further, so that by 1997 only 13 per cent of them could be described as working class (see table 6.1).[31]

To a certain extent, this shift reflected Britain's changing occupational structure and, in particular, the growth of non-manual jobs in the public sector and the expansion of higher education. Thus, a considerable proportion of Labour MPs (about 25 per cent in the 1997 intake) are

Table 6.1. *Occupation of Labour candidates, 1997*

	Elected	Defeated
Professions		
Barrister	12	7
Solicitor	17	11
Doctor/dentist/optician	3	2
Architect/surveyor	–	–
Civil/chartered engineer	3	2
Accountant	2	2
Civil service/local government	30	19
Armed services	–	–
Teachers:		
university	22	4
polytechnic/college	35	17
school	54	37
other	3	4
Scientific/research	7	2
Total	188	107
	(45%)	(48%)
Business		
Company director	7	3
Company executive	9	13
Commerce/insurance	2	9
Management/clerical	15	8
General business	4	7
Total	37	40
	(9%)	(18%)
Miscellaneous		
Miscellaneous white collar	69	29
Politician/political organiser	40	9
Publisher/journalist	29	10
Farmer	1	2
Housewife	–	–
Student	–	4
Total	139	54
	(33%)	(24%)
Manual workers		
Miner	12	–
Skilled	40	20
Unskilled/semi-skilled	2	–
Total	54	20
	(13%)	(9%)
Grand total	418	221

Source: D. Butler and D. Kavanagh, *The British General Election of 1997* (London, Macmillan, 1997).

Table 6.2. *Education of Labour candidates, 1997*

Type of education	Elected	Defeated
Elementary and secondary	2	–
Secondary	48	19
Secondary and polytechnic/college	86	54
Secondary and university	216	120
Public school	2	–
Public school and polytechnic/college	5	4
Public school and university	59	24
Total	418	221
Oxford	41	11
Cambridge	20	16
Other university	214	117
All universities	275	144
	(66%)	(65%)
Eton	2	–
Harrow	–	–
Winchester	1	–
Other public school	63	28
All public schools	66	28
	(16%)	(13%)

Source: D. Butler and D. Kavanagh, *The British General Election of 1997* (London, Macmillan, 1997).

teachers and lecturers (table 6.1). The PLP is now much more middle class than British society as a whole. In the 1997 intake, for instance, sixty-six Labour MPs (16 per cent) had been to public school compared with about 5 per cent of the British population. In 1997, similarly, 275 Labour MPs (66 per cent) had been to university, a much higher proportion than the population as a whole, and even more significantly, no less than sixty-one (15 per cent) had graduated from Oxford or Cambridge (table 6.2). Whether the unrepresentative nature of Labour MPs is a negative or positive feature of British politics is open to question.

Ethnic minorities and women are similarly under-represented in the PLP. After the 1997 election, there were four Asian and four black Labour MPs which, at 2 per cent of the total, is a significantly lower proportion than in British society. One inequality which has begun to be corrected is the gender imbalance among Labour MPs. Up to the end of the 1980s, no more than about 5 per cent of Labour MPs had been women. In 1992, however, women constituted 14 per cent of the successful Labour candidates and in 1997, mainly due to the imposition of all-women short-lists, a total of 101 female Labour MPs were elected, 24 per cent of the total. Despite this, there is still a considerable gender imbalance among Labour MPs and the discrepancy in the Commons as a whole is greater still.

Before 1980, the Labour leader (and deputy leader), as with the Conservative leader since 1965, was elected by MPs alone although, unlike the Conservative party, there was no formal procedure to challenge the leader when Prime Minister (see table 6.3). This changed when the 1980 conference agreed to a widening of the franchise and to end the anomaly preventing a challenge to a Labour Prime Minister. The procedure adopted in 1980 was then substantially altered again in 1993.

To force a challenge to a Labour leader in opposition or a Labour Prime Minister, it is necessary for the challenger to receive the support of 20 per cent of the PLP (increased from 5 per cent in 1988 after Benn's unpopular challenge to Kinnock). If the challenger is intent upon unseating a Labour Prime Minister an additional hurdle has to be overcome. In this situation, the contest must be approved by a two-thirds majority at the annual conference. After John Smith's election in 1992, there were complaints that the 20 per cent hurdle was too high and, in response, the 1993 conference agreed that when a vacancy occurs (as it did after John Smith's untimely death in 1994) the support of only 12.5 per cent of Labour MPs was required for nomination. The 20 per cent barrier, however, was retained for challenges to an incumbent.[32]

Once the contest is approved, the electoral college comes into play. At a special conference in Wembley in 1981, it was decided that the votes should be weighted so as to give 40 per cent to affiliated societies (the vast majority being trade unions) and 30 per cent each to CLPs and Labour MPs. If no candidate receives 50 per cent of the vote at the first attempt, a second ballot is held in which the second preferences to the bottom-placed candidate are redistributed. As table 6.4 shows, only one contest (when Healey beat Benn in the 1981 deputy leadership election) has necessitated a second ballot. By 1992, many were dissatisfied with the system which, it was argued, was too lengthy, gave too much influence to unions and not enough to rank-and-file members. As a result, proposals were made for reform which were accepted by the 1993 conference. Smith favoured the introduction of OMOV but, unlike the reform to the procedure for the selection of parliamentary candidates, union opposition prevented him from getting his way.[33] Instead, the reform represents a compromise, in some ways unsatisfactory.

As box 6.2 demonstrates, sectional voting was retained but the formula was altered to give each section an equal share of the votes. As a result, it remains possible for someone to cast more than one vote and the value of each vote is still unequal, with Labour MPs (and MEPs) exercising more influence than levy payers and individual members. The most important change was the scrapping of the block vote for affiliated organisations. Before 1993, some unions balloted their levy payers but even then their

Table 6.3. *Labour leadership contests, 1922–80 (PLP ballot)*

Year	Candidate	Votes in favour		
Leadership contests				
1922	R. MacDonald	61		
	J. R. Clynes	56		
1935	C. Attlee	(58)	88	
	H. Morrison	(44)	48	
	A. Greenwood	(33)		
1955	H. Gaitskell	157		
	A. Bevan	70		
	H. Morrison	40		
1960*	H. Gaitskell	166		
	H. Wilson	88		
1961*	H. Gaitskell	171		
	A. Greenwood	59		
1963	H. Wilson	(115)	144	
	G. Brown	(88)	103	
	J. Callaghan	(41)		
1976	J. Callaghan	(84)	(141)	176
	M. Foot	(90)	(133)	137
	R. Jenkins	(56)	–	–
	T. Benn	(37)	–	–
	D. Healey	(30)	(38)	–
	A. Crosland	(17)		
1980	M. Foot	(83)	139	
	D. Healey	(112)	129	
	J. Silkin	(38)	–	
	P. Shore	(32)	–	
Deputy leadership contests				
1952*	H. Morrison	194		
	A. Bevan	82		
1953*	H. Morrison	181		
	A. Bevan	76		
1956	J. Griffiths	141		
	A. Bevan	111		
1960	G. Brown	(118)	146	
	F. Lee	(73)	83	
	J. Callaghan	(55)	–	
1961*	G. Brown	169		
	B. Castle	56		
1962*	G. Brown	133		
	H. Wilson	103		
1970	R. Jenkins	133		
	M. Foot	67		
	F. Peart	48		
1971*	R. Jenkins	(140)	140	
	M. Foot	(96)	126	
	T. Benn	(46)		
1972	E. Short	(111)	145	
	M. Foot	(89)	116	
	A. Crosland	(61)	–	
1976	M. Foot	166		
	S. Williams	128		

*Denotes challenge to incumbent.
Parentheses denote inconclusive ballot.

Table 6.4. *Labour leadership contests, 1981–92 (electoral college) (%)*

	TU	CLP	PLP	Total
Leader				
1983				
N. Kinnock	29.04	27.45	14.77	71.27
R. Hattersley	10.87	0.57	7.83	19.28
E. Heffer	0.04	1.97	4.28	6.3
P. Shore	0.03	0.0	3.1	3.13
1988*				
N. Kinnock	38.96	24.36	24.9	88.64
T. Benn	1.04	5.64	5.1	11.78
1992				
J. Smith	38.51	29.31	23.16	91.02
B. Gould	1.48	0.69	6.82	8.98
Deputy leader				
1981*				
First ballot				
D. Healey	24.69	5.36	15.30	45.36
T. Benn	6.41	23.48	6.37	36.62
J. Silkin	8.09	1.15	7.95	18.00
Second ballot				
D. Healey	24.99	5.67	19.75	50.42
T. Benn	15.00	24.32	10.24	49.57
1983				
R. Hattersley	35.23	15.31	16.71	67.26
M. Meacher	4.73	14.35	8.80	27.88
D. Davies	0.0	0.24	3.28	3.52
G. Dunwoody	0.03	0.09	1.19	1.32
1988*				
R. Hattersley	29.2	13.8	22.8	66.8
J. Prescott	12.7	8.4	2.6	23.7
E. Heffer	0.07	7.2	2.3	9.5
1992				
M. Beckett	25.39	19.04	12.87	57.30
J. Prescott	11.63	7.10	9.41	28.13
B. Gould	2.98	3.87	7.72	14.57

*Denotes challenge to incumbent.
Electoral college gives trade unions (TU) 40 per cent, CLPs 30 per cent and the PLP 30 per cent.

entire vote was cast in a block for one candidate or another. Now, the choice of each levy payer is recorded in the final count. As a result, the 1994 leadership contest, the first to be conducted under the new procedure, involved four and a half million eligible voters and represented the largest ever ballot organised by a British political party.

Box 6.2. Electing a Labour leader: procedures since 1993

Candidates seek nomination from 12.5 per cent of PLP[a]

Electoral college[b]
PLP (271 MPs and 62 MEPs)
One-third of votes: each member's vote = 0.1 per cent of electoral college
CLPs (260,039 constituency members)
One-third of votes: each member's vote = 0.00013 per cent of electoral college
Levy payers (4.1 million members from thirty-eight affiliated unions and twelve socialist societies)
One-third of votes: each member's vote = 0.000008 per cent of electoral college[c]

Ballot papers dispatched, collected and counted by Electoral Reform Society and Unity Balloting Services

[a]When the electoral college was set up in 1981, a candidate needed only 5 per cent backing from fellow Labour MPs, raised to 20 per cent after Benn's unpopular challenge to Kinnock in 1988. Complaints that the 20 per cent figure precluded a desirable number of candidates in 1992 led to the 12.5 per cent figure being approved at the 1993 conference. A challenge to an incumbent, however, still needs 20 per cent PLP backing. If there is a challenge to a Labour Prime Minister, the contest must be agreed to in principle by a two-thirds majority at the annual conference.
[b]These figures refer to the contest in 1994. They will, of course, vary depending upon the size of the PLP and the party membership. Until 1993, the electoral college's composition had been 40 per cent trade unions and 30 per cent each for the PLP and CLPs. Block voting for CLPs was abolished in 1989 and for the unions in 1993. The 1994 contest was the first in which union and CLP votes were aggregated nationally – no weight was attached to the result within one union, CLP or affiliated society.
[c]Following their conferences to discuss the contest, only a minority of unions (e.g., TGWU) recommended support for a particular candidate.

Source: R. Kelly, 'Labour's Leadership Contest and Internal Organisation', *Politics Review*, February 1995, p. 9.

The new system has come in for some criticism. It is an extremely lengthy and costly procedure. Two unions (Union of Construction, Allied Trades and Technicians, and the National Union of Mineworkers (NUM)), unwilling to spend money on balloting their members, chose not to participate in the 1994 contest and the legitimacy of the process might be questioned in the event of other unions taking this option in a future

Table 6.5. *The 1994 Labour leader and deputy leader election*

	Blair	**Prescott**	**Beckett**
Leader			
PLP nominations	154	46	42
Electoral college			
PLP	60.5%	19.6%	19.9%
CLPs	58.2%	24.4%	17.4%
Levy payers	52.3%	28.4%	19.3%
Total	57.0%	24.1%	18.9%
Deputy leader			
PLP nominations	–	101	106
Electoral college			
PLP	–	53.7%	46.3%
CLPs	–	59.4%	40.6%
Levy payers	–	56.6%	43.4%
Total	–	56.5%	43.5%

Turnout:

PLP: 327 (98.2%).

CLPs: 172,356 (69.1%).

Levy-payers: 779,426 (19.5%) – many ballot papers from trade unionists were spoilt on account of failure to tick the box indicating support for the Labour party (8,000 in one of the communications unions).

Total number of eligible votes cast: 952,109 (21.8%).

election. The participation of levy payers is also problematic. In the first place, the turnout, as shown in table 6.5, was very low (under 20 per cent) compared to nearly 70 per cent for individual members. In addition, many levy payers play no part in Labour's affairs – some may not even vote for the party – and yet there is little to stop them from participating in the election. Finally, the procedure creates a dilemma for a deputy leader interested in challenging for the leadership, since the cost of running a separate deputy leadership election in the event of an incumbent successfully competing for the leadership is likely to deter party members from supporting the aspirant. Margaret Beckett's fate in 1994, when she failed to win either contest, will obviously act as a warning to future deputy leaders with their eyes on the top job.[34]

The distribution of power in the Labour party

We have now sketched out the bare bones of Labour's organisation. It seems appropriate at this juncture, particularly given the surfeit of organisational reforms in recent years, to consider the relationship between the different organs of the party. Locating where power lies in a complex, pluralistic structure like the Labour party is no easy task. The major debate has surrounded the relationship between the PLP leadership and the extra-parliamentary party. Clause 5 of Labour's 1918 constitution (reflecting the fact that the party originated as a mass movement outside parliament) states that 'the work of the party shall be under the direction and control of the party conference.' A contrary view was provided by Robert McKenzie's major study of political parties written in the 1950s. For McKenzie, power in the Labour party, as with the Conservatives, rested with the parliamentary leadership. 'No major Parliamentary party in the modern period,' he argued, 'has allowed itself to be relegated to the role of spokesman or servant of its mass organisation.'[35]

The validity of both of these two diametrically opposed positions can be questioned. The constitutional emphasis on the sovereignty of the extra-parliamentary party quite clearly overestimates its actual influence. The parliamentary leadership consists of full-time, experienced politicians permanently engaged in defining party policy on the national stage and reacting to day-to-day events. In such circumstances, and particularly when Labour is in government, it is impossible to refer every decision to conference or the NEC and, more often than not, these bodies can only pass retrospective judgements on the parliamentary leaders, who are, of course, skilled in the art of defending the decisions they have made through the media or to the party directly.

Labour leaders, in any case, have usually been able to 'manage' the party in such a way that it follows their broad preferences. In the past, the leadership has only had to secure the agreement of a small number of unions with large block votes to ensure victory at conference and ensure the election of a supportive NEC. This was graphically illustrated at the 1989 conference, when Kinnock was able to muster enough support from trade union delegations to secure the abandonment of unilateralism against the wishes of many CLPs and the delegation from the TGWU, led by Ron Todd. Such 'management' of conference votes is far from new. Indeed, throughout the period 1949–60, conference voted against the platform on only one occasion, as the triumvirate of moderate trade union leaders, Williamson (General and Municipal Workers' Union), Lawther (NUM) and Deakin (TGWU), delivered their block votes into the leader's hands time after time.[36] It should also be remembered that, as we commented in the last chapter, there are times when the unions desperately need a Labour government to legislate in their interests, and this gives the parliamentary leadership the opportunity to demand, in return, a large degree of independence to pursue their electoral strategy. In these circumstances, too, loyalty and discipline can be invoked (as it has been by recent Labour leaders), since any internal party conflict will hinder the achievement of success at the polls.

If conference or NEC decisions are made which are contrary to the wishes of the leadership there is the option of ignoring or diluting them. Labour leaders have traditionally denied they are the mere spokespeople of the party in the country. As early as 1907, for instance, Keir Hardie, Labour's first parliamentary leader, refused to take instructions from conference over the women's suffrage question.[37] Clement Attlee, too, despite writing in 1937 that the PLP must carry out the instructions of conference, reneged on this in 1945 when he refused to accept the NEC's claim that Labour would not be bound by foreign policy commitments he had made while deputy leader of the wartime coalition government.[38] Hugh Gaitskell, similarly, reacted to the conversion of the 1960 conference to unilateral nuclear disarmament by remarking: 'What sort of people do you think we [the PLP] are? Do you think we can simply accept a decision of this kind?'[39]

It was during the period of Harold Wilson's leadership, however, that the rejection of conference decisions became a regular occurrence. As Lewis Minkin points out: 'Rarely in modern times can a parliamentary leadership have appeared so impervious to the policy preferences of its extra-parliamentary supporters.'[40] There are numerous examples. In 1968, for instance, the government ignored a conference vote of five to one against its prices and incomes policy; in 1975, the government supported Britain remaining in the European Economic Community despite conference's opposition (a referendum was held on the issue because the cabinet was split, but official government policy was in favour of staying in); in 1978, the conference voted against the government's economic strategy by 3.6 million to 2.8 million.[41] Wilson, of course, was not chosen by the electoral college system, the aim of which was to make a future Labour Prime Minister more accountable to the party outside parliament. But, ironically, it can be argued that in some ways the electoral college system actually makes Labour leaders more secure. In the first place, leaders chosen by this system have greater authority, since they are elected by all sections of the party and not just MPs. Furthermore, as we have seen, the process of challenging the leader is cumbersome and prevents Labour MPs from quickly deposing a leader, a possibility which exists within the Conservative party – as the fate of Thatcher showed (see chapter 4).

Finally here, the leader has enormous influence over what goes in the party manifesto. By convention, the NEC and the shadow cabinet decide which parts of the party's programme approved at conference should be included. In practice, the leader holds all the aces. Callaghan illustrated this in 1979, when he apparently threatened to resign if what he regarded as unacceptable proposals – such as the abolition of the House of Lords – were included. As a result, the Prime Minister was able to veto 'the most extreme of the NEC's proposals as contained in the Labour's Programme 1976 document' and fudge 'phraseology dealing with their more moderate proposals.'[42] Even in 1987, with a leader who had been elected by the whole party, the manifesto was a pale reflection of the policies carried by conference. On defence, for instance, although unilateralism remained there was no recognition of conference's desire to cut spending on conventional defence.

Does all of this mean, then, that the extra-parliamentary party has little or no influence? Was, in other words, McKenzie right? The answer must be no. No leader can ignore conference. Its proceedings are extensively publicised in the media and, if its decisions are regularly contrary to the wishes of the leadership, this can only damage the party's electoral prospects, as well as the leader's personal position. Thus, the important feature of Gaitskell's denunciation of unilateralism in 1960 was not that he threatened to ignore it but that he went back a year later and got the decision reversed.[43] Similarly, it would have been inconceivable for Kinnock to have abandoned unilateralism in 1989 without the backing of conference. To have done so would have made his position untenable.

In addition, it is worth mentioning that, unlike their Conservative counterparts' relationship with their extra-parliamentary party, the PLP does not have a privileged position at conference or on the NEC – where, although the leader and deputy leader are automatically members, there is no PLP section as such. Conference has traditionally been marked by the lack of deference shown to the party's parliamentarians, symbolised by the reservation of the platform for NEC, rather than PLP, members – the latter do not even have a right to vote unless they are acting as delegates of affiliated organisations. Traditionally, even senior members of the shadow cabinet or – if Labour is in office – the cabinet itself, were not entitled to sit on the platform or make a keynote speech unless they were also members of the NEC – although in recent years front-benchers have played an increasingly high-profile role at conference. This deference to senior parliamentarians, however, is unusual in Labour party politics. Thus, to give the classic example of the traditional lack of deference, Denis Healey, Chancellor in the Wilson and Callaghan governments between 1974 and 1979, was given the floor for five minutes at the 1976 conference, as any other ordinary delegate would be, to explain and defend, with much heckling, the government's acceptance of a loan from the International Monetary Fund.[44]

As we intimated, the conference has been effectively 'managed' by the leadership in the past. But the very fact that it requires 'managing' demonstrates it has some importance and if the leadership loses control it can spell trouble. This became patently obvious in the period between the late 1960s and the early 1980s when the traditional consensus between the parliamentary leadership and the major union delegations broke down. This resulted, as we saw, in a growing divergence between what conference voted for and what Labour governments were doing. After Labour's defeat in the 1979 election, the conflict engendered by this dichotomy exploded as the conference demanded that future Labour leaders be made more accountable to the extra-parliamentary party. The consequence was that conference accepted, in 1980, the electoral college system for choosing the leader and mandatory reselection of MPs. The third proposal on the agenda, that the NEC have the final say in the drawing up of the manifesto, was narrowly rejected.

The adoption of the reforms was the culmination of nearly a decade of campaigning by various left-wing groups. A small group of Labour activists, provoked by Wilson's rejection of the left-wing programme approved by conference in 1973, formed the Campaign for Labour Party Democracy, which, initially, worked virtually alone to promote change.[45] Its campaign was expertly organised. By circulating 'model resolutions' on mandatory reselection to CLPs and unions it was able to co-ordinate effectively the left's conference challenge. In addition, although in favour of a left-wing programme of policies, it was able to achieve a broad base of support by focusing exclusively on the case for greater intra-party democracy without reference to policies which may have alienated it from many.[46] The movement for constitutional change was strongly associated with Tony Benn. Benn, however, played little part in the early part of the campaign, only joining once Labour had been defeated in 1979. By this time, the Campaign for Labour Party Democracy had garnered significant support from other left-wing groups, CLPs and union branches. In May 1980, it joined together with various other left-wing groups, including Militant and the Labour Co-ordinating Committee, to form the Rank and File Mobilising Committee.[47]

It was clear why the left should want to impose controls on a right-wing leadership. But they had no chance of success unless they could persuade enough unions to use their block votes to back the proposals. They managed to achieve this for a variety of reasons. First, from the late 1960s onwards, a number of large unions began to move to the left. This was obviously crucial since the leadership's success in 'managing' conference had been based upon the support of key right-wing union leaders. Increasingly bereft of this support, the parliamentary leadership was in trouble. The move left began as early as 1956, when Frank Cousins replaced Arthur Deakin as general secretary of the TGWU, a vital factor in the union's 'conversion' to unilateralism at the 1960 conference. The extensive drift to the left did not really begin, however, until the mid to late 1960s. With the election of Hugh Scanlon as president of the AUEW in 1967 and Lawrence Daly as general secretary of the NUM in 1968, the parliamentary leadership had lost their key conference allies. Although in the 1970s some unions remained loyal and some (such as the AUEW, which moved back to the right with the election of Terry Duffy as president in 1978) had shifting alliances, the party's leadership could no longer rely on enough solid support to get their way consistently. They were not helped by changes in employment patterns which increased the block votes of traditionally left-led unions such as NUPE and the Association of Scientific, Technical and Managerial Staffs.[48] The consequence of this was that increasingly left-wing proposals were carried by conference.

The leftwards move, though, is only a partial explanation for the trade union disenchantment with the parliamentary leadership which led to support for the constitutional changes. Even many moderate union leaders were disturbed about the way in which the Labour governments of Wilson and Callaghan had interfered in industrial relations. They remembered the 1969 white paper *In Place of Strife* – introduced by the Wilson government to limit union powers – and the centrality of pay restraint to the economic strategy of Labour governments in the 1960s and 1970s (Frank Cousins, Minister of Technology in Wilson's government, resigned in 1966 to lead the union opposition to the government's prices and incomes policy). There was initial agreement with and, for some (such as Jack Jones, leader of the TGWU), enthusiasm for the 'social contract', whereby unions moderated pay claims in return for the government's maintenance of a range of social benefits.[49] By 1978, however, most unions regarded the imposition of a rigid 5 per cent ceiling on wage rises coupled with cuts in public spending as unacceptable.[50] Finally, it should be remembered that some unions were still willing to side with the leadership in the debates on constitutional reform, fearing the increase in power for the left that was likely to accrue. Indeed, there was much good fortune associated with the campaign for party reform. At the special conference in 1981 the choice was between the eventual vote distribution of 40 per cent, 30 per cent, 30 per cent and the leadership's favoured option giving the PLP 50 per cent and the unions and CLPs 25 per cent each. This option, giving the PLP considerably more influence, failed only because the AUEW, adopting a principled position, abstained rather than vote for a proposal which failed to give the PLP a majority of the vote.[51]

Changes to the ideological balance within trade unions also inevitably affected the composition of the NEC, which moved gradually leftwards during the 1970s. As a result, the social democratic leadership was isolated further. The left's control of the NEC meant that it was able to develop its policies within NEC sub-committees (Benn being chair of the influential Home Policy Committee at this time) and put them before conference from the platform, thus giving the policies an air of authority which they had not had when tabled, often by CLPs, from the floor of the conference. The left's control of the NEC also meant that the parliamentary leadership was no longer able to use procedural mechanisms to prevent issues being debated.

Finally, the way in which the party outside parliament was managed by the NEC changed fundamentally in the 1970s. From the 1930s to the 1960s, in what Shaw describes as a period of 'social-democratic centralism', the party's rank and file were rigorously controlled from the centre and its authority to exercise this control was largely recognised by Labour activists.[52] In the 1970s, however, this authority structure broke down. A much more liberal regime was introduced – symbolised by the abolition, in 1973, of the proscribed list of ideologically incompatible organisations (resulting in the Militant 'problem' in the 1980s) and the unwillingness of the NEC to intervene to 'save' right-wing Labour MPs who had been deselected by their CLPs. Furthermore, Labour activists were much less willing to accept the edicts of the centre. This was partly because the new breed of middle-class activists was not as deferential as the party's working-class membership. Equally important was that the previous loyalty of the rank and file had been based upon an acceptance of majority decisions taken at conference, but when conference decisions were blatantly ignored by the Wilson and Callaghan governments, the legitimacy of direction from the centre took a severe mauling.[53]

By the end of the 1970s, then, the 'elite consensus' among the PLP, NEC and major trade unions that had been a feature of Labour party politics in the social democrat centralist era had crumbled and the ensuing conflict centred on the attempts to restrict constitutionally the autonomy of the parliamentary leadership. It is important to understand the significance of this for the debate about the location of power in the Labour party. The assertion of conference authority after 1979 did not so much shift the balance of power in the party away from the PLP leadership as confirm the power that the conference, or to be more accurate the biggest unions, already possessed. It was not necessary to exercise that power previously because of the essential agreement between leading unions and the parliamentary leadership, both of whom were committed to the social democrat consensus. But, as Minkin has pointed out, this 'bond of mutual confidence was a contingent and not an endemic feature of the pattern of power within the Party.'[54] Thus, while conference has never been sovereign in the sense that it can dictate to Labour parliamentarians, its constituent elements, particularly the trade unions, have always had more power than McKenzie realised.

Kinnock's organisational legacy

The election of Neil Kinnock as leader, after Labour's election defeat in 1983, precipitated another era of organisational change. Indeed, Kinnock will be remembered not for his ill-fated attempts to remove Thatcher and Major from Downing Street, but for his party management skills. As a man steeped in the traditions of the labour movement and, initially at least, trusted and respected by all sections of the party, he was probably the only senior Labour politician who could have persuaded the party to adopt the organisational and policy changes required to make it electable again. These very traits, however, made Kinnock a transitional figure, too rooted in Labour's traditions to appeal successfully to the wider electorate. Kinnock's inheritance – and, to a lesser extent, John Smith's too – made Blair's task easier than it otherwise might have been.

There were two facets to the Kinnock strategy. First, under his leadership, central authority was restored – seen in the greater involvement of parliamentary leaders, and particularly Kinnock, in policy making at the expense of conference and the NEC, and the greater intervention of the national party in the affairs of CLPs.[55] This came about partly, as we pointed out above, because the leader was able to rely on a new generation of moderate trade union leaders.[56] In addition, the disastrous defeat in 1983 dented the aspirations of the left and enabled Kinnock to use the electoral imperative to justify greater centralised control.

Secondly, and rather paradoxically, Kinnock used the leader's greater authority within the party to initiate a series of reforms to widen the involvement of ordinary members in the party's affairs. These changes have interesting implications for the distribution of power in the Labour party. We have suggested that, while it would be an exaggeration to describe Labour's extra-parliamentary organisation as sovereign, McKenzie's thesis underestimates its influence. This is not to say, however, that the party's organisation is much more democratic than McKenzie led us to believe. Indeed, as McKenzie well understood, power in the extra-parliamentary party has traditionally rested with small elite groups in the trade unions and the CLPs. This is far removed from the intra-party democracy envisaged in Labour's constitution.[57]

Despite the fact that their political levy keeps the party financially afloat, the views of ordinary trade union members have not been represented adequately in decisions made at Labour conferences or in the election of the party leader. In the latter case, as we saw, rank-and-file trade unionists do now have a say but ordinary conference voting is far from democratic. Unions are not obliged to consult their members and a 'bewildering and generally unrepresentative range of methods' are used to decide how a delegation will cast its vote. Some ballot their members, some are mandated by their own conferences, some by their executives and some take decisions immediately before or during the conference itself.[58] It would be wrong to suggest, therefore, that no consultation takes place and that union delegations are immune from grass-roots pressure but it is common for union leaders to play a decisive role. The TGWU delegation, for instance, supported Benn in the second ballot in the deputy leadership election in 1981 despite the fact that a survey of members' views revealed support for Healey.[59]

In the CLPs, too, small cliques on general committees have traditionally taken the most important decisions – on candidate selection and reselection, NEC elections and conference votes. In the past, ordinary individual members who were not particularly active in their local parties were not consulted and neither were affiliated members in local union branches. This enabled union activists to use the influence provided by their branches' vote on the general committee to get their own views adopted.

Of course, this lack of democracy in the trade unions and the CLPs suited the left. As trade union leaders moved to the left in the 1960s and 1970s, the block vote was, as we have seen, increasingly used to back left-wing policies. Similarly, those extremely active in CLPs tended to be more left wing than ordinary party members and the more liberal regime of the left-controlled NEC gave them much greater autonomy.

It is in this context that the left's support for the electoral college and mandatory reselection should be seen. When the former was used for the first time in 1981, no less than 83 per cent of the CLPs voted for Benn compared with 28 per cent of his parliamentary colleagues.[60] The intro-duction of the latter offered the prospect of an increasingly left-wing PLP. True, between 1981 and 1983 the relatively small number of eight, mainly right-wing, Labour MPs were deselected and there were fewer in the 1983–7 parliament, but these figures do not give the full picture of the reform's impact. Many of the twenty-eight Labour MPs who defected to the SDP faced deselection, as did a number who chose retirement rather than going through with the procedure. A survey at the end of 1981 of twenty-five Labour MPs who had announced their intention of standing down at the next election showed that seventeen had voted for Healey in the deputy leadership election and that all twenty-five were replaced by candidates further to the left.[61] Finally, some Labour MPs no doubt took more notice of the opinions of their local parties and modified their behaviour in order to avoid deselection.[62] It was not just the left who tended to pay lip service to intra-party democracy. The 'gang of three' who left the Labour party to set up the SDP after the Wembley conference in January 1981 were highly critical of the influence given to the unions in the electoral college but they were not quite so vocal when the votes of the leading union leaders protected the PLP against the more left-wing demands of the CLPs.

Since 1983, as we have seen, some of the more undemocratic aspects of the party organisation outside parliament have been eradicated. Just as the left sought organisational change to further their ideological goals, Kinnock and his successors have seen political benefits in this strategy of democratisation. Thus, the strategy of giving more influence to ordinary affiliated and individual members was based on the seemingly accurate assumption that they are more likely to support the moderation of the party's objectives than the committed activists. An example of this effect is the selection of more moderate parliamentary candidates. In 1989, for instance, John Hughes – the left-wing Labour MP for Coventry North East – was deselected. For the first time, under the electoral college system, individual members were entitled to a vote in a secret ballot and Hughes, the sitting left-wing MP who was a member of the Campaign Group, won only 87 out of the 283 votes they cast.

The effect of the widening franchise has also been noticeable in elections to the constituency section of the NEC. This has resulted in the election of an unprecedented number of shadow cabinet members and the defeat of left-wingers. Thus, by 1993, the foremost opponents of the modernisation of the party and long-standing members of the NEC – Dennis Skinner and Tony Benn – had both lost their seats (although the former has since been re-elected) while moderates such as Gerald Kaufman, Gordon Brown, Tony Blair and, after resigning as leader, Neil Kinnock were elected.[63] It is also revealing that John Smith and Tony Blair (the moderate candidates) won as much as 90 per cent and 60 per cent respectively of the CLP vote in the 1992 and 1994 leadership elections – figures which were surely boosted by the participation of ordinary members. Since becoming leader, Blair has taken party plebiscites a stage further. In 1995, he encouraged CLPs to ballot their members on the adoption of a revised version of clause 4 (see chapter 5) and, after appealing over the heads of party activists to ordinary party members in a series of meetings up and down the country, he secured the support of 85 per cent of those taking part.[64] A year later, similarly, party members were balloted on Labour's pre-election manifesto *Road to the Manifesto*, no less than 95 per cent, not surprisingly, voting in favour.[65]

The effect of the organisational reforms set in train by Kinnock on the power relationship between the parliamentary and extra-parliamentary wings of the party is unclear. For some, they have reinforced the power of the parliamentary leadership. Dunleavy, for instance, remarks that the development of greater central control under recent Labour leaders seems 'decisively to rehabilitate' the McKenzie thesis, and Shaw concurs, suggesting that:

> By the 1990s, the dispersal of power at the centre which had so complicated the work of Kinnock's three predecessors had been replaced by a tightly integrated system in which control was effectively concentrated in the hands of the Parliamentary elite.[66]

The problem with these interpretations, however, is that they negate the potential impact of the greater influence given to ordinary party members in the selection of candidates as well as in the election of the leader and the constituency section of the NEC. Shaw, in response, has argued that the introduction of OMOV is 'likely to contribute towards oligarchical control' precisely because it removes influence from elites in the general committees of CLPs and trade union branches which have acted as a counterbalance to the parliamentary leadership. Thus, these 'autonomous ancillary or intermediary organisations' can operate as centres of opposition, alternative sources of communication, agencies for mobilising the rank and file and suppliers of candidates to challenge senior office holders.[67]

There is a great deal to be said for Shaw's interpretation. The new 'selectorate' created by organisational reform is much more difficult for oppositional groups on the left to organise, and ordinary party members who play no part in a local party organisation are more likely to be swayed by the media and by appeals from the party leadership.

Shaw's interpretation is not entirely satisfactory, however, not least because he ignores the contingent nature of power relationships within the party. There is no doubt that the leadership has been able to get its way most of the time in the last decade or so. The circumstances – of an overwhelming desire to reverse Labour's electoral fortunes – were conducive to party loyalty, however, and it is not clear how far this, rather than organisational and procedural reform, was the primary reason for the leadership's control over the party. Should there be internal party dissent over the direction of Blair's government, the organisational reforms might be used to exercise control over the leadership. Crucially, here, is the – so far uncompleted – reform of ordinary conference procedures. Consistency demands that union delegations should be mandated to follow the wishes of their levy payers and if this were to happen, coupled with a further increase in the party's individual membership which would reduce the voting power of unions, it would be increasingly difficult for the leadership to use the union's vote to manage conference.

That the leadership has recognised the potential problem of managing a more pluralistic conference, and an NEC which could provide a forum for opposition to the government (as it did during the Labour governments of the 1960s and 1970s), is revealed by their enthusiasm for the further development of the Policy Forum structure. Initially approved with little controversy by the 1990 conference, the Policy Forum was originally envisaged as an advisory talking shop, providing an additional arena for party members to discuss policy. After the 1997 election, as we saw above, the party leadership proposed that the role of the Policy Forum be expanded at the expense of the conference and the NEC, and conference accepted this. There is little doubt that the aim of this reform is to ensure that policy differences will be ironed out by the Policy Forum, in which the parliamentary leadership has a decisive role. As a result, the conference could then take on the characteristics of the traditional Conservative model as a media-friendly gathering designed to promote the leadership rather than make difficult policy choices.[68]

In conclusion, it will have become apparent that Labour's organisation is extremely complex and locating where power lies in the party is no easy task, particularly given the state of flux that has existed in recent years. Arguments about intra-party democracy are inextricably interwoven with ideological positions and electoral strategies as different groups have sought to impose their version of Labour's 'true purpose'. Describing the constitutional position provides only a partial picture of power relationships within a political party. These relationships will alter depending, not least, on the external political environment within which a party must react. In this sense, the quietism which has characterised Labour's rank and file in the recent past was, first and foremost, a product of the unity necessary for electoral victory. If the new Labour government fails to live up to the expectations of party members, however, renewed internal conflict may well occur, and only then will the implications of recent organisational reforms become clearer.

Notes

1   H. Pelling, *Origins of the Labour Party* (Oxford, Clarendon Press, 1964), ch. 10.
2   E. Shaw, *Discipline and Discord in the Labour Party* (Manchester, Manchester University Press, 1988), pp. 1–2.
3   *Labour Party News*, March–April 1989, pp. 20–1.
4   P. Seyd, *The Rise and Fall of the Labour Left* (Basingstoke, Macmillan, 1987), pp. 40–1.
5   *Independent*, 12 September 1989.
6   H. Pelling, *A Short History of the Labour Party*, 11th edn (Basingstoke, Macmillan, 1995), p. 191; *Guardian*, 4 January 1997.
7   Jenkins quoted in Shaw, *Discipline and Discord*, p. 361. For the decline of working-class involvement see P. Whiteley, *The Labour Party in Crisis* (London, Methuen, 1983), pp. 53–80; and B. Hindess, *The Decline of Working Class Politics* (London, MacGibbon and Kee, 1971).
8   P. Seyd and P. Whiteley, *Labour's Grass Roots* (Oxford, Clarendon Press, 1992).
9   See M. Crick, *Militant* (London, Faber and Faber, 1984).
10 Shaw, *Discipline and Discord*, p. 248.
11 See Seyd and Whiteley, *Labour's Grass Roots*; P. Seyd, 'Why the Red Rose Must Tend its Grassroots and Branches', *Guardian*, 16 June 1992; and P. Whiteley and P. Seyd, 'Labour's Vote and Local Activism: The Impact of Local Constituency Campaigns', *Parliamentary Affairs*, October 1992.
12 A. Geddes, J. Lovenduski and P. Norris, 'Candidate Selection', *Contemporary Record*, April 1991, p. 20; R. Kelly, 'Labour's Leadership Contest and Internal Organisation', *Politics Review*, February 1995, p. 11; R. Turner, 'The Politics of Parliamentary Candidate Selection', *Politics Review*, November 1996, pp. 30–1.
13 R. Kelly and S. Foster, 'Power in the Labour Party', *Politics Review*, September 1991, p. 29; *Guardian*, 17 May 1989. For a critical perspective on the imposition of candidates see R. Heffernan and M. Marqusee, *Defeat from the Jaws of Victory* (London, Verso, 1992), pp. 265–77, 281–2.
14 *Guardian*, 27 July 1991; *Sunday Times*, 12 July 1992.
15 Kelly, 'Labour's Leadership Contest', pp. 10–11.
16 A. Ball, *British Political Parties* (Basingstoke, Macmillan, 1987), p. 207; Shaw, *Discipline and Discord*, ch. 9.
17 Kelly and Foster, 'Power in the Labour Party', p. 29.

18   C. Crouch, 'The Peculiar Relationship: The Party and the Unions', in D.
      Kavanagh (ed.), *The Politics of the Labour Party* (London, Allen and Unwin,
      1982), pp. 176–7.
19   L. Minkin, *The Contentious Alliance* (Edinburgh, Edinburgh University Press,
      1991).
20   *Guardian*, 26 April 1990.
21   *Guardian*, 4 October 1995.
22   Kelly, 'Labour's Leadership Contest', pp. 11–12.
23   E. Shaw, *The Labour Party Since 1979: Crisis and Transformation* (London,
      Routledge, 1994), p. 110.
24   *Democracy and Policy Making for the 1990s*, statement by the NEC (London,
      1990). One of the main proponents of this reform was Tom Sawyer, at the
      time the deputy general secretary of NUPE and chair of the NEC's Home
      Policy Committee. Sawyer, who replaced Larry Whitty as the party's general
      secretary, also proposed the creation of the policy review. See his 'After the
      Policy Review', *Labour Party News*, July–August 1989, p. 7.
25   *Guardian*, 30 January 1997.
26   Shaw, *Discipline and Discord*, pp. 280–5; Hefferman and Marquesee, *Defeat
      From the Jaws of Victory*, pp. 261–5, 277–90.
27   P. Mandelson, 'Marketing Labour', *Contemporary Record*, winter 1988, pp.
      11–13; see also C. Hughes and P. Wintour, *Labour Rebuilt* (London, Fourth
      Estate, 1990) for a fascinating account of the transformation of the Labour
      party under Kinnock's leadership; and Shaw, *Labour Party Since 1979*, pp.
      53–80, 124–51, 167–99.
28   *Guardian*, 7 June 1991. For a critical account of Labour's increasing reliance
      on image makers see Hefferman and Marquesee, *Defeat From the Jaws of
      Victory*, pp. 205–32.
29   Seyd, *Rise and Fall*, pp. 77–83.
30   Seyd, *Rise and Fall*, pp. 163–70; Shaw, *Labour Party Since 1979*, pp. 161–3.
31   P. Norris, *Electoral Change Since 1945* (Oxford, Blackwell, 1997), p. 179.
32   Kelly and Foster, 'Power in the Labour Party', p. 27; Kelly, 'Labour's Leadership
      Contest', p. 10.
33   R. Kelly, 'Choosing Labour Leaders: Reforms and Surprises', *Politics Review*,
      September 1993, pp. 11–15.
34   Kelly, 'Labour's Leadership Contest', pp. 9–11.
35   R. T. McKenzie, *British Political Parties* (London, Heinemann, 1955).
36   L. Minkin, *The Labour Party Conference* (Manchester, Manchester University
      Press, 1980), p. 321.
37   I. McLean, 'Party Organisation', in C. Cook and I. Taylor (eds), *The Labour
      Party* (London, Longman, 1980), p. 44.
38   Pelling, *A Short History of the Labour Party*, p. 93.
39   Minkin, *Labour Conference*, p. vii.
40   Minkin, *Labour Conference*, p. 316.
41   Minkin, *Labour Conference*, p. 359.
42   S. E. Finer, 'The Organisation of the Labour and Conservative Parties', in
      M. Burch *et al.* (eds), *Three Political Systems* (Manchester, Manchester
      University Press, 1985), p. 45.
43   See Minkin, *Labour Conference*, pp. 278–89.
44   P. Whitehead, *The Writing on the Wall* (London, Michael Joseph, 1985), pp.
      189–90.
45   M. Kogan and D. Kogan, *The Battle for the Labour Party* (London, Kogan Page,
      1982), pp. 23–4.
46   Kogan and Kogan, *Battle for the Labour Party*, pp. 27–9.

47 Seyd, *Rise and Fall*, p. 115.
48 Crouch, 'Peculiar Relationship', p. 180; Minkin, *Labour Conference*, pp. 322, 343.
49 A. Fenley, 'Labour and the Trade Unions', in Cook and Taylor, *Labour Party*, pp. 75–8.
50 Crouch, 'Peculiar Relationship', pp. 81–2; see also Kogan and Kogan, *Battle for the Labour Party*, pp. 54–5.
51 Seyd, *Rise and Fall*, pp. 320–1.
52 Shaw, *Discipline and Discord*, pp. 26–152.
53 Shaw, *Discipline and Discord*, pp. 153–253.
54 Minkin, *Labour Conference*, p. 321.
55 Shaw, *Discipline and Discord*, pp. 254–83; Shaw, *Labour Party Since 1979*, pp. 110–23.
56 Hefferman and Marquesee, *Defeat From the Jaws of Victory*, pp. 147–65.
57 McKenzie, *Political Parties*, pp. 485–516. It should also be noted that McKenzie regarded intra-party democracy itself as undesirable since, in his view, it is incompatible with parliamentary democracy. See R. McKenzie, 'Power in the Labour Party: The Issue of "Intra-party Democracy"', in D. Kavanagh (ed.), *Politics of the Labour Party* (London, Allen and Unwin, 1982), pp. 191–201.
58 Kogan and Kogan, *Battle for the Labour Party*, p. 79.
59 Seyd, *Rise and Fall*, p.135.
60 Kogan and Kogan, *Battle for the Labour Party*, p. 146.
61 Kogan and Kogan, *Battle for the Labour Party*, p. 150.
62 Seyd, *Rise and Fall*, pp. 129–33.
63 Shaw, *Labour Party Since 1979*, p. 118.
64 *Sunday Times*, 30 April 1995.
65 *Guardian*, 5 November 1996.
66 P. Dunleavy, 'The Political Parties', in P. Dunleavy *et al.* (eds), *Developments in British Politics 4* (Basingstoke, Macmillan, 1993), p. 142; Shaw, *Labour Party Since 1945*, p. 191.
67 Shaw, *Labour Party Since 1979*, p. 119.
68 See R. Kelly, 'The Tory Way is the Better Way', *Political Quarterly*, July 1997, pp. 241–4.

7

The centre of British party politics

Before 1981, an examination of the centre ground of British party politics would have been concerned exclusively with the Liberal party. Outflanked by Labour early in the present century, the last Liberal government folded in 1915 and the last Liberal Prime Minister (David Lloyd George), heading a Conservative-dominated coalition government, left office in 1922. Between 1945 and 1981, despite hanging on to life tenaciously and, indeed, threatening a major revival at times, the party was very much on the periphery of British politics. This seems reason enough for providing a more limited treatment of the centre than that proffered for both Labour and the Conservatives in this book. Such a treatment, however – relatively truncated though it may be – is important.

First, an analysis of the realignment of the party system involving the replacement of the Liberals by Labour tells us a great deal about twentieth-century British politics. Secondly, the Liberal party – during both its heyday and its period of decline – pioneered many of the ideas that later became part of the British political mainstream. Furthermore, the Liberal revival in the 1970s, boosted by the creation of the Alliance with the newly formed Social Democratic party in 1981, seemed, for a while at least, to have broken the back of the two-party system, with Labour's future as a major party looking decidedly shaky in the early 1980s. Finally, a political force which has been able to attract, for nearly twenty years, an average of six million votes (around 20 per cent of those who voted) at general elections, and whose failure to become a party of government can be put down to the workings of a grossly unfair electoral system, deserves not to be neglected.

In the past two decades, the politics of the centre in Britain has been in a state of considerable flux. In order to explain the long-term causes of these events (the social democratic split from the Labour party, the formation of the Alliance between the Liberals and Social Democrats, and the eventual merger which produced the Social and Liberal Democratic party in the late 1980s) it is necessary to examine the nature of the nineteenth-century Liberal party and its replacement as a party of government by Labour early in the present century.

Classical liberalism

The Liberal party emerged from a meeting of Peelites, Whigs and Radicals on 6 June 1859[1] and, from 1868 (with the election of Gladstone's first government) until the outbreak of war in 1914, alternated in power with the Conservatives. Although always a coalition of diverse interests – representing such causes as Irish home rule, free trade, nonconformity and temperance – the party was, above all, the vehicle of the new middle class of manufacturers and merchants created by the industrial revolution. In addition, although – as chapter 3 has shown – this was disputed by the Conservatives (and later by Labour), the party also regarded itself as the natural home of the industrial working class.

Not surprisingly, given that the wealth and power of the new industrial middle class rested upon it, the party's ideology (described variously as Gladstonian, Manchester, economic, Victorian or classical liberalism) was based around a belief in the efficacy of *laissez-faire*. According to this doctrine, the state's role should be limited to the creation and maintenance of the free market, both internally and between nations. Thus, interference by the state, for example to alleviate poverty, should be minimal, since this would hinder the process of wealth creation by diverting resources required for investment. By allowing the unfettered play of market forces, the greater prosperity generated would benefit the working class in terms of higher wages for those in work and more employment for those presently idle.[2] This economic analysis was reinforced by an individualistic philosophy. Individuals were responsible for their own actions and those who did not benefit from the new industrial age had only themselves to blame. The poverty and squalor in Britain's cities were particularly blamed on the corrupting influence of drink, which prevented men (and women) from seeking work and wasted already limited resources. Thus, the temperance movement, an important group within the Victorian Liberal party, made great efforts to 'liberate' the poor from the clutches of 'evil' (mainly Conservative-supporting) landlords.[3] Self-help and thrift, therefore, were the answers to urban deprivation, not a change in the state's role.

The free market was not only the most economically efficient method of production, it also promoted individual liberty, a central tenet of liberalism. The seminal work here was J. S. Mill's *On Liberty*, published in 1859. Mill, in what is still regarded as a central text by Liberals today, provides the classic case for individual freedom. 'The sole end', he argues:

> for which mankind are warranted, individually or collectively, in interfering with the liberty of action of any of their number, is self protection. That

the only purpose for which power can be rightfully exercised over any member of a civilised community, against his will, is to prevent harm to others.[4]

Thus, the state or society has no right to intervene in what Mill describes as 'self-regarding' actions. Liberty, for Mill, was crucial because it promoted individual self-development. Only if individuals were allowed to find their own way in the world would they become intelligent, self-motivated people able to participate fully in the political and economic life of the community.

The new liberalism

The roots of the Alliance between the Liberals and the Social Democrats can be traced back to the crisis which enveloped classical liberalism towards the end of the nineteenth century. This ideological crisis was the consequence of a variety of factors. The extent of the poverty and degradation in late-Victorian Britain became much more visible as a result of major social surveys by philanthropists such as Booth and Rowntree and it became apparent that much of it was beyond the control of the victims.[5] This was symbolised by the realisation of many opinion formers that unemployment and poverty were not so much the effect of excessive drinking but its cause. Of course, it was recognised that, for some, personal failure was the key factor, but it became widely recognised (not least by many associated with the Liberal party) that something had to be done for the so-called 'deserving poor' and that public authorities (initially local authorities, but increasingly central government) would be the major agencies. Social compassion was only part of the reason for this change of attitude. There was also a general feeling that Britain could not compete industrially or militarily if many of its population were unhealthy and unfit. This was driven home in stark fashion by the Boer War (1899–1902), when many of those who attempted to enlist for military service were found to be in poor physical condition. Finally, there was a fear of serious social unrest if something was not done to help the dispossessed. The period from 1880 to 1900 saw the revival of trade union militancy and organisations such as the Fabian Society and the ILP were created to promote the doctrine of socialism, which emerged as a serious rival to the prevailing liberalism.

The factors described above led to the reformulation of classical liberalism. The 'new' or 'social' liberalism which resulted derived in particular from the work of intellectuals such as J. A. Hobson and L. T. Hobhouse, who were themselves influenced by the Oxford philosopher T. H. Green.[6] These intellectuals emphasised that individual self-development through the exercise of freedom was the goal of liberalism but that it was necessary for the state to intervene in order to create the conditions for individual self-development. Thus, state action was justified as a mechanism whereby freedom could be enhanced. This reformulation, then, recognised that the conditions of life for many were such that the freedom they 'enjoyed' was a legal entity with no foundation in reality. For the new liberals, therefore, the two concepts – liberty and equality – were not, as in classical liberalism, totally incompatible since, as Hobhouse pointed out, 'the manifest teaching of experience' told that 'liberty without equality is a name of noble sound and squalid result.'[7] P. F. Clarke sums up the significance of the new liberalism in the following way:

> it meant the end of laissez-faire. The death of the old individualism was pronounced – whatever good it might have done in the nineteenth century. The market was now exposed as neither fair nor expedient in its workings; and in particular the entitlement of the poor to the state's active assistance was explicitly claimed.[8]

This ideology, of course, was to provide the basis for what we have described in earlier chapters as the social democratic consensus which dominated British politics for much of the period after the Second World War. Social democracy – as we pointed out in chapter 5 – had a Marxist connotation in the nineteenth century, however, and (although after the Russian revolution in 1917 it began to be used to describe those socialists who sought change through existing democratic institutions[9]) the term did not become widely used, at least in Britain, until after 1945. However, before that, Hobhouse, in particular, had claimed the term for the new liberals. The old liberalism had achieved political democracy, he argued, which had 'paved the way for what, if the term were not limited to a rather narrow theory, we might call a social democracy', which was the aim of the new liberals.[10]

It is important to recognise that there was a good deal of ideological compatibility between this reformulated liberalism and the newly formed Labour party. As we pointed out in chapter 5, it would be correct to describe many leading Labour party socialists as social democrats and there was a good deal of personal contact between early Labour socialists and the exponents of the new liberalism. MacDonald, for instance, was involved in the Rainbow Circle, a society set up in 1893 to propagate the ideas of the new liberalism, while many Liberals were members of the Fabian Society. The pre-war electoral pact (negotiated by Herbert Gladstone, the Liberal chief whip, and Ramsay MacDonald, the secretary of the Labour Representation Committee, in 1903) symbolised the common ground between the parties. The aim of many Liberals was to create a progressive alliance whereby the Liberals headed a coalition of the centre-left, absorbing the interests of the trade unions within its ranks.[11] The success of such a strategy was vital for the long-term prospects of the Liberals and as long as the Labour party remained merely a trade union pressure group in parliament and the Liberal party in general was prepared to accept its new role as the leader of radical social reform in Britain, thus attracting working-class votes, it stood a chance of surviving as a major party of government.

The downfall of the Liberal party

It is not clear how far the ideas of the new liberals permeated the Liberal party in the early part of the twentieth century nor how far the party's electoral performance up to 1914 was based upon an attraction to these ideas. Such questions are inextricably bound up with the historical debate about the decline of the Liberal party. The speed of this decline has long fascinated historians and the reasons for it have a great bearing on the character of twentieth-century British politics. In the 1906 election, the Liberals were returned with 400 seats, nearly 50 per cent of the votes cast and a majority of 130 over all the other parties combined. Even in the two elections held in 1910, the party, although deprived of an overall majority in the Commons, was still polling well over 40 per cent of the vote. By contrast, the Labour party before 1914 made little progress at the parliamentary level, increasing their thirty seats gained in 1906 to only forty-two in December 1910. After the 1924 election, however, this pattern had been reversed. Labour was now the major opposition party with 151 seats and over five million votes while the Liberals were reduced to a rump of forty seats and about 18 per cent of the vote.

This dramatic decline has been the subject of a concerted debate among historians.[12] All agree that politics in Britain at the beginning of this century was becoming increasingly dominated by a cleavage based upon social class and that the Liberal party's chances of surviving depended upon adapting to this new environment. The extent to which it was able to do so is a matter of dispute. P. F. Clarke, for instance, in his study of Liberalism in Lancashire, suggests that the Liberals had adapted to the new class-based society by promoting a radical programme of social reform, based on the ideas of the new liberals, which was proving attractive to working-class voters.[13] Clarke places a great deal of importance on the performance of the Liberal government elected in 1906. The landslide victory achieved by the party in that election had more to do with traditional Liberal causes than a campaign for social reform. Nevertheless, the reforms carried out by the radical Liberal governments led by Asquith from 1908 to 1914 (competently aided by Lloyd George and Winston Churchill) – including the introduction of old-age pensions and a national insurance scheme – involved exactly the kind of redistributive state action called for by the new liberals.[14] For Clarke, then, the Liberal party was – although not without some serious problems – reasonably healthy before 1914. What finished it off was the First World War, which produced severe divisions within the party and the sacrifice of a number of cherished Liberal principles. Continuing with this medical metaphor, Trevor Wilson has argued that:

> The Liberal party can be compared to an individual who, after a period of robust health and great exertion, experienced symptoms of illness.... Before

a thorough diagnosis could be made, he was involved in an encounter with a rampant omnibus [the First World War], which mounted the pavement and ran him over. After lingering painfully, he expired.[15]

Other historians question the strength of the Liberal party before 1914 and emphasise that the war only hastened a process which was already well under way. They point to the fact that although, superficially, Labour did not appear to be making much progress before 1914, this disguised the underlying strength of the party, in particular, the extent to which trade unions were affiliating to it (crucially important was the accession of the Miners' Federation in 1909), symbolising growing class divisions which were always going to benefit Labour.[16] In addition, it is argued that the new liberalism did not take a firm grip on the Liberal party at the national or local level. Middle-class Liberals in constituency parties (with the possible exception of parts of Lancashire which were, in any case, not typical) tended to be hostile to the new creed and to Labour, which they saw as a threat to their interests.[17] Finally, the ability of the Liberals to attract working-class support was never really tested before 1914 because of the limited franchise. Labour's electoral success after 1918 was based upon the introduction of universal male suffrage which, had it been introduced earlier, would have spelt trouble for the Liberals.[18]

The years in the wilderness

Whatever the reason, from the 1920s to the late 1950s, the Liberal party played an extremely minor role in British politics. After the 1931 election the party split into three distinct factions: the official party (led by Samuel), with thirty-three MPs, the National Liberals (led by Simon), with thirty-five MPs, and the four MPs in the Lloyd George faction. This disguises the true extent of the party's malaise, since many Liberal candidates faced no opposition from the Conservatives. A better guide is the share of the vote which – at 11 per cent – spelt disaster for the party. The 'Samuelites' and 'Simonites' joined the national government formed after the election but the former group left after a year. The National Liberals ultimately merged with the Conservative party.[19] The following twenty-five years saw a further decline in the party's fortunes, culminating in the abyss of the 1951 election, which saw the Liberal share of the vote crumble to 2.5 per cent, only large enough to secure the election of six MPs. At this point the party came close to extinction. Had Clement Davies, the Liberal leader, accepted Winston Churchill's offer of a place in his cabinet in 1951, the party would probably have formally merged with the Conservatives.[20] As it was, the party soldiered on, achieving a similar poor result in the 1955 election.

The reasons for the insignificance of the Liberal party during this period have already been explored both earlier in this chapter and elsewhere in this book and therefore do not need much elaboration here. In an era when social class was the key determinant of voting behaviour, a party which had no claims on any particular class, and no financial and logistical support from interests created to promote class interests, was always going to struggle.

In the late 1920s, the Liberal party had been reasonably confident of making some kind of comeback. It was united under the leadership of Lloyd George and had developed a set of radical policies to deal with unemployment, the key political issue of the time. Indeed, the Liberals offered a far more imaginative approach to the unemployment problem than either of the two major parties. The party published, in 1928, *Britain's Industrial Future*, better known as the *Yellow Book*, which was the result of the Liberal Industrial Enquiry set up in 1925. This was to form the basis of the 1929 manifesto, *We Can Conquer Unemployment*. The proposals 'were firmly placed in the bedrock of Keynesian economics' (Keynes himself being heavily involved in drawing them up),[21] prefiguring much of the economic strategy of the social democratic consensus by advocating a measure of public ownership together with a massive scheme of public works to relieve unemployment. By contrast, the two major parties stuck with the traditional economic policy known as the 'Treasury view' which held that, in the event of depression, governments should maintain a balanced budget, reducing public spending when the income from taxation declined.[22] Despite the radical nature of the Liberal proposals, it was far too late for them to aid a recovery in the party's electoral fortunes. Indeed, arguably, ideology mattered little compared with the representation of class interests, where the Liberals had already been overwhelmed.

A related aspect of the Liberal decline should be mentioned here. The failure to attract support concentrated in certain areas, itself a product of the lack of disproportionate support from a particular class, meant that the Liberals suffered under the rules of the first-past-the-post electoral system. Thus, in the 1924 election, Labour won less than twice as many votes as the Liberals (33.1 per cent to 17.6 per cent) yet won over three times as many seats (151 to 40). Such figures are a familiar feature of British elections and it is hardly surprising that, since 1922, a central plank of Liberal policy programmes has been electoral reform.

Another important factor that contributed to the decline of the Liberal party (also explored in more detail elsewhere in this book) was the post-war 'Butskellite' consensus itself. The Liberals were firmly in support of the basic tenets of this consensus: 'as committed as social democracy to the values of community, fraternity and social equality and as determined to use the power of the state to redistribute resources to the disadvantaged.'[23] The problem was that so were the two major parties. As Vernon Bogdanor has pointed out, in 'the era of centrist politics, there was no room for a centre party.'[24] Liberals had played a significant role in the creation of this consensus. It had much in common with the new liberalism discussed earlier, which had an important impact on the 1906 Liberal government. In addition, the Liberals were the first party to advocate, as part of their election programme in 1929, demand management techniques which became commonplace after 1945. Finally, the key architects of the post-war consensus (Keynes and Beveridge) were both Liberals.

It is important to recognise that, in the inter-war years, the similarity between much of what Labour was offering and the political standpoint of the new liberals was such that many of the latter found it easy to transfer their allegiance to the former.[25] Many remaining Liberals, particularly in the 1920s, recognised the similarity and used it to campaign for a renewal of the pre-war progressive alliance between the two parties. Hobhouse was one who recognised that party was now getting in the way of principle, seeing a division between progressives ('true' Liberal and 'moderate' Labour) and conservatives ('old' Liberals and Tories).[26]

Of course, the moderate Labour referred to by Hobhouse consisted of those with what might be called a social democratic outlook. As we saw in chapter 5, though, Labour also contained a fundamentalist socialist wing whose commitment to public ownership was an article of faith and not, as for the new liberals, something to be considered case by case. J. A. Hobson summed up the difference between the two doctrines by distinguishing what he called 'practical' socialism from 'theoretic' or 'full' socialism. The former, the employment of collectivism where appropriate, he regarded as consistent with the new liberalism. The latter, though, was inappropriate to the new liberalism since it involved the indiscriminate application of collectivism without reference to its usefulness. Thus, the aim of the practical socialism was:

> not to abolish the competitive system, to socialise all instruments of production, distribution and exchange ... but rather to supply all workers ... with all the economic conditions requisite to the education and employment of their personal powers for their personal advantage and enjoyment.[27]

In addition, the class-based 'labourism' of the trade unions (also described in chapter 5) sat uneasily with the new liberal attempt 'to be the party of social reform with a classless base'.[28] Keynes, for instance, remained a Liberal because Labour 'is a class party, and the class is not my class. If I am going to pursue sectional interests at all, I shall pursue my own ... I can be influenced by what seems to me to be justice and good sense; but the class war will find me on the side of the educated bourgeoisie'.[29] Despite these differences, however, many new liberals did find their way into the Labour party in the inter-war years as it became apparent that Labour, and not the Liberals, was the more effective vehicle for the promotion of new liberal or social democrat ideas. Only when the fundamentalist socialists began to assert themselves did the social democrats begin to question their allegiance to the Labour party.

The Liberal revival and the road to Limehouse

On 25 January 1981, three senior Labour figures (David Owen, Shirley Williams and Bill Rodgers) together with a former Labour cabinet minister (Roy Jenkins) met in Owen's Limehouse residence to take a key step in the formation of a new social democratic party. The resulting 'Limehouse Declaration', which committed them to the formation of the Council for Social Democracy (CSD), was followed, on 26 March, by the formal launch of the SDP and, by the autumn, the electoral Alliance with the Liberals.[30] This was to alter fundamentally the nature of centre party politics in Britain.

This, though, is to get ahead of ourselves. The formation of the SDP, and the greatly improved chances of the centre parties 'breaking the mould' of British politics, was the result of earlier developments which must be considered. In the first place, it is inconceivable that the so-called 'gang of four' would have risked forming a new party without some confidence of electoral success. Central to the formation of the SDP, therefore, was the revival of the Liberal party.

As we saw, the Liberals, by the mid-1950s, were in some disarray. Towards the end of the decade, though, there were signs of a modest recovery. The party, benefiting from Conservative unpopularity – particularly after the Suez fiasco – came close to winning a by-election in Rochdale (February 1958), gained a Conservative seat at Torrington the following month and had made thirty-one net gains in the local elections of the previous year. This improvement was confirmed in the 1959 general election, when the party doubled its 1955 share of the vote and fought many more seats.[31] The recovery continued in the 1960s as the Liberals were able to capitalise on Labour divisions and the growing problems of Macmillan's Conservative government. The party's membership increased from 150,000 in 1959 to 350,000 in 1963 and after Eric Lubbock's sensational by-election victory at Orpington in 1962 (in which a 14,000 Conservative majority was turned into a 9,000 Liberal lead), the Liberals briefly led in the opinion polls. Although, not surprisingly, this level of support was not maintained, the 1964 and 1966 general elections, in which the party polled 11.2 per cent (nine seats) and 8.5 per cent (twelve seats) of the vote, respectively, showed that the revival was no flash in the pan.[32]

After Wilson's second Labour government (1966–70), the Liberal advance was halted and apparently reversed in the 1970 election, with the party's share of the vote reduced to 7.5 per cent and the number of seats to six. This was to be the prelude, however, to another major advance during Heath's Conservative government. Between October 1972 and November 1973, the party won five by-elections, including two (Ripon and the Isle of Ely) on the same day, and in the February 1974 election secured their highest share of the vote (19.3 per cent – fourteen seats) since 1929 and, with other minor parties, deprived either of the two major parties of an overall majority. In retrospect, this was a missed opportunity for the party. As Michael Steed points out, Liberals had avoided discussing what their response would be in the event of a hung parliament, concentrating instead on the highly optimistic aim of winning an overall majority, and were, therefore, totally unprepared for what happened.[33] Jeremy Thorpe, the Liberal leader, took the initiative and accepted Heath's invitation to discuss the situation after the election but was offered only a seat in the cabinet, with no policy commitments attached. The breakdown of these talks, of course, allowed Wilson to form a minority Labour administration.[34]

Had the Liberals been united on the strategy to be adopted – for instance, either a national government (Thorpe's favoured option) or a set of agreed policies as a basis for negotiation with one of the two major parties – then their chances of participating in government would have been greatly improved. Moreover, even if such negotiations had failed, the party would have been in a much stronger position to fight the October 1974 election, since they could have campaigned effectively along the lines that it was the negative attitude of the two major parties which had led to political instability. As it was, the Liberals could not keep the momentum going and won a reduced share of votes (18.3 per cent – thirteen seats) in October.

The period 1974–9 marked a further decline. The Liberals were severely embarrassed by the Thorpe court case[35] and, even though the party had a sniff of power during the 'Lib–Lab pact' (when the party agreed to maintain Labour in office), precious little was gained in return. David Steel, elected leader in 1976, regarded it as crucial that the Liberals took every opportunity to show they could share in government but the experiment backfired, particularly as the party was alienating Conservative waverers by supporting 'socialism'. In the 1979 election, the party's share of the vote reduced further to 13.8 per cent (eleven seats), still well up on the catastrophic 1950s but seemingly as far away as ever from making the big breakthrough.

The revival of the Liberal party was the product of a reversal of the factors which had engineered the two-party system in the post-war period. First, as we saw in chapter 2, the 1970s witnessed the breakdown of the social democratic consensus. Its apparent failure to deliver (both economically and politically) led to the search for alternative solutions and the consequent polarisation of the Labour and Conservative parties. This in turn left an ideological gap in the centre which the Liberals could exploit. Secondly, and relatedly, the decline of class as the key determinant of voting behaviour relaxed the grip the two major parties previously had on their blocks of class support, thereby producing a dealigned electorate much more likely to consider voting for a 'classless' party like the Liberals.

Both these factors were present as early as the late 1950s and formed the basis of Jo Grimond's strategy as Liberal leader. Grimond hoped for a realignment on the left whereby the Liberals would become the major challenger to the Conservatives by absorbing the moderates in the Labour party. This new radical, but non-socialist, force would take its place in a new two-party system, with a small socialist party relegated to minor party status. As Bogdanor writes, this would have reversed what had happened in the 1920s. 'Instead of Labour, with the aid of left-wing Liberals, replacing the Liberals, the Liberals, with the aid of right-wing Labour, would replace Labour.'[36] This seemed a plausible scenario for a while as the left were beginning to make a challenge to Labour's social democratic leadership. In addition, Labour's three successive election defeats in the 1950s seemed to confirm Labour's inability to attract an increasingly prosperous electorate. Thus, in Grimond's view, the old working class, to whom Labour appealed most, would 'disappear with universal education, television, cars and a middle-class wage.'[37] Of course, Grimond's hopes were not fulfilled at the time but in the 1970s and 1980s they were to be reawakened.

Labour and the Social Democrats

The realignment Grimond had hoped for received a boost in the 1970s with the mounting crisis in the Labour party. As the decade wore on, the position of the social democrats in the party was becoming increasingly untenable. As we saw in chapter 5, ideological divisions in the Labour party had surfaced almost as soon as Attlee's government lost office in 1951. In the 1950s, the revisionists (or social democrats) and the fundamentalists fought for the right to dictate Labour's future direction. As Peter Clarke remarks: 'In retrospect, the road to Limehouse appears better signposted than anyone noticed at the time'.[38] Indeed, the split could have come earlier. With Gaitskell's failure to persuade his party to remove clause 4 from its constitution in 1959, and the victory for the unilateralists in 1960, social democrats (including such familiar names as Brian Walden, Dick Taverne, Denis Howell and William Rodgers) organised around the Campaign for Democratic Socialism.[39] By the time Wilson became Prime Minister in 1964, however, the social democrats had regained control and, devoid of purpose for the time being, the Campaign was dissolved in 1963.

During the 1970s, though, conference votes began to swing the left's way and the social democrats were again forced to fight their corner. They organised in several factions operating within the Labour party. Some Labour councillors formed the Social Democratic Alliance in 1975, the social democrats in parliament created the Manifesto Group in 1974 and in 1977 the Campaign for Labour Victory was launched to gather support from the party in the country. All of those who were to be prominent in the formation of the SDP (including Williams, Rodgers and Owen) were active in this latter faction.[40]

A crucial, but often neglected, issue in the conflict within the party was Britain's position in Europe. The Labour conference had voted by a large margin in 1975 to end Britain's membership of the European Economic Community (EEC), despite the opposition of the social democrats. Wilson, faced by a serious split in his cabinet, called a referendum to decide the issue. During the campaign, many Labour social democrats for the first time came into contact and worked closely with those of similar views in other parties.[41] It is interesting to note, in addition, that so important was the issue for the social democrats that Dick Taverne (a former Labour MP and founder member of the SDP) has claimed that he, together with Bill Rodgers and Roy Jenkins, seriously considered forming a social democratic party in 1971 during the passage of the European Communities Bill, which Labour MPs were ordered – on a three-line whip – to oppose.[42] The issue of Europe was also the cause of the split between Taverne and his anti-EEC CLP in Lincoln. Taverne's deselection as Labour candidate in 1972 and his subsequent victories as an 'independent social democrat' in the 1972 by-election and February 1974 general election exemplified both the splits within the Labour party and the ability of 'social democracy' to attract electoral support.[43]

Most social democrats in the 1970s thought, though, that Labour could still be 'saved' from the left. It was only after the 1979 election that they became gradually more disillusioned about this prospect and more enthusiastic about breaking away. An important intervention was made by Roy Jenkins, who, in his Dimbleby lecture 'Home Thoughts from Abroad' (delivered in November 1979) advocated a realignment of British politics. In Hugh Stephenson's words, the lecture 'proved to be the single most important event in placing on the agenda for serious discussion the idea of some new party or grouping in the middle ground of British politics.'[44] In the lecture, Jenkins, who had resigned from the Labour government in 1976 to become President of the European Commission, decried the growing extremism of the two major parties (Jenkins himself had let his Labour party membership lapse and had not voted for the party in the 1979 election) and called for electoral reform to represent more accurately the moderate centrist views of the bulk of the electorate. To achieve this a strengthening of the 'radical centre' was required.[45]

At the time, Jenkins was not firmly committed to forming a new party. Indeed, he strongly considered joining the Liberals. The impetus for a new party came first from David Steel, who persuaded Jenkins that a new party, separate from the Liberals, would stand a better chance – in alliance with the Liberals – of achieving the realignment both sought.[46] Even then, a new party would never have got off the ground without the defection of the 'gang of three' from Labour. Since the 1979 election things, for them, had gone from bad to worse. The resignation of Jim Callaghan and his replacement by Michael Foot (rather than Denis Healey, their preferred candidate), who proved unable to halt the tide of the left, was a severe blow. The final straw, though, was the decision of the special conference at Wembley in January 1981 to introduce the electoral college for the election of a future Labour leader (see chapter 6). A key power had been taken out of the hands of the PLP and the influence this gave to the left in the trade unions and the CLPs was unacceptable to the social democrats. The Limehouse Declaration was issued the following day.

The rise and fall of the Liberal–SDP Alliance

In retrospect, the Alliance between the Liberals and the SDP – enthusiastically endorsed by the Liberal party assembly at Llandudno in September 1981 – was a failure in that the 'mould' of British politics was not, ultimately, broken. For a time, though, it appeared likely to succeed. The positive response to the creation of the CSD was so great that the formation of a new party was put beyond doubt. In addition to Owen and Rodgers (the only two of the gang of four in parliament at the time) nine Labour MPs immediately announced their intention of joining the breakaway, and, by the middle of 1982, the parliamentary strength of the SDP had increased to thirty. This included further defections by Labour MPs (and Christopher Brocklebank-Fowler, the only Tory MP to join the SDP) and by-election gains.

The response from the electorate was even more sensational. An advertisement in the *Guardian* asking for support and donations for the CSD produced, within a month, 80,000 letters and £175,000 in donations.[47] Furthermore, opinion polls suggested that an alliance between a social democratic party and the Liberals would win the votes of a majority of the electorate.[48] These polls were translated into real votes in a number of by-elections. In July, a safe Labour seat at Warrington was turned into a marginal by Roy Jenkins and this was followed by victory for candidates of the newly created Alliance at Croydon in October (Bill Pitt), Crosby in November (where Shirley Williams won with a 34 per cent swing from the Conservatives) and Glasgow Hillhead in March 1982 (Jenkins winning in more fertile territory).

This unprecedented surge of support, however, was not maintained. The outbreak of the Falklands war in April 1982, coupled with an improvement in the economic environment and a more united Labour party, burst the Alliance bubble. The SDP turned inward, focusing on a leadership contest between Jenkins and Owen, won – although by a smaller margin (26,300 to 20,900) than had been expected – by the former. Despite the downturn (and it is difficult to believe anyone really thought that the level of support achieved in the heady early days would be maintained) the Alliance came within a whisker (27.6 per cent to 25.4 per cent) in the 1983 election of pushing Labour into third place in terms of votes won. This was a larger share than any Liberal performance since 1923. In terms of seats, however, the Alliance won only twenty-three (seventeen of these going to the Liberals) and most of those MPs who had defected to the SDP lost their seats (including Rodgers and Williams). In the final analysis it was the electoral system which, by granting Labour ten times more seats than the Alliance (despite the closeness of the votes), put paid to their hopes of holding the balance of power. With Labour recovering rapidly under Kinnock's leadership after the debacle of the 1983 campaign it seemed that the Alliance had lost their chance and this was confirmed by the 1987 result, which saw their share of the vote drop to 23 per cent.

The impact of the Alliance

Accurately evaluating the impact of the SDP and the Alliance on British politics is not an easy task. Crewe and King argue that it was negligible.[49] Labour's transformation, they suggest, 'owed almost nothing to the SDP' since it occurred largely after the Alliance's demise in 1987 and was a response to election defeats in 1983 and 1987 which would have happened regardless of the SDP's existence. Furthermore, the existence of the SDP did not prevent Conservative election victories nor did it alter the policies pursued by the Thatcher governments. Finally, the party which arose after the merger between the Liberals and the SDP differed little, in character or electoral performance, from the old Liberal party.

There is an alternative, more generous, interpretation of the SDP's contribution to British politics in the 1980s. First, although the Alliance failed to break the mould of British politics, it failed to do so only because of the electoral system which, above all, gave Labour the time to reorganise after the 1983 election. The fact that the large number of votes won by the Alliance (fractionally fewer than Labour in 1983) were not converted proportionately into seats brought the issue of electoral reform firmly on to the political agenda, where it has remained. Secondly, there is no doubt that the organisational structure of the new Liberal Democratic party was influenced by the SDP. The old, rather chaotic – and sometimes amateurish –

Liberal party organisation has been replaced by one (characteristic of the SDP) which is much more centralised and efficient (see below).

It is largely true that the Alliance's direct electoral impact on Labour was minimal. The formation of the SDP raised the prospect of a viable attack on Labour strongholds, something which the Liberals (with one or two exceptions such as Leeds and Liverpool) had been unable to do. The Alliance, therefore, hoped to fulfil the Grimond strategy of a realignment on the left with a new centre-left party replacing Labour. This strategy had failed in the past because the electoral strength of the Liberal party had been concentrated in Conservative areas. Liberal revivals, therefore – in the early 1960s and between 1970 and 1974 – had occurred largely as a result of discontent with Conservative governments. The effect was to benefit the Labour party (the opposite of what the Grimond strategy intended), such as in February 1974.

The SDP never looked likely to fulfil the task of realigning the left. Like the Liberals before them, the electoral strength of the Alliance was in – primarily southern – Conservative seats. Indeed, survey evidence suggested that, as Ivor Crewe remarks:

> SDP supporters place not only their party but themselves in the centre; they are, in fact, fractionally to its right. Typically SDP supporters do not see themselves as moderate but left of centre-voters abandoned by a leftwards-drifting Labour Party. They see themselves as 'middle-of-the-roaders'.[50]

Ironically, then, the Alliance was a bigger threat to the Conservatives, coming second in about two-thirds of seats won by that party in 1983, and had the Alliance achieved marginally better results in 1983 and 1987, a hung parliament at the very least could have resulted, with Labour being the likely beneficiary. Despite this, however, many in the Labour party perceived the Alliance as a threat and its existence, therefore, provided one incentive for hastening the speed of the party's transformation. Furthermore, had Labour not begun the process of transforming its image and policies, it is plausible to speculate that the Alliance would have become a serious threat to Labour's position as the major party on the centre-left of British politics.

David Owen and the demise of the SDP

Immediately after the 1987 election, David Steel called for the formal merger of the two parties or 'democratic fusion' as he called it. For many in the Alliance, this seemed the natural step. In most constituencies, SDP and Liberal activists worked closely and amicably together, with the joint selection of candidates taking place in seventy-eight constituencies.[51]

Furthermore, the joint leadership of Owen (who had become the unopposed leader of the SDP upon Jenkins' resignation in 1983) and Steel had proved to be a hindrance. Owen, though, was opposed to any such move and, despite his party's eventual approval for merger and the launch of the new Social and Liberal Democratic party (SLD) in March 1988, an Owenite rump (including the MPs John Cartwright and Rosie Barnes) continued with the SDP. At first, the SDP threatened to be a serious thorn in the side of the new merged party, pushing the SLD, for instance, into third place in the Richmond by-election in February 1989. The resources of Owen's party were, however, severely strained and, after a poor showing in the local elections in May 1989 – where the party ended up with only fifteen of the 3,509 seats in England and Wales – and a fall in membership to around 10,000, it was announced that the SDP would no longer be a national party, engaging instead in 'selective campaigning'.[52] Finally, after finishing seventh (behind even Screaming Lord Such's Monster Raving Loony party!) in the Bootle by-election in 1990 it was decided to wind up the party's affairs.[53]

It is worth considering Owen's reasons for refusing to contemplate the merger of the two parties, since they go to the heart of the problems faced by the Alliance. The creation of a merged party was not, for Owen, part of his long-term strategy. In contrast to Grimond and Steel's 'realignment' strategy (whereby a new centre party would replace Labour in a new two-party system) Owen envisaged the Alliance as a short-term device to achieve electoral reform, after which the two parties could go their separate ways, competing in a viable multi-party system. It is questionable, therefore, whether Owen would – under any circumstances – have entertained the idea of a merger.

Added to Owen's general doubts, though, were his negative feelings towards the particular merger being considered. He feared that the SDP would be submerged in a merged party. This view was largely correct. The Liberals had more MPs, a bigger, and much more politically experienced, membership and were an old and established party with a clearer identity than the SDP. This would not have mattered so much had Owen not thought that the two parties had significant policy differences. A key area here was defence. The Liberals had a strong unilateralist wing, the party's assembly consistently voting against the siting of American cruise missiles and the replacement of Polaris by Trident as Britain's independent nuclear deterrent. This was totally unacceptable to Owen, who had left the Labour party partly because of its conversion to unilateralism. A joint commission of the two parties came to the compromise position that Polaris would be retained for ten years until a decision about its future could be taken, with Trident being cancelled in the meantime. This was immediately attacked by Owen as a 'fudge' and, particularly given that the 1987 manifesto broadly took the commission's position, Owen was far from happy with the situation.[54] By 1987, too, Owen had moved to the right on economic policy, symbolised by his reluctance to rule out a coalition with the Conservatives after the election. His idea of the 'social market', which put greater emphasis on the need for wealth creation than wealth distribution, put him at odds with the bulk of the Liberal party in addition to Jenkins and his followers in the SDP who were more sceptical about the market and more interested in the traditional social democratic concern with equality (Jenkins having been a leading Croslandite in the 1950s and 1960s – see chapter 5).[55]

The Owenite faction believed also that the Liberal party organisation was too fragmented, decentralised and undisciplined to be a serious competitor for power. Much of this, too, was true. At the national level there was a great overlap of functions between the various organs of the Liberal party, making it extremely difficult for the leadership to gain control and for effective and speedy decision making. The party was federal in nature, giving a good deal of autonomy to the regional and national parties, and there was little central intervention in the selection of candidates. The Liberals were also the first of the mainstream parties to involve their extra-parliamentary party in the election of the leader, adopting a complicated system of weighted votes in 1976 before introducing a OMOV system in 1981.[56] Liberal conferences were often as rowdy and disorganised as the Labour party at its worst. This was graphically illustrated in the 1986 defence debate, when it was far from clear who was entitled to vote.[57]

The organisation of the Liberal party reflected its lack of parliamentary success. For a considerable time, the focus of much Liberal activity had been based upon building up support at the local level. This 'community politics' strategy, developed in the late 1960s, involved 'electioneering tactics which concentrated on local issues, intensive leaflet distribution and the involvement of Liberal candidates and councillors in day-to-day popular grievances'.[58] For those Liberals brought up on such a strategy (which proved to be very successful in areas such as Liverpool and Leeds – both of which elected Liberal MPs) a suspicion of centralised control developed. The party's tendency towards a lack of discipline reflected, too, the fact that the Liberals had not (for some time) had to portray themselves as a party of government. It should also, finally, be noted that the party contained many radicals, often associated with fringe causes, who were ideologically indisposed in any circumstances to accept centrally imposed direction.[59]

In contrast, the factors which led to decentralisation in the Liberal party were not present in the SDP. As Mick Moran points out: 'Central control is the natural product of the way the Party was born', as an 'initiative by politicians with an established reputation'.[60] As such, the leadership could retain control, both through institutional devices and the inexperience of rank-and-file members, the majority of whom had never been active in a party before. The CSD, consisting mainly of the party's rank and file, was in theory the sovereign body of the party. In practice, however, it had no power to initiate policy but could only reject proposals put before it in the form of white papers by the party's National Committee, a body dominated by MPs. Furthermore, the parliamentary party was not obliged to accept decisions made by the CSD. Finally, although the leader was elected by a ballot of the whole membership, once elected he was difficult to remove. Only if the leader was not also the Prime Minister and if a motion calling for an election was passed by more than half the parliamentary party within a month of the beginning of a new session could a challenge be made.[61]

There were obviously important differences between the Liberals and the Social Democrats. Nevertheless, they can be exaggerated. The policy differences were relatively minor and there have been few problems in ironing them out in the merged party. What united them was far more important – a commitment to the mixed economy, to constitutional change (involving proportional representation, a bill of rights and devolution) and opposition to the class-based fundamentalist socialism of the Labour left. Likewise, the organisation of the new party has, as we shall see below, taken on some of the centralised practices of the SDP. The fact that the bulk of the SDP had few problems with merger demonstrated that what united the two parties was more important than what divided them. Owen's decision, then, should be seen partly in terms of his own personal characteristics – his dislike for compromise and co-operation[62] – partly in terms of a certain organisational loyalty to the party he and others had put so much work into creating and partly because of his divergent long-term political strategy. What is clear is that his decision to oppose merger was to have serious initial consequences for the prospects of the centre.

The Liberal Democrats

The SLD (now known by the shortened title of Liberal Democrats after a ballot of the party's membership in October 1989) was launched on 3 March 1988, after the merger terms were accepted by the memberships of both parties (by 87.9 per cent in the case of the Liberals and 65.3 per cent in the case of the SDP). A leadership election was set for July and, after David Steel announced he would not be standing, the contest was between two other Liberals – Paddy Ashdown and Alan Beith – the former winning with 72 per cent of the vote.

The organisation of the Liberal Democrats is an attempt to reconcile the centralised structure of the SDP with the decentralised, pluralistic Liberal party.[63] Thus, the Liberal Democratic party has a federal structure with a certain amount of autonomy given to the party organisations in the English regions and Scotland and Wales. These constituent units have responsibility for choosing candidates as well as having their own conferences and policy committees. The twice-yearly national conference, made up of representatives from every constituency, is in theory the sovereign body of the party, having, according to the party's rules, 'the power to determine the definitive policy of the party having implications for Great Britain or the United Kingdom as a whole'.

In practice, though, the power of the conference is limited. The majority of policy proposals are put before conference in the form of green and white papers by the party's Federal Policy Committee. Final decisions can only be made once the Committee has considered any amendments made by conference to the green papers. Conference then has the opportunity to consider the revised proposals. This is clearly a more democratic procedure than the one that operated in the SDP, where decisions made by the CSD applied only if agreed to by the Policy Committee. But it does prevent the conference from reaching decisions quickly, and gives the Policy Committee the chance to argue against a decision that they dislike. This is particularly important given that the parliamentary party (in the form of the leader, the president, four MPs and one peer) are well represented on the Committee and only thirteen members (out of twenty-seven) are elected by the conference – the other members being three councillors and two Scottish and two Welsh representatives.

In addition, although members of the conference are able to propose motions on policy issues for debate, the Policy Committee has the power to insist that a final decision be deferred to give more time for consultation and thought and, in addition, it has the responsibility – in consultation with the parliamentary party – for drawing up the election manifesto. Finally, article 8 of the constitution gives the federal executive of the party (responsible for the party's organisation and consisting of fourteen elected members and, ex-officio, the president, three vice presidents, the leader, three MPs, one peer and two councillors) the power to initiate a ballot of the whole membership on any issue which it considers to be important. One can see that the leadership, well represented on the executive, could utilise this device to overturn a conference decision with which they disagreed.

The constitution puts into practice the principle of OMOV for the election of leader and president (a post initially held by Charles Kennedy and, since 1994, by Robert Maclennan), the selection of parliamentary candidates and the election of conference representatives. The process for electing a leader owes more to the Liberals than the SDP. The latter's leader was, as we have seen, relatively secure if he held the support of most MPs. In the new party, a leadership election, conducted by single transferable vote, is held two years after each general election or if a majority of the party's MPs or seventy-five local parties demand it.

The two parts of the constitution which caused most controversy were the party's new name and the preamble. Initially the constitution stipulated that the party's title was to be the New Liberal and Social Democratic party, shortened to the Alliance. This was unacceptable to many in both parties and was changed to the SLD, the shortened version – Liberal Democrats – being adopted in 1989. The preamble to the constitution includes a commitment, insisted upon by SDP negotiators, that Britain should play a full and constructive role in NATO. For many radical Liberals this was unacceptable, being a current policy rather than an enduring statement of values. The SDP negotiators, with the shadow of Owen's submersion charge hanging over their heads, knew full well that such a commitment, enshrined in the constitution, would be difficult for Liberals to alter given the need for two-thirds support from conference representatives.

A brighter future?

The prospects of a realignment of the left, seemingly dead and buried with the demise of the Alliance and Labour's recovery, suddenly reappeared on the political agenda following the 1997 election. Such a possibility (discussed further below) seemed a long way off in the immediate aftermath of the merger between the Liberals and the SDP. The new party's problems were a product of the acrimonious merger debate (which was little short of a disaster for a political force which based its appeal on deriding the 'old style' confrontational politics practised by the two major parties[64]) and the inexperience of Paddy Ashdown, who found it difficult to establish a high public profile. As a result, the Liberal Democrat poll ratings rapidly slumped into single figures and in the 1989 European elections it seemed that the Greens had replaced it as the natural receptacle of the protest vote. A financial crisis ensued, with most of the national staff laid off amidst a rapidly declining membership. In February 1988, 155,000 members of the two parties participated in the merger ballot yet in July 1990 the Liberal Democrats claimed a membership of only 82,400.[65]

Gradually, however, the Liberal Democrats began to recover. The party won three seats in by-elections from the Conservatives (Eastbourne in October 1990, Ribble Valley in March 1991, and Kincardine and Deeside in October 1991), polled over 20 per cent of the vote in the 1991 local elections, winning control of fifteen new councils and, in the run-up to the 1992 election, were back well into double figures in the opinion polls. Such was the recovery that in 1992 the Liberal Democrats helped to make a hung parliament (for the first time since 1945) the assumption among most commentators during an election campaign.

Seen in the context of the immediate post-merger problems, the Liberal Democrats' electoral showing in the 1992 and 1997 elections was surprisingly healthy. The six million votes (17.8 per cent) and twenty seats secured by the party in the 1992 election represented, if not a triumph, then certainly not the disaster that looked, for a time, on the cards. Of course, seen in a longer-term perspective, and particularly in the light of the hopes and aspirations of the early 1980s, the 1992 result was a big disappointment. For the second consecutive election, the gap between Labour and their opponents in the centre (in terms of vote share) widened. While securing a higher share of the vote than in 1979, the Liberal Democrat performance was similar to that of the pre-Alliance Liberals, with electoral strength limited to traditional Liberal heartlands such as the South West. In the 1997 election, the Liberal Democrats won a similar share of the vote. This time, however, because their votes were more concentrated in the constituencies that mattered, the party won forty-six seats, far and away the best centre party result in any post-1945 election.

Both elections revealed how much the fortunes of the Liberal Democrats (and their predecessors in the centre ground) are dependent on the voters' perceptions of the two major parties. In 1992, one of the major reasons that the Liberal Democrats were deprived of the influence a hung parliament would have given them was that not enough voters were prepared to risk a Labour government, which could have resulted from voting for the centre party candidate in vulnerable Conservative seats. In the last week or so of the campaign, Major made a great deal of this fear factor, describing the Liberal Democrats as 'Labour's Trojan horse'. In 1997, on the other hand, disillusionment with the record of the Conservative government, coupled with Labour's rehabilitation, persuaded many voters to opt for Liberal Democrat candidates in order to defeat the Conservatives. This had the effect of maximising the number of Liberal Democrat MPs but at the cost of increasing Labour's majority. As a result, immediately after the election at least, it appeared that the party's influence in the Commons was as limited as ever.

The Liberals had traditionally been the vehicle for those who wanted to protest against either or both of the two major parties, but they consistently failed to attract enough positive support. As Crewe and King point out, their vote:

> resembled a modest hotel, with large numbers of short-stay guests coming and going through its ever-revolving door. By comparison the Conservative and Labour hotels were not only larger but also had far more long-stay residents.[66]

The Liberal Democrats have not solved this problem. Like its predecessors, in a political system which encourages the major parties to gravitate towards the centre of the ideological spectrum, the party has found it difficult to carve out a distinct identity for itself. This problem is compounded by the Liberal Democrats' inability to appeal to any particular interest within society. It is no accident, therefore, that Labour's modernisation and moderation has resulted in the return to the party of many of those who originally defected to the SDP in the early 1980s.

The Liberal Democrats have made some attempt to be associated with a 'big idea' which would attract voters. Before the 1992 election, for instance, the party flirted with the idea of 'citizenship'. The notion of citizenship involves giving individuals a stake in society through the granting of formal rights and increased opportunities for participating in the political system. Constitutional reforms are central to this approach, although they are not seen merely as a means to the end of greater citizen involvement but also as an essential device for effective economic policy making.[67] In addition, the emphasis upon participation and community is aimed at carving a distinctive space for the Liberal Democrats between the top-down corporate collectivism which failed to 'mobilise consent' for government policy in the 1970s and the 'selfish' individualism of the Thatcherite market approach.

This 'populist' agenda was emphasised by a policy paper, 'Our Different Vision', published by the party in February 1989 and has also been taken on board by Ashdown in his book *Citizens' Britain*.[68] The ideals of citizenship, though, have proved to be insufficiently distinctive to enthuse Liberal Democrat activists, let alone voters, not least because the two major parties moved decisively away from the extreme positions that the citizenship approach was designed to attack. Indeed, both Labour and the Conservatives (by the promotion of the stakeholder society and the citizens' charter, respectively) have adopted many of the citizenship themes themselves. In the 1992 and 1997 elections, traditional economic issues predominated and, even though in this area the Liberal Democrats did offer an alternative approach (in 1992 by promising to create an extra 600,000 jobs through a 'prudent' increase in borrowing and in both elections committing a Liberal Democratic government to a 1p increase in income tax, the proceeds of which would be spent on education), it never became a pivotal part of the campaign.

After the 1992 election, the Liberal Democrats could, with Labour's fourth successive election defeat, still hope for some kind of pact which might give the party significant influence after a future election. In 1997, however, these hopes appeared to disappear and another five largely frustrating years seemed on the cards.[69] This initial assessment, though, seems to have totally underestimated Tony Blair's desire for a rapprochement with the centre. On their way back from witnessing the handing over of Hong Kong to China in July 1997, Blair invited Ashdown to join, along with his senior colleagues, a newly formed cabinet committee which will discuss constitutional reforms, upon which the two parties are largely agreed.[70] In addition, the Labour government is intent upon introducing proportional representation for elections to the European parliament, for the planned strategic London authority and for the new assemblies in Scotland and Wales. This, of course, will be greatly beneficial to the Liberal Democrats.

Blair's intentions are not entirely clear. Some regard his initiative as merely a ploy to reduce the Liberal Democrats' capacity to criticise the government. Thus, although Ashdown and his colleagues on the cabinet committee will not be subject to collective responsibility, it would be politically difficult for them to be seen openly criticising a government with which they have been in close co-operation. Blair, in addition, has been careful to ensure that Labour has a majority on the committee and that he controls the agenda. A further point is that, despite the manifesto commitment to a referendum on the issue, Blair has not been particularly enthusiastic about the introduction of proportional representation for Westminster elections, and yet this is an essential requirement for the Liberal Democrats. Some commentators, on the other hand, have gone as far as to suggest that Blair's overtures are the first steps towards the realignment of the centre-left, either through an eventual merger with the Liberal Democrats, or through the introduction of proportional repre-sentation for Westminster elections, with the intention that an electoral pact – such as the one that existed in West Germany between the Social Democrats and the FDP – would keep the centre-left parties in office for the foreseeable future.[71]

The realignment strategy is consistent with Blair's political approach. He has long eschewed a tribal, party-based, view of politics and is ideologically sympathetic to a centrist position, no doubt seeing a long-term agreement with the Liberal Democrats as a means of further isolating the left in his own party.[72] The formal invitation to Ashdown to participate in a cabinet committee is not a flash in the pan but is rather the product of a series of meetings both before and since the election. Significantly, Roy Jenkins has been an important source of advice for Blair since becoming leader and he has played an important role in organising meetings between the Labour and Liberal Democrat leaders. There is more than a touch of irony in the fact that way back in the early 1980s, Jenkins and the 'gang of three' toyed with the idea of New Labour before adopting the SDP as the name of their new party.[73]

Even if Blair was intent on a realignment strategy, it should be remembered that, despite the leader's increasing hold on the party, he would still face fierce internal resistance to closer ties with the Liberal Democrats. The two parties have worked closely together in the Scottish Constitutional Convention but only for very narrow purposes. Any form of electoral pact under the existing electoral system would require not only a joint policy platform but also agreement on seat allocation. Conflict between the two parties would be extremely likely to be the result. At the national level, for instance, some senior Labour figures are strongly opposed to proportional representation. Further, local activists in both parties, who have spent years fighting against each other, are unlikely to be keen on campaigning for candidates standing under another party's banner. Finally, it is doubtful whether a formal electoral pact, even concluded under a reformed electoral system, would benefit Labour and the Liberal Democrats electorally. Any such pact is based on the dubious assumption that those inclined to vote Liberal Democrat naturally prefer Labour to the Conservatives. In the 1997 election, it was clear that the prospect of a future Labour government held little fear for defecting Conservative voters (and allowed Ashdown, in 1995, to drop the traditional emphasis on the Liberal Democrats' 'equidistance' between the two major parties) but the experience of elections between 1979 and 1992 demonstrates that this is not always the case.

Conclusion

One of the key aims of this chapter has been to show that the development of the centre parties has been, and continues to be, inextricably linked with the two major parties, and particularly with Labour. Ideologically, the Liberals have been, throughout the twentieth century, in the mainstream of British political life. Unfortunately for them they have, at key times, been excluded from government both because the other parties have gravitated towards their position in the centre of the political spectrum and because of their lack of a solid class base. This does not mean, however, that the centre parties have not been influential. Events have shown that they serve as a permanent reminder to both Labour and the Conservatives that if they stray too far from this mainstream they risk severe electoral consequences. This has ensured, in particular, that Labour retains a commitment to the ideals which persuaded many Liberals to transfer their allegiance in the early 1900s and which still, despite the partial realignment of the early 1980s and the closer ties forged between Labour and the Liberal Democrats since the 1997 election, keeps social Liberals and social democrats apart.

Notes

1   J. Vincent, *The Formation of the British Liberal Party 1857–68* (London, Penguin, 1972).
2   H. V. Emy, *Liberals, Radicals and Social Politics 1892–1914* (Cambridge, Cambridge University Press, 1972), ch. 1.
3   B. Harrison, *Drink and the Victorians* (Staffordshire, Keele University Press, 1971).
4   J. S. Mill, *On Liberty* (1859) (Oxford, Oxford University Press, 1991), pp. 72–3.

5   M. Pugh, *The Making of Modern British Politics 1867–1939* (Oxford, Blackwell, 1982), p. 112.

6   See L. T. Hobhouse, *Liberalism* (1911) (Oxford, Oxford University Press, 1964); and J. A. Hobson, *The Crisis of Liberalism* (London, P. S. King, 1909). See also M. Freeden, *The New Liberalism: An Ideology of Social Reform* (Oxford, Clarendon Press, 1978).

7   Quoted in R. Behrens, 'The Centre: Social Democracy and Liberalism', in L. Tivey and A. Wright (eds), *Party Ideology in Britain* (London, Routledge, 1989), p. 81.

8   P. F. Clarke, 'Liberals and Social Democrats in Historical Perspective', in V. Bogdanor (ed.), *Liberal Party Politics* (Oxford, Clarendon Press, 1983), p. 31.

9   Behrens, 'The Centre', p. 75.

10   Clarke, 'Liberals and Social Democrats', p. 28. See also P. Clarke, *Liberals and Social Democrats* (Cambridge, Cambridge University Press, 1978).

11   K. O. Morgan, *The Age of Lloyd George* (London, Allen and Unwin, 1971), pp. 32–5.

12   For a summary of the debate see P. Adelman, *The Rise of the Labour Party* (Harlow, Longman, 1972), pp. 83–90; A. Ball, *British Political Parties* (Basingstoke, Macmillan, 1987), pp. 82–4; K. Laybourn, *The Labour Party 1881–1951* (Gloucester, Sutton, 1988), pp. 1–12.

13   P. F. Clarke, *Lancashire and the New Liberalism* (Cambridge, Cambridge University Press, 1971).

14   Morgan, *Lloyd George*, ch. 2; Emy, *Social Politics*, chs 5–7.

15   T. Wilson, *The Downfall of the Liberal Party* (London, Collins, 1966), p. 18.

16   H. Pelling, *Popular Politics and Society in Late Victorian Britain* (London, Macmillan, 1968); P. Thompson, *Socialists, Liberals and Labour* (London, Routledge, 1967); R. McKibbin, *Evolution of the Labour Party, 1910–1924* (Oxford, Clarendon Press, 1974).

17   Ball, *British Political Parties*, pp. 81–2.

18   H. Matthew, R. McKibbin and J. Kay, 'The Franchise Factor in the Rise of the Labour Party', *English Historical Review*, February 1976.

19   Morgan, *Lloyd George*, pp. 104–5.

20   R. Douglas, *The History of the Liberal Party 1895–1970* (London, Sidgwick and Jackson, 1971), pp. 262–6.

21   Ball, *British Political Parties*, p. 80.

22   R. Skidelsky, *Politicians and the Slump* (London, Macmillan, 1967), pp. 31–51.

23   David Marquand, quoted in Behrens, 'The Centre', p. 92.

24   Bogdanor, *Liberal Party*, p. 8.

25   See C. A. Cline, *Recruits to Labour: The British Labour Party 1914–31* (New York, Syracuse University Press, 1963).

26   Clarke, 'Liberals and Social Democrats', p. 36.

27   Hobson, *Crisis*, pp. 133–4.

28   Ball, *British Political Parties*, p. 81.

29   Quoted in Clarke, 'Liberals and Social Democrats', p. 35.

30   The most thorough account of the SDP is by I. Crewe and T. King, *SDP: The Birth, Life and Death of the Social Democratic Party* (Oxford, Clarendon Press, 1995). For an account of the SDP's formation see I. Bradley, *Breaking the Mould? The Birth and Prospects of the Social Democratic Party* (Oxford, Clarendon Press, 1981).

31   W. Wallace, 'Survival and Revival', in Bogdanor, *Liberal Party*, pp. 47–8.

32   Wallace, 'Survival and Revival', pp. 50–9.

33   M. Steed, 'The Liberal Party', in H. M. Drucker (ed.), *Multi-party Britain* (London, Macmillan, 1979), p. 102.

34   Wallace, 'Survival and Revival', pp. 67–9.
35   See L. Chester, M. Linklater and D. May, *Jeremy Thorpe. A Secret Life* (London, Fontana, 1979).
36   Bogdanor, *Liberal Party*, p. 276.
37   Quoted in Bradley, *Breaking the Mould?*, p. 51.
38   Clarke, 'Liberals and Social Democrats', p. 40.
39   Bradley, *Breaking the Mould?*, pp. 46–7.
40   Bradley, *Breaking the Mould?*, pp. 58–63.
41   Bradley, *Breaking the Mould?*, pp. 31–9.
42   Bradley, *Breaking the Mould?*, pp. 53–4.
43   G. Williams and A. Williams, *Labour's Decline and the Social Democrats' Fall* (London, 1989), pp. 102–3. Taverne launched the national Campaign for Social Democracy, which put up four candidates in the February 1974 election.
44   H. Stephenson, *Claret and Chips. The Rise of the SDP* (London, Michael Joseph, 1982), p. 20.
45   Stephenson, *Claret and Chips*, pp. 20–2.
46   Stephenson, *Claret and Chips*, p. 29; Crewe and King, *SDP*, pp. 52–70.
47   Stephenson, *Claret and Chips*, p. 50.
48   Bradley, *Breaking the Mould?*, pp. 90–1.
49   Crewe and King, *SDP*, pp. 465–70.
50   I. Crewe, 'Is Britain's Two-Party System Really About to Crumble? The Social Democratic–Liberal Alliance and the Prospects for Re-alignment', *Electoral Studies*, January 1982, pp. 301–2.
51   S. Ingle, 'Liberals and Social Democrats: End of a Chapter or End of the Book?', *Talking Politics*, winter 1988–9, p. 48.
52   *Sunday Times*, 14 May 1989.
53   *Sunday Times*, 3 June 1990.
54   Behrens, 'The Centre', pp. 88–9; see also Williams and Williams, *Labour's Decline*, who emphasise the importance of defence in the Labour split and in Owen's opposition to the merger.
55   Behrens, 'The Centre', pp. 89–91.
56   D. Kavanagh, 'Organisation and Power in the Liberal Party', in Bogdanor, *Liberal Party*, pp. 123–42.
57   Ingle, 'Liberals and Social Democrats', p. 48.
58   Steed, 'The Liberal Party', p. 101; see also S. Mole, 'Community Politics', in Bogdanor, *Liberal Party*, pp. 258–74.
59   A number of radical Liberals opposed merger precisely because the SDP was too centralised. Thus, Claire Brooks, a well known Liberal activist, commented that the SDP constitution is 'oligarchical, centralist, authoritarian, deliberately disguised to preserve power in the hands of an elite'. *Guardian*, 18 September 1987.
60   M. Moran, *Politics and Society in Britain* (London, Macmillan, 1985), p. 97.
61   H. Drucker, '"All the King's Horses and All the King's Men": The Social Democratic Party in Britain', in W. E. Paterson and A. H. Thomas (eds), *The Future of Social Democracy: Problems and Prospects of Social Democratic Parties in Western Europe* (Oxford, Clarendon Press, 1986), pp. 108–26; Crewe and King, *SDP*, pp. 226–37.
62   Crewe and King, *SDP*, pp. 303–8.
63   Details of the Liberal Democrat's constitution can be found in the *Guardian*, 18 December 1987. See also B. Jones *et al.*, *Politics UK* (Hemel Hempstead, Harvester Wheatsheaf, 1991), pp. 261–2.
64   For details of the torturous merger negotiations see D. Denver, 'The Centre',

in A. King, *Britain at the Polls 1992* (Chatham, Chatham House, 1993), pp. 109–15; Crewe and King, *SDP*, ch. 21. We now know that the Alliance suffered from debilitating personality clashes right from its inception. See the revelations, for instance, in R. Jenkins, *A Life at the Centre* (London, Macmillan, 1992), D. Owen, *Time to Declare* (London, Penguin, 1992), and Crewe and King, *SDP*, part I.

65   J. Stevenson, *Third Party Politics Since 1945* (Oxford, Blackwell, 1993), p. 107.

66   Crewe and King, *SDP*, p. 286. See also J. Curtice, 'Liberal Voters and the Alliance: Realignment or Protest?', in Bogdanor, *Liberal Party*, pp. 105–6.

67   This 'new' thinking has been particularly associated with David Marquand, an academic political scientist, former Labour MP and founder member of the SDP. See D. Marquand, *The Unprincipled Society* (London, Fontana, 1988); D. Marquand, 'So What's the Big Idea About Citizenship?', *Guardian*, 16 August 1990. Marquand was one of those who rejoined Labour before the 1997 election.

68   P. Ashdown, *Citizens' Britain: A Radical Agenda for the 1990s* (London, Penguin, 1989).

69   See M. Kettle, 'Who Needs Paddy', *Guardian*, 28 June 1997.

70   *Guardian*, 23 July 1997.

71   The realignment interpretation has been expressed by Hugo Young, 'Why Tony and Paddy Are Stepping Out', *Guardian*, 24 July 1997; and by D. Draper, *Blair's Hundred Days* (London, Faber and Faber, 1997).

72   See Tony Wright, 'Why Diversity is a Dirty Word', *Guardian*, 2 October 1995.

73   Crewe and King, *SDP*, p. 100.

8

The parties of Scotland, Wales and Northern Ireland

Michael Cunningham

Introduction

The electoral significance of national parties in Scotland and Wales in recent history dates from the late 1960s. In the 1966 general election, the SNP gained 128,474 votes and in 1970 this figure increased to 306,802. The figures for Plaid Cymru are 61,071 and 175,016, respectively, and in February 1974 both parties gained breakthroughs in terms of seats gained (for more details see below).[1] The most recent election, that of May 1997, indicates a plateau of support, with both parties' share of the vote increasing only marginally over that of 1992 (see tables 8.1 and 8.2). However, the 1997 election may prove to be of great significance because the Conservatives, the only party to oppose some form of regional or devolved government for the two countries, lost their remaining seats and thus every seat in Scotland and Wales is held by a party either committed to recasting the constitutional structure of Great Britain and/or to a referendum on the issue. With Labour's large majority, the relationship between the nations of Great Britain will become a central policy issue for the first time since the late 1970s. Whether the new structures will meet the aspirations of the nationalist parties, especially given Labour's frequent contradictory statements concerning a Scottish parliament, remains to be seen.

The Scottish National party

Introduction: a brief history

The SNP was founded in 1934, a merger of the right-of-centre Scottish party and the more left-wing National party. These two parties were the product of a revival of independence and home-rule sentiment in the 1920s. The moving figure behind the merger was John MacCormick, who had been a founding member of the National party, and by 1936 the new party had come to assume a leftist orientation following the departure of many who joined from the Scottish party and was committed to a policy of 'a Parliament which shall be the final authority on all Scottish affairs'.[2]

Nationalist activists engaged in campaigns of civil disobedience in the 1930s and a wider, if less militant, sentiment was demonstrated by the two million signatures in support of the Home Rule Covenant of 1949–50. Nonetheless, a sense of 'Scottishness', however articulated, and support for home rule did not necessarily translate into electoral support for the SNP. The party generally faired poorly in the 1940s and 1950s despite their first MP being elected in a by-election in 1945. It is the party's own opinion that 'Scotland was a much more "British" country than it is now, with a relatively low level of teaching and awareness of Scottish history and culture'.[3]

The 1960s marked the evolution of the SNP into a fully fledged political party. One commentator has noted that at the beginning of the decade it had the characteristics of a sect rather than a party,[4] but by the late 1960s it was firmly established in the Scottish party system, symbolised by the by-election victory of Winifred Ewing in 1967 and a massive rise in membership (see below). This rise in fortunes was related to a wider British pattern of partisan dealignment and increasing dissatisfaction with the major parties, the relative economic decline of Scotland and also the efforts of Ian Macdonald, the first full-time organiser, which massively expanded the grass-roots structures of the SNP. A former leader of the party, Gordon Wilson, according to a recent history, 'locates the beginning of modern nationalism not in North Sea Oil but in industrial decline, political disillusionment and Scotland's resentment at being used as a range for weaponry and as a NATO "aircraft carrier"'.[5]

The discovery of North Sea oil, exploited under the slogan 'It's Scotland's Oil', provided an additional boost to the campaign for independence, since it appeared to address concerns that an independent Scotland would not be a viable economic unit, though it should be recorded that, as now, it is difficult to obtain reliable and objective projections of the state of the Scottish economy outside the larger political unit of Britain. However, the electoral march of the SNP was halted by its confused position and internal differences over Labour's devolution proposals in the late 1970s; the poor performance of the SNP in the 1979 general election was followed by factionalism and expulsions from which it has slowly recovered.[6]

Party ideology

The SNP has faced a problem common to all nationalist parties operating within an electoral system in which the principal ideological cleavage is of 'left' and 'right': namely, how to locate itself to maximise support from potential voters whose position on that axis may be very different. There may be a *prima facie* assumption that the Downsian model – which argues that a 'centrist' position is likely to maximise a party's support – would best serve the SNP to appeal to potential defectors from Labour and the Conservatives. The history, and indeed the foundation, of the SNP would indicate that tensions between right and left have been evident, although the recent and current policies of the party would position it on the centre-left.

It is commonplace to examine divisions and tensions within the SNP in terms of 'left' and 'right' and also along the axis of 'gradualist' versus 'fundamentalist'. Oversimplifying somewhat, gradualists are those who would accept a constitutional settlement short of independence – the most obvious example being devolution – and perhaps form tactical alliances with other parties in order to effect it. Fundamentalists are likely to consider anything other than independence a sell-out rather than a stepping-stone to Scottish freedom. Having said this, all wings of the party are conscious of the risks of being outflanked by involvement in cross-party activity or of being split in responding to agendas set by other parties. The painful lessons of 1978–9 have been learnt and help to account for the SNP's decision in 1989 not to participate in the Constitutional Convention which, with Labour and Liberal Democrats participating, was searching for an 'agreed scheme for an Assembly or Parliament for Scotland'.[7]

In addition to these two divisions Mitchell has identified a third, which he characterises as 'party' versus 'movement', which overlaps with that between right and left. In a passage that supports the contention above that the SNP is a left-of-centre party, Mitchell states:

> the lack of anything approaching a right-wing prospectus and the existence of agreement on most policy issues suggests that many described in internal SNP debates and beyond as 'right-wing' are more accurately 'cultural nationalists.' Their aims are principally the maintenance of a sense of Scottish identity, not necessarily defined in terms of political institutions or citizenship.[8]

As with many 'left' parties, the SNP has perhaps moved to a position of a pragmatic acceptance of markets in recent years, albeit regulated ones. This can be contrasted with the strands of thought found in the '79 Group' in the period of factionalism after the devolution debacle, which included both a 'shop-floor' quasi-syndicalist approach and a more old-fashioned labourism.[9] It can thus be argued that the party has moved rightwards but only in the sense that former strategies of the left have become implausible. However, opposition to pit closures in the mid-1980s campaign, support for a campaign of civil disobedience against the poll tax in the late 1980s and opposition to nuclear weapons locate the party on the left and the election of Alex Salmond as leader in 1990, the first self-professed socialist, symbolised this orientation.

An important recent policy innovation is that concerning the European Union. As with Labour, the SNP has transformed itself from advocating withdrawal to being pro-European, although a wholehearted endorsement has been tempered more recently with some 'sceptical' statements. The idea of 'independence in Europe', formulated by the left-wing member Jim Sillars, emerged in the mid-1980s and was adopted at the party conference in 1988. Independence from Britain within a large, supra-national political union has the advantage of reducing concerns of those outside the party who felt that independence could imply isolationism and also provides a way of evading what is sometimes perceived as a practical and psychological dependence on England. Despite the misgivings of some, including the 'Sovereignty '90' Group, which believes that European Union membership also constitutes an unacceptable erosion of Scottish sovereignty, this pro-European policy is firmly entrenched, even if some of the more optimistic claims for its implications for Scotland are questionable.[10]

In her discussion of the European dimension, Lindsay identifies four strands of Scottish nationalism: first, a romantic, semi-mystical form which stresses history and a shared communal experience; secondly, 'small state' nationalism with a decentralised and 'green' ethos; thirdly, a left-wing variant which sees nationalism as a route to a more socialist state; and, finally, nationalism as a modernising project which is a response to uneven development and may manifest itself in left- or right-wing forms. She contends that membership of the European Union is in potential conflict with the first three forms; however, the fourth variant was dominant in the SNP of the late 1980s.[11] This perhaps suggests that Europe is seen as a way to improve Scotland's economic performance, through a more direct representation rather than relying on an over-centralised British state, as well as a means of asserting a national identity outside Britain.

Support and electoral performance

The left-wing profile of the SNP indicated above is explicable in part by a more collectivist political culture, compared with England, in Scotland in the 1980s and a tactical attempt to challenge the hegemony of the Labour party among the working class of the west of Scotland. However, the success among this grouping has proved limited and spectacular by-election victories, for example Hamilton in 1967 and Govan in 1988, and other impressive showings have not translated into consistent gains. Despite a solid body of support, the SNP depends, more than the other parties, upon a residue of 'protest votes'. The competition with Labour, often marked by much acrimony between the parties, is made difficult because Labour's present commitment to devolution appears sufficient to satisfy much of its 'natural' voters' sense of Scottish identity and it would appear to have a lead in addressing material concerns.

The SNP runs an electoral risk in an over-concentration on the Labour vote, since it needs to maintain support in the more rural and middle-class north-east. Commentators have noted the historic cross-class and dispersed nature of the SNP's support. Gallagher states, 'no institution, no region of the country, no section of society has clearly been won over to their cause. Traditionally, the SNP has drawn its support more evenly across the spectrum than any of its competitors.'[12] In the period from the party's rise in the late 1960s until the late 1970s decline, there was some evidence of disproportionate support among the socially mobile, the geographically mobile, including those who had moved to the new towns, the 'new' working class and young voters.[13] The last local elections for the unitary authorities would seem to provide evidence of the SNP's problems in dislodging Labour, as it fared relatively poorly in Glasgow but won Moray, Angus and Perth and Kinross.[14] This is also borne out by the results of the 1997 general election. The SNP came second in all ten Glasgow seats, behind Labour, and all but one witnessed small swings from the SNP to Labour. All six seats won in 1997 were predominantly rural ones, and the three gains since the 1992 election, Perth, Tayside North, and Galloway and Upper Nithsdale, were from the Conservatives. Nationally, the SNP came second in forty-one of the seventy-two seats and its distribution of support meant that winning 22 per cent of votes resulted in winning only

Table 8.1. *Electoral performance of the SNP, 1979–97*

	Percentage of vote	*Number of seats*
1979 (G)	17.3	2
1979 (E)	19.4	1
1983 (G)	11.7	2
1984 (E)	17.8	1
1987 (G)	14.0	3
1989 (E)	25.6	1
1992 (G)	21.5	3
1994 (E)	32.6	2
1997 (G)	22.0	6

G = general election; E = European election.
Sources: J. Bochel and D. Denver, 'The 1989 European Elections in Scotland', in A. Brown and R. Parry (eds), *The Scottish Government Yearbook 1990* (Edinburgh, Unit for the Study of Government in Scotland, 1990), p. 97; A. Seldon (ed.), *UK Political Parties since 1945* (Hemel Hempstead, Philip Allan, 1990), p. 129; D. Butler and D. Kavanagh, *The British General Election of 1992* (London, Macmillan, 1992); Dod's Parliamentary Companion, *Guide to the Parliamentary and European Elections 1994* (London, Dod's Parliamentary Companion Ltd, 1994), p. 59; *Times*, 3 May 1997.

8.33 per cent of seats (table 8.1). The recent unpopularity of the Conservatives in Scotland has given the SNP inroads into sections of the middle class; however, much of the larger financial and commercial sectors remain concerned about the economic implications of devolution, and especially independence, and are unreceptive to the SNP message.

A more optimistic trend is the decline of the salience of religion in Scottish elections. In the 1950s and 1960s, the SNP had virtually no support from Catholics; in 1992, 20 per cent of this cohort supported the SNP, leading some commentators to believe this could facilitate a challenge in Labour's traditional heartlands.[15]

Membership and organisation

In 1960, membership of the SNP was approximately 1,000 and by the end of the decade had risen to 125,000. This high figure could not be sustained and had fallen to around 75,000 by 1976 and, following the factionalism and infighting of the early 1980s, to 20,000 by 1983. In 1992, one estimate put membership at around 12,000.[16]

The branch is the primary unit of party organisation and each must consist of a minimum of twenty members. The next tier is the constituency association, based on parliamentary boundaries and comprised of a number of branches. The annual conference is formally the supreme governing body of the party, but shares general policy making and party direction with the National Council. The National Executive Committee, a smaller body which includes representatives of the student, trade union and Young Scottish Nationalist sections, is elected by conference and is responsible for the day-to-day affairs of the party.[17] The party, like many which have experienced past and overt factionalism, contains tensions between the perceived need for self-discipline and debate, and there is evidence that there is some dissatisfaction with leadership discipline.[18]

Plaid Cymru

Introduction: a brief history

Plaid Cymru was founded in 1925 by Saunders Lewis and in the pre-war period was a cultural and intellectual movement principally dedicated to the defence and preservation of the Welsh language rather than a political party, having only a rudimentary organisation and making only occasional forays into electoral politics. In 1932, it adopted a policy of self-government for Wales as the best means to preserve the language. Unlike the contemporary party, it had a conservative ethos, with Saunders, a Catholic, being heavily influenced by the right-wing, anti-industrial, romantic French nationalism of Maurras and Barrès.[19]

The post-war period saw the gradual evolution of the party under the long presidency of Gwynfor Evans, from 1945 to 1981, with the development of social and economic policies. The influx of younger, more radical members in the 1960s moved the party in a social democratic direction and the foundation of the Welsh Language Society in 1962 provided Plaid Cymru with the space to develop both organisationally and ideologically. The mid-1960s roughly marks the consolidation of the evolution from cultural and somewhat elitist movement to party status, bolstered by its first parliamentary seat captured in the Carmarthen by-election of 1966.

Party ideology

The general ideological leanings of Plaid Cymru and recent developments can be usefully examined through a comparison of two versions of the party's constitution. The 1976 version contained the aim 'to secure self-government for Wales', which in a version dated July 1995 read 'to secure self-government for Wales within the European Union'. Secondly, the later version was committed to safeguarding and promoting the environment of Wales as well as the earlier commitment to its cultures, languages, traditions and economic life.

The changing attitude towards the European Community (now Union) closely parallels that of the SNP. From a position of hostility, as with many left-of-centre and nationalist parties, Plaid Cymru has come to view the European Union as a political unit which has the potential, even if not currently realised, to develop into a federal structure which both supersedes the obsolete nation state and allows full expression of the economic and cultural interests of smaller states and areas – a 'Europe of the regions'. This has obvious attractions for Plaid Cymru; it permits the possibility of breaking a dependence on Westminster and what is regarded as the latter's failure to promote Wales' interests in the Union, and provides linkages with a larger political and economic unit, thus reducing concerns of isolationism or the economic unfeasibility of a self-governing Wales.[20]

There is a degree of overlap with the second change highlighted above. The inclusion of the environment signals the important 'green' element in Plaid Cymru thinking. This is meant in the broader sense of not only an environmental emphasis but the need for decentralised decision making (hence the support for subsidiarity above) and the promotion of small-scale economic activity. Along with the promotion of self-government (not necessarily independence) and the language issue, an advocacy of decentralisation has been a key theme in Plaid Cymru ideology. Birch notes that 1960s nationalist support for workers' co-operatives and community-based activity indicated that the party owed more to Proudhon and Morris than Marx and the Webbs.[21] In recent years statist and centralised forms of socialism have become largely discredited, so this would seem to have vindicated and perhaps accelerated the decentralising ethos of Plaid Cymru, as found in its attack on the 'quangocracy' which it argues governs Wales.[22] The close affinity to green politics is also highlighted by the joint contesting of three seats in the 1992 general election with the Green party.

The 1997 general election manifesto indicated the leftist and green tendencies of Plaid Cymru. The creation of a public works programme to provide 100,000 jobs was advocated. This would be funded by a 2p rise in the basic rate of income tax, a 50p higher band and a 'polluter pays' environmental tax. On the constitutional issue, the manifesto supported a Welsh parliament with responsibility for education, housing, health, employment policy, agriculture, transport and the environment. This would be succeeded, after a five-year transitional period, by full self-government in Europe, subject to ratification by referendum.[23]

Support and electoral performance

Plaid Cymru has tended to gain greatest support in rural and Welsh-speaking Wales, particularly the north-west, and has fared poorly in the industrial areas of the south, although local and by-election results in the latter area suggest that it can frequently benefit from 'protest' votes. This failure parallels the problems the SNP has had in dislodging the working class from its traditional Labour affiliations. With reference to denominational divisions, Plaid Cymru gains disproportionate support from nonconformists and is under-represented in the Anglican electorate.

There are potential limitations in the two keystone policies of Plaid Cymru. First, only approximately 20 per cent of the population are Welsh-speaking and it is questionable how much salience the issue has for monoglot English-speakers. Also, ironically, the successful campaign to have Welsh recognised as an official language and thus used in public administration and the establishment of a Welsh television channel may have convinced the electorate that the battle to defend it had been won. Secondly, the 80 per cent 'no' vote in the devolution referendum of 1979 was a severe blow, indicating that self-government was not a pressing concern for the majority of the Welsh. It remains to be seen if the reworking of the campaign within the European context described above can resurrect this.

Although the party gained a fourth seat in the 1992 general election, the losing of deposits in twenty-five of the thirty-eight Welsh seats indicates the limited geographical and social appeal of Plaid Cymru. In the 1997 general election, the party won the same four seats, with a slight rise in the share of the vote (see table 8.2), and its concentrated support was again highlighted by the fact that it polled less than 10 per cent of the

Table 8.2. *Electoral performance of Plaid Cymru, 1979–97*

	Percentage of vote	Number of seats
1979 (G)	8.1	2
1979 (E)	11.7	0
1983 (G)	7.8	2
1984 (E)	12.2	0
1987 (G)	7.3	3
1989 (E)	12.9	0
1992 (G)	8.8	4
1994 (E)	17.1	0
1997 (G)	10	4

G= general election; E= European election.
Sources: D. Butler and D. Kavanagh, *The British General Election of 1992* (London, Macmillan, 1992) ; J. G. Kellas 'Scottish and Welsh Nationalist Parties since 1945', in A. Seldon (ed.), *UK Political Parties since 1945* (Hemel Hempstead, Philip Allan, 1990), p. 129; Dod's Parliamentary Companion, *Guide to the Parliamentary and European Elections 1994* (London, Dod's Parliamentary Companion Ltd, 1994); *Times*, 3 May 1997.

votes cast in thirty of the forty Welsh seats. Its social democratic orientation precludes support from the principal financial and commercial sectors and its relative weakness in industrial (or post-industrial) areas indicates a predominantly rural and petit bourgeois base of support.

Membership and organisation

Membership of Plaid Cymru in 1997 was 5,695 'paid up', or 16,000 including those who had not paid their current subscription.[24]

The primary level of organisation is the branch, which must have a minimum of ten current members. Rhanbarth committees, based on larger geographical units, co-ordinate branch activity, help to establish new branches and co-ordinate the party's electoral activity. The conference is the highest authority of Plaid Cymru, although detailed policy development is the responsibility of the National Council, which also has the role of determining party strategy and approving manifestos. The National Council is a large body, composed of, *inter alia*, all candidates for Westminster and European elections, all current MPs and MEPs, all national officers and two representatives from each branch and Rhanbarth committee. The smaller National Executive Committee, of approximately fifteen members, controls the day-to-day running of the party, ensuring that the decisions of conference and the National Council are implemented and co-ordinating the work of the national officers elected by conference.[25]

The political parties of Northern Ireland

Introduction

The parties of Northern Ireland operate in a fundamentally different political and electoral environment from the territorially based parties considered above. First, whereas in Scotland and Wales the principal electoral cleavage is socio-economic, in Northern Ireland it remains that of religion and national identity made manifest in the division over the constitutional status of Northern Ireland. Secondly, Northern Irish parties are not in competition with the major UK parties. The British Labour party neither contests elections nor accepts members from Northern Ireland. Since 1989 the Conservative party has grudgingly recognised local Conservative associations following grass-roots support for their affiliation but offers little practical support to them.[26]

Another feature of the contemporary party system is its youthfulness. Most of the contemporary parties were founded in the period of violence and constitutional upheaval of the late 1960s and early 1970s. For the entire period of devolved government from 1921 to 1972, the Ulster Unionist party (UUP) formed the government, with the majority of nationalist support going to the Nationalist party, which for much of the period did not act as the official opposition party owing to its denial of the legitimacy of Northern Ireland as a political unit. It should also be noted that, despite the point above concerning the principal cleavage, there were attempts to mobilise the electorate around socio-economic issues, the Northern Ireland Labour party in the late 1950s and early 1960s being the most successful example. Bearing this in mind, the following sections classify parties within the principal divide.

Unionist parties

The larger of the two established unionist parties is the UUP, often referred to as the Official Unionist party (OUP). In its current form it can be traced back to the reconsolidation of that section of the UUP opposed to the institutionalised power-sharing arrangements of 1974 which the then party leader, Brian Faulkner, had endorsed. The OUP reflects its origins, in that support for Northern Ireland's continuation as part of the UK is its primary policy. Although it is commonly seen as a more 'establishment' and less populist party than the Democratic Unionist party (DUP), it is more meritocratic than its predecessor. The UUP elite before direct rule was re-imposed in 1974 was heavily influenced by the 'landed' and 'county family' element but this social stratum's influence has been much reduced.

Also, because of the predominance of the constitutional question and a desire to win support across the unionist community when there is a direct rival for this support, explicit conservatism is not as evident as in earlier periods. The 'broad church' nature of the party is personified in two of its former MPs: Enoch Powell, who was a proponent of economic liberalism, and Harold McCusker, whose politics were of a broad social democratic complexion. To generalise, most party members and MPs would probably be classified as right of centre, though the relative weakness of the Northern Ireland economy tends to preclude espousal of unchecked market forces.

Although the party is united in opposition to a united Ireland and rejected the Anglo-Irish Agreement of 1985, the last ten years have witnessed a lack of consensus about the most suitable constitutional arrangements for Northern Ireland. This is an area of much complexity, but three broad positions can be highlighted. First, James Molyneaux, the leader from 1979 to 1995, saw both full legislative devolution and integration into the UK polity as unrealistic, and favoured an emphasis on improving the machinery of direct rule and restoring the powers of local government. A second grouping in the period after the Anglo-Irish Agreement favoured devolution, partly on the grounds that a local assembly, particularly with the support of the Social Democratic and Labour party (SDLP), would be the best strategy for marginalising Sinn Fein and the IRA. A third position, cogently argued by Powell, was that the fullest integration into the UK was the best strategy for protection of the union. Some members of the OUP extended this to support for the Campaign for Equal Citizenship, which advocated that British parties should contest Northern Ireland elections. This could obviously conflict with the electoral interests of the OUP and the tensions within the party led to expulsions in 1987.

The accession to the leadership in September 1995 of David Trimble has led to a change of style, though not obviously to one of substance. Many unionists felt that the quiet diplomacy of Molyneaux, centred on building support at Westminster, failed to check the political tide flowing against unionists. Trimble has attempted to articulate the unionist case to a wider audience, including Dublin and the USA, and raised the possibility of a modernising strategy for the OUP by playing down links with the Protestant Orange Order. However, qualitative shifts in unionism seem unlikely in the sense that while Trimble will endorse limited co-operation with the Republic of Ireland on a cross-border basis, he rejects the institutional structures which seem implicit in the Framework documents signed by the British and Irish governments in February 1995.

The other major unionist party is the DUP. It was founded in 1971 by Ian Paisley, who had earlier formed the Protestant Unionist party and won a Stormont by-election in 1970 on a platform of opposition to reforms of that period. Like the OUP, the DUP is fundamentally opposed to a united Ireland and favours the maintenance of the union. However, there are clearly identifiable differences between the parties. First, as founder of his own Free Presbyterian Church, Paisley is a representative of fundamentalist Protestantism, rooted in Calvinism, which espouses a robust anti-Catholic theology and an opposition to ecumenism. The overlap between membership of the Free Presbyterian Church and the DUP should not be over-emphasised; fewer than one-third of Free Presbyterian ministers are members of the DUP. However, the DUP does gain support from those for whom Protestantism, rather than the British link, is the defining factor in what it means to be a 'loyalist'.[27]

Secondly, as well as fundamentalism, the DUP has gained electoral support from working-class unionism, for example in North and East Belfast. This ties in with the point above about the more populist flavour of the DUP; historically, much of the unionist working class was uneasy with, or hostile to, the 'establishment' domination of the UUP, and the DUP has had some success in tapping into this constituency.

Thirdly, the DUP has, for most of its existence, been committed to devolution. This reflects both Paisley's distrust of Westminster and the electoral dominance of the OUP in Westminster elections in Northern Ireland; therefore the establishment of a local forum offers the best hope of challenging the OUP's hegemony. Hence, the DUP was an active supporter of the last such body, the Assembly created by James Prior in 1982.

Recent research confirms that the basis of support for the two main unionist parties is different. The OUP is disproportionately supported by economically active Protestants while the DUP has less support among professional classes and greater support among those aged sixty or over.[28]

The future of unionist politics is difficult to predict given the uncertainties of the current period. In recent years the established unionist parties have been widely criticised for failing to check what is widely perceived to be the development of an agenda favourable to nationalists and for failing to represent adequately the concerns, in particular the material ones, of working-class unionists. The latter critique has manifested itself in the higher profile of two newer parties, the Ulster Democratic party and the Progressive Unionist party, both of which have links with loyalist paramilitary groups. Their limited excursions into local politics do not suggest a realignment in unionist politics, at least in the short term, and the paramilitary links may preclude a widening of support. The record of their predecessors suggests that they will find it difficult to gain major party status.[29]

Nationalist parties

The principal nationalist party is the SDLP, which was formed in 1970 and quickly superseded the previously dominant Nationalist party. As its name suggests, the SDLP was not intended to be a narrowly confessional party. It adopted a broadly social democratic and pro-civil rights programme and joined the Socialist International. Its founders were a diverse group, including those from the labourist tradition of Belfast politics (e.g. Paddy Devlin and Gerry Fitt), independents and a former member of the Nationalist party. The independent power base of many of the MPs who joined and the inclusion of nationalist and socialist elements was to cause tensions; Devlin and Fitt later left the party partly because of its focus on 'green' rather than 'red' issues.

By 1973, the SDLP had become the dominant nationalist party, winning nineteen assembly seats as, for the first time in a Northern Ireland election, the Nationalist party failed to win any. Despite its non-sectarian roots, the SDLP's commitment to eventual unification ensured that virtually all its support would come from the Catholic community.

From its inception, the SDLP supported the creation of a devolved administration with power-sharing structures. The failure of such initiatives gradually moved the party's focus from an 'internal' settlement to one which embraced the construction of all-Ireland institutions with a significant role for the Irish Republic. Its leader since 1979, John Hume, has proved adept at promoting this vision on the international stage and he was a major force in the engineering of both the Anglo-Irish Agreement and the Downing Street Declaration. While the ideal of the party remains a re-unified Irish state, Hume currently invokes the concept of an 'Agreed Ireland', which may prove different and less than this. The institutions and form of such an 'Agreed Ireland' remain somewhat hazy; what does seem clear is that it is premised on the inadequacy of present constitutional arrangements and thus it is likely to prove unacceptable to unionists.

The other nationalist party of significance is the current incarnation of Sinn Fein, often termed the political wing of the IRA. It dates from a split within the IRA in 1970, although the original Sinn Fein was founded in 1905 to fight for Irish independence. Sinn Fein entered electoral politics in 1982, overturning a policy of abstentionism determined by non-recognition of the Northern Ireland state. This was a strategy partly inspired by the mobilisation around the hunger strikes of the previous year, the belief that the economic and social marginalisation of sections of the Catholic working class could be channelled into electoral support for Sinn Fein, and the limitations of the 'armed struggle' used in isolation. The most obvious difference between the two parties is that Sinn Fein did not (and does not) question the right of the IRA to use violence to end or reduce British influence in Ireland.

Since 1982, Sinn Fein has been formally committed to the establishment of a thirty-two-county socialist republic. This replaced the position set out in the 1972 document *Eire Nua*, which advocated a federal Ireland with four regional assemblies based on the four historic provinces of Ireland. Despite the secular tradition in republicanism (invoked by both parties), and a 'leftward' shift in the mid-1980s, Sinn Fein is foremost a nationalist

Table 8.3. *Electoral performance of the principal Northern Ireland parties,*
1979–97: percentage of vote (number of seats won)

	OUP	*DUP*	*SDLP*	*Sinn Fein*
1979 (G)	36.2 (5)	10.1 (3)	18.0 (1)	*
1979 (E)	21.9 (1)	29.8 (1)	24.6 (1)	*
1982 (A)	29.7 (2)	23.0 (21)	18.8 (14)	10.1 (5)
1983 (G)	34.0 (11)	20.0 (3)	17.9 (1)	13.4 (1)
1984 (E)	21.5 (1)	33.6 (1)	22.1 (1)	13.3 (0)
1987 (G)	37.8 (9)	11.7 (3)	21.1 (3)	11.4 (1)
1989 (E)	22.2 (1)	29.9 (1)	25.5 (1)	9.1 (0)
1992 (G)	34.5 (9)	13.1 (3)	23.5 (4)	10.0 (0)
1994 (E)	23.8 (1)	29.2 (1)	28.9 (1)	9.9 (0)
1997 (G)	32.7 (10)	13.6 (2)	24.1 (3)	16.1 (2)

G= general election, E= European election, A = Assembly election, *did not contest election.
Sources: W. D. Flackes, *Northern Ireland: A Political Directory 1968–83* (London, BBC, 1983);
J. McGarry and B. O'Leary (eds), *The Future of Northern Ireland* (Oxford, Oxford University
Press, 1990), p. 343; *Irish Political Studies*, 1995, p. 207; *Irish News*, 3 May 1997; *News
Letter*, 3 May 1997.

party whose support comes entirely from the Catholic community. Its
policies reflect this and its radicalism is employed pragmatically, since its
bedrock of support comes from what is, generally speaking, a morally and
socially conservative constituency.

As indicated above, Sinn Fein has found support among younger, urban
Catholics, many of whom were previously abstainers, and the economically
disadvantaged. Compared with the SDLP, its support is more likely to be
non-home owning, unemployed or, if in employment, not self-employed.
'On the nationalist side, the SDLP and Sinn Fein electorate are characterised
as economically active and socially disadvantaged respectively.'[30] However,
Knox *et al.* believe the combined Hume–Adams contribution to the peace
process is likely to make the divisions less stark. As with the Ulster
Democratic party and Progressive Unionist party mentioned above, it may
require a long period of peace and a greater distancing from the IRA for
Sinn Fein to expand its electoral base, although it performed well in both
the Forum elections of May 1996 and the general election of May 1997.

The 1997 general election confirmed the pre-eminence of the constitutional question. Of the non-confessional parties, the Alliance fared
best, with 8 per cent of the vote, 0.7 per cent down on its 1992 result.
Of the nationalist parties, Sinn Fein's 16 per cent was its most successful
result to date; however, the SDLP gained more votes and a higher percentage
share than it had in 1992. Of the unionist parties, the DUP vote was
depressed as it contested only nine of the eighteen seats owing to electoral

pacts with the OUP, despite considerable tensions between the parties. Northern Ireland Conservatives contested eight seats; their best performance was in Antrim East, where they gained 6.8 per cent but gained only 1.2 per cent of the popular vote overall compared with 5.7 per cent in 1992.

There were seventy-eight seats in the 1982 Assembly. There were twelve Westminster seats up to and including 1979, seventeen from 1983 to 1992 and eighteen in the 1997 general election. The highest support gained by a party not listed is 10 per cent, for the Alliance party. Conservative candidates gained 5.7 per cent of the vote in the 1992 general election, 1 per cent in the 1994 European election and 1.5 per cent in the 1997 general election. In the 1979 general election two seats were gained by independent unionists and one by an independent nationalist. Since 1983 one seat has been held by an independent unionist. The SDLP gained one seat in the by-elections of early 1986 when unionists resigned them and fought them again as part of the campaign against the Anglo-Irish Agreement. The relatively low vote for the DUP in the 1987, 1992 and 1997 general elections is a result of electoral pacts with the OUP. The Progressive Unionist party received 1.4 per cent of the overall vote in 1997.[31]

Notes

1   Figures from A. H. Birch, *Political Integration and Disintegration in the British Isles* (London, George Allen and Unwin, 1977), p. 123.
2   For more details of the history of the SNP see J. G. Kellas, *The Scottish Political System*, 4th edn (Cambridge, Cambridge University Press, 1989); J. Brand, *The National Movement in Scotland* (London, Routledge and Kegan Paul, 1978); and R. J. Finlay, *Independent and Free: Scottish Politics and the Origins of the Scottish National Party 1918–1945* (Edinburgh, John Donald, 1994).
3   SNP Research Department, *A Short History of the Scottish National Party* (Edinburgh, SNP, 1994), p. 2.
4   A. Marr, *The Battle for Scotland* (London, Penguin, 1992), p. 95.
5   A. Kemp, *The Hollow Drum: Scotland Since the War* (Edinburgh, Mainstream, 1993), p. 97.
6   For details see Kemp, *The Hollow Drum*, chs 8–19.
7   Cited in Marr, *Battle for Scotland*, p. 205.
8   J. Mitchell, 'Factions, Tendencies and Consensus in the SNP in the 1980s', in A. Brown and R. Parry (eds), *The Scottish Government Yearbook 1990* (Edinburgh, Unit for the Study of Government in Scotland, 1990), pp. 51–2.
9   For a fuller discussion of the '79 Group see I. O. Bayne, 'The Impact of 1979 on the SNP', in T. Gallagher (ed.), *Nationalism in the Nineties* (Edinburgh, Polygon, 1991).
10 For more on the debates around this policy see I. Lindsay, 'The SNP and the Lure of Europe', in Gallagher (ed.), *Nationalism in the Nineties*, and A. Macartney, 'Independence in Europe', in Brown and Parry (eds), *Scottish Government Yearbook 1990*.

11   Lindsay, 'The SNP and the Lure of Europe', p. 87.
12   T. Gallagher, 'The SNP Faces the 1990s', in Gallagher (ed.), *Nationalism in the Nineties*, p. 18
13   See, for example, D. McCrone, *Understanding Scotland: The Sociology of a Stateless Nation* (London, Routledge, 1992), pp. 164–5.
14   *New Statesman and Society*, 14 April 1995.
15   D. Seawright and J. Curtice, 'The Decline of the Scottish Conservative and Unionist Party 1950–92: Religion, Ideology or Economics?', *Contemporary Record*, 1995, p. 330.
16   Reliable figures for party membership are difficult to obtain. The figures cited for the 1960s are from Kemp, *The Hollow Drum*, p. 98, for 1976 from J. Mercer, *Scotland: The Devolution of Power* (London, John Calder, 1978), p. 141, for 1983 from R. Levy, *Scottish Nationalism at the Crossroads* (Edinburgh, Scottish Academic Press, 1990), p. 5, and for 1992 C. Harvie, *Scotland and Nationalism: Scottish Society and Politics 1707–1994*, 2nd edn (London, Routledge, 1994), p. 266.
17   This summary of the formal structure of the SNP is taken from a party information handbill of July 1994.
18   See *New Statesman and Society*, 29 September 1995.
19   For details of the early years of Plaid Cymru see D. Hywel Davies, *The Welsh Nationalist Party 1925–1945* (Cardiff, University of Wales Press, 1983).
20   For a discussion of Plaid Cymru's views on the obsolescence of the contemporary nation state, its advocacy of 'subsidiarity' and a 'Europe of the regions', see the 1994 European election manifesto *Making Europe Work for Wales*.
21   Birch, *Political Integration and Disintegration*, p. 125.
22   See, for example, *Governing Locally for Wales*, the manifesto for the 1995 unitary authority elections.
23   *Guardian*, 9 April 1997.
24   Telephone information from Plaid Cymru, 13 November 1997.
25   This section is adapted from sections 5–11 of the July 1995 copy of 'Constitution of Plaid Cymru'.
26   For a short review of this question see M. Cunningham and R. Kelly, 'Standing for Ulster', *Politics Review*, November 1995, pp. 20–3.
27   See J. Todd, 'Two Traditions in Unionist Political Culture', *Irish Political Studies*, 1987, pp. 1–26, for more on differences within unionism.
28   C. Knox, C. McIlheney and R. Osborne, 'Social and Economic Influences on Voting in Northern Ireland', *Irish Political Studies*, 1995, p. 90.
29   For more details see S. Bruce, *The Red Hand: Protestant Paramilitaries in Northern Ireland* (Oxford, Oxford University Press, 1990).
30   Knox *et al.*, 'Social and Economic Influences', p. 94.
31   Accurate membership figures for Northern Ireland parties appear to be unavailable. (The comprehensive data section of *Irish Political Studies* does not include them.)

9

The 'problem' of party finance

During the last twenty years, there has been a mounting belief that the funding of political parties represents another serious problem in British politics. This view has been expressed by the government-backed Houghton report of 1976, by the independent Hansard Society report of 1981 (box 9.1), by academics such as Keith Ewing, by large sections of the Labour and Liberal Democrat parties and more recently by the Nolan Commission, set up by Major's administration in 1994 following concern about moral standards in politics.

This chapter will elucidate the supposed problem, look at some of the supposed solutions and examine finally whether party finance really is the problem many suggest – or just another symptom of a much deeper malaise affecting our political culture.

Defining the problem

Among those who acknowledge a problem, it is widely agreed that it has two interlocking features: first, that our parties have insufficient revenue to carry out their 'essential' tasks; secondly, that they rely excessively upon corporate and institutional support.

Insufficient revenue

For parties, the cost of electorally effective activity has soared since 1970 and continues to rise. At the same time, they have had acute problems raising the necessary additional income.

Causes
Three reasons seem to exist for this combined difficulty. First, the electorate has undergone what psephologists term 'dealignment' (see chapter 10). The reasons for this development have already been touched upon in this book

201

Box 9.1. Recommendations of Houghton Committee[a] and Hansard Society[b]

Houghton
It was recommended that the state's subsidies to British political parties be increased, and that this should mainly take the form of annual grants paid by the Exchequer into the parties' central organisations. To qualify for a grant, a party at the previous general election must have saved the deposits of at least six parliamentary candidates *or* had at least two candidates elected *or* had one candidate elected, with the party receiving not less than 150,000 votes nationwide. The size of grant would be calculated on the basis of 5p for each vote cast for its candidates at the previous general election. It was estimated that the cost of these grants would amount to an average of £2.25 million a year, which would include £360,000 worth of additional reimbursement to candidates' election expenses.

Hansard
It was proposed that the state's subsidies to British political parties be increased and that this should take the form of ongoing payments by the Exchequer into the parties' central organisations. To qualify for such payments, a party at the previous general election must have met the same criteria as those defined by the Houghton report (see above). The state's payments would be calculated on the basis of £2 for every £2 subscription or donation given by an individual supporter to a constituency party. The constituency party would then claim a matching sum from the party's central organisation, which would then reclaim it from the Exchequer. It was proposed that, under this scheme, the state should make available a total of £1 million per annum; to achieve its maximum payment, it was calculated that each party would have to secure a £2 contribution from almost one in twelve of those who had voted for it at the previous general election – judged a 'not unreasonable' expectation in the light of recent psephological surveys.

[a]Cmnd 6601, August 1976 (London, HMSO).
[b]'Paying for Politics', July 1981.

and, though fairly complex, have two blistering effects upon party finance in Britain. To begin with, the more diverse and cynical electorate created by dealignment makes it hard for the main parties (especially those rooted in traditional class loyalties) to recruit and sustain a large membership; the Conservative and Labour parties had a combined membership of under one million by the mid-1990s, it having been over four million in the 1950s.

Fewer members mean fewer subscriptions and a sharp fall in revenue. Yet dealignment deals the parties a 'double whammy' by depriving them of members and revenue at the very moment when more members and revenue are needed: dealignment, after all, produces a less reliable electorate, which begs a greater degree of campaigning from parties anxious for its support (the 1997 campaign lasted almost six weeks, twice as long as that of 1979). In other words, parties have to devote more resources to the arts of persuasion just as those resources are harder to come by.

Seyd *et al.*'s research confirms that the most electorally effective parties in recent years have been the most active and high profile at constituency level. Indeed, in the case of the Tories, there was a quite explicit link to the amounts spent, with 75 per cent of those local Tory parties which spent a 'high amount' polling over 40 per cent of votes in 1987.[1] While recognising that more is likely to be spent on winnable seats, Seyd *et al.* still calculate that, if local Tory campaigns had spent 30 per cent less overall, fifty-two seats would have been lost – with devastating effects upon the outcome of the 1987 election.

The second reason for the increased strain upon party finances relates to technological change. The 1980s and early 1990s saw a revolution in information technology which the parties, keen to communicate in the most up-to-date manner possible, were obliged to respect. Getting themselves on to the 'information superhighway' – through the purchase of computers, fax machines and desktop publishing – has therefore put additional strains upon party resources. Geoffrey Harper, responsible for training the Tories' constituency agents, recalled that a 'huge slice' of CCO's budget in the late 1980s went on sending agents to computer training courses.[2] In the long term, new technology may well prove an economy for the parties, but in the short term it has certainly compounded their financial worries.

Thirdly, the parties must not only campaign more intensely, but more frequently. European elections since 1979 have added to the parties' bills, while the centralisation of local government in the 1980s meant that local elections are now fought nationally as well as locally. The greater likelihood of hung parliaments (another effect of dealignment), allied to Britain's lack of fixed-term parliaments, could also mean more general elections: it was no coincidence that the parties' finances hit a particular crisis in the mid-1970s after fighting two general elections in 1974.

Manifestations
These financial pressures have revealed themselves in a number of ways during the past decade. Sir Norman Fowler's survey of the Tory organisation in 1993 (see chapter 4) acknowledged an accumulated deficit of £19 million and ordered a 40 per cent reduction in CCO costs over the next three years. Being largely separate, this did little to ease the plight of the constituency associations. A full-time constituency agent is traditionally seen by the Tories as the benchmark of an efficient constituency party. Yet, at the start of 1994, only 207 associations had one (a 30 per cent drop since 1992),

including only five in the thirteen most marginal seats. The Tories' problems were worsened by the tail-off in company donations during the last, crisis-ridden Tory government, forcing them to spend about £3 million less on advertising during the 1997 election than they had during the election of 1992 – despite the 1997 campaign being twice as long.[3] After the 1997 election, one of the new party chairman's first tasks was to 'cancel his own salary and sort out redundancy notices at Central Office'.[4]

The Tories' financial problems had echoes in other parties. Labour's debts at the start of the 1990s were in excess of £2 million, forcing heavy redundancies at Labour headquarters and the closure of two regional offices in the re-organisation of 1993. At the 1992 general election, only 100 constituency Labour parties had a full-time constituency agent at a time when a slight increase in the pace of Labour's local campaigns just might have forced a hung parliament.[5] The Liberal Democrats also claimed to be 'living on a shoestring' in 1995, with a central income of only £7 million in 1992–3 (while the Tories considered their own revenue of £26 million insufficient under modern circumstances).[6]

Effects

The Hansard report of 1981, *Paying For Politics*, noted that one of the most worrying effects of under-funding was the parties giving less energy to policy research when the complexities of government demanded the exact opposite. In the 1980s, the Conservative Research Department shed almost a quarter of its staff and was reduced to 'providing cheap jokes for Tory councillors'.[7] Labour rebels during the Kinnock regime, like Tony Benn and Eric Heffer, complained that the party had forsaken serious policy work in favour of vapid sloganising. The feared outcome is that parties in office are even less likely to match voter expectation with performance, thus eroding membership further and exacerbating their financial plight.

Perhaps the most alarming effect the dearth of funds has upon a party is desperation, out of which come tactics that diminish further the stature of British political parties. In recent years, this charge has been levelled particularly at the Conservatives, whose ardour for funds produced various accusations of 'sleaze' within their organisation. The party's willingness to accept donations from dubious business people was the most spectacular illustration of this tendency, as with the £450,000 accepted from Asil Nadir in 1987 (Nadir was later charged with fraud and fled the country). Nadir's was not an isolated example. John Latsis, a shipping magnate linked to the Greek military dictatorship of the early 1970s, gave the party £2 million in 1986; Octav Botnar gave £1 million in the early 1980s and later evaded £97 million in taxation; Hong Kong banker Li Ka Shing donated £500,000 in 1991 just five years after being censured for alleged insider dealing.

It has also been suggested that the enfranchisement of expatriate Britons in 1984 and 1989, through two separate Representation of the People

Acts, was the trade-off for their continued donation to Tory funds, a point conceded by the 'Chairman of the South of France Conservatives' in 1990. It was further alleged that at least one aspect of the government's tax reforms, exemption from capital gains for those working in Britain for less than six months a year, was an invitation for those affected to contribute generously to the party – as many could certainly afford to do. That these charges may be groundless is almost irrelevant: their very existence sullies the public's faith in the party system.[8]

However, the most serious effect of under-funding is in fact the second dimension to the 'problem' of party finance.

Reliance upon institutional funding

The parties' need for greater income at a time of falling membership highlights their reliance upon institutional donations (figures 9.1 and 9.2). Such donations refer to trade union funding of the Labour party and company monies given to the Tories (table 9.1). These donations are at the heart of concern expressed about the probity of political parties and were indeed mentioned by Lord Nolan's report on ethics in public life in May 1995.

Manifestations
The parties' reliance upon this sort of income is always marked in election years, when donations are more eagerly sought and more readily given. As the seeking is usually done by the parties' national treasurers, most of the donations are paid into the parties' central accounts. Accordingly, donations amounting to £19 million were paid into CCO in 1991–2 (over three-quarters of its income that year), while £7.7 million in trade union donations were paid into Labour headquarters at Walworth Road in 1996 (45 per cent of its income that year). One of William Hague's first tasks as Tory leader was to secure £2 million from various 'Yorkshire tycoons' to help the party stay afloat until the 1997 Tory conference.[9]

Institutional donations normally outstrip those of any constituency party. The highest quota paid by any Tory association in 1994, for example, was £16,062 (from Chelsea), whereas the donation from the P&O group was £100,000 – without this being the most generous (see table 9.1). Neither is it any coincidence that parties without much institutional funding – notably the Liberal Democrats – have revenue which is but a fraction of their principal rivals'.

Effects
The most common complaint about institutional funding is that it 'lowers the tone' of British politics, raising ethical questions about the conduct of party politicians. It is said to do this in three ways. First, there is a strong

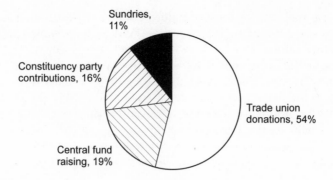

Figure 9.1. *Income of Labour party headquarters, 1995.* Source: *Guardian, 7* September 1996.

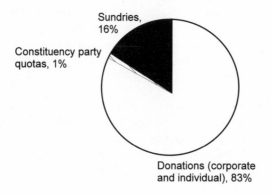

Figure 9.2. *Income of Conservative Central Office, 1995.* Source: CCO accounts.

Table 9.1. *Top ten company donations to the Conservative party, 1994*

Company	Donation
Hanson	£115,000
P&O	£100,000
Forte	£80,000
Glaxo Wellcome	£72,000
Pearson	£60,000
Caledonia Inverness	£56,000
Tomkins	£52,000
Guardian Royal	£50,000
Scottish and Newcastle	£50,000
Sun Alliance	£50,000

Source: *Sunday Telegraph,* 7 May 1995.

whiff of secrecy, and a distinct lack of accountability, surrounding donations to the Conservative party. Parties receiving individual or corporate donations do not have to reveal their source and CCO chooses not to do so. Under the Companies Acts of 1967 and 1985, firms donating more than £200 to political parties must declare them in their accounts. But many companies side-step this by giving money to 'filter' organisations like British United Industrialists, which claims to be directing subsidies only for 'free enterprise' purposes. (It is revealing that in 1991–2 only £3.7 million of the Tories' £19 million of donations were traceable at Companies House.) It is also worth recalling that companies are under no legal obligation to consult shareholders before making such donations, nor do shareholders have the facility to 'contract out' of such indirect contributions to party funds.

Secondly, as hinted earlier, there is a perception among voters that such donations affect the parties' policies – hence the perennial complaint of centre parties that 'the big two' are 'in the pockets' of organised labour and big business. Such complaints are not entirely groundless. Following the Monopolies and Mergers Commission report of 1989, the Thatcher government was minded to liberalise the licensing trade by restricting the number of pubs a single brewery could own – a move that would have chimed with Thatcherism's stress upon competition and consumer choice. This view was not as easily shared by several of the major breweries donating to Tory funds, and the subsequent U-turn by the Department of Trade and Industry left many with a cynical view of policy making in Britain. Such cynicism has also shrouded the government of Tony Blair, his opponents claiming that the decision to exempt motor racing from the ban on tobacco sponsorship was linked to the £1 million donation Labour had received from Formula 1 chief Bernie Ecclestone (the donation was returned, but by then the damage was done).

Yet it is in connection with trade union funding that Labour policy has attracted most criticism. Trade union funding has been directly linked to union strength inside Labour's organisation. For most of Labour's history, the unions accounted for the vast majority of votes cast at Labour's conference and a plurality of seats on its NEC (see chapter 6). It is hardly surprising that the union view has been crucial to the development of policy during previous Labour governments. Indeed, the 'social contract' between unions and the 1974–9 government was officially at the heart of economic strategy. The unions' capacity to frustrate Labour leaders was shown vividly in 1968 when the white paper *In Place of Strife* had to be shelved after lobbying from union-sponsored MPs and a party treasurer (James Callaghan) concerned at the possible loss of union subsidies in the run-up to an election.

All this – the parties' own version of 'insider dealing' – fuels public scepticism and does not abet membership recruitment. Many of those who drifted from Labour after 1970 to 'progressive' pressure groups like Amnesty and Greenpeace claimed that their own particular interests had been swamped inside the party by monolithic union influence.[10]

Thirdly, institutional donations are thought to have demeaned the honours system by inviting the idea that honours are 'for sale'. This, of course, has been a recurrent complaint ever since the premiership of Lloyd George (1916–22), but has been particularly prevalent since 1979. The *Guardian* revealed that between 1979 and 1992, 50 per cent of the honours awarded to business went to the 6 per cent of companies donating to the Tory party. The claim that Tory finances had 'an atmosphere of sleaze and an odour of corruption' doubtless rang true for many voters.[11]

As well as 'lowering the tone', institutional funding is also thought to have created unfair electoral competition. Institutional donations to the Conservatives have usually been more generous than those given to Labour – £6 million more generous in 1992. This allowed the Tories to spend more on the campaign at a time when electoral volatility gives it greater importance (according to MORI, 25 per cent of voters in 1992 made up their minds only during the official campaign). In 1992, the Tories duly spent £10.1 million (£5,800 per candidate), Labour £7.1 million (£5,100 per candidate), and the Liberal Democrats £2.1 million (£3,100 per candidate). In other words, as in 1987, the Tories spent more than their main opponents combined. As pointed out earlier, Seyd *et al.* have spotted a link between a party's constituency vote and the strength of its constituency organisation; and as this chapter has suggested, a local party's efficiency is helped by the presence of a full-time professional organiser. Here again, superior revenue may have helped prolong Tory government, with the Tories in 1992 having 200 more full-time constituency agents than Labour.

The situation at constituency level is a reminder that figures from CCO and Walworth Road do not reveal the full extent of the Tories' advantage. Their *overall* income (central *and* constituency level) for 1991–2 was put at £39 million, compared with Labour's £20 million; many companies and their executives donate at local as opposed to, or as well as, national level. When harnessed to the support given by most newspapers during most general elections, described by Martin Linton as '£37m worth of free propaganda', it could be argued that the Tories in 1992 had a financial advantage over Labour of about £50 million.[12] Although it would be rash to say this determined the 1992 result, it would be equally rash to claim it had no effect, given the nearness of a hung parliament.

Solving the problem

Party finance was the subject of an inquiry by the Home Affairs Select Committee between 1993 and 1994, an inquiry later used by the Major

Table 9.2. *The majority and minority reports of the Commons' Home Affairs Select Committee Enquiry into the Funding of British Political Parties (1993)*

Majority	Minority
No changes to the way parties raise funds	Limited state funding for parties
State funding for parties is expressly ruled out	
No curbs on secret donations	Donations above £5,000 to be legally declarable
No curbs on foreign donations	Foreign donations to become illegal
No disclosure of sources	See the second point above
No legal protection for shareholders if they object to a political donation	Shareholders' right to reject directors' decision to donate to become legally enforceable
Accounts to be published and audited. However, sources will not have to be divulged	Full accounts to be published though donations in kind can be excluded
No limit to the amount an individual can donate	No limit to the amount an individual can donate
A voluntary code of practice to be established to guide parties in their fund raising	Funding to be regulated by statute. An electoral commission to be set up to assist

The Conservatives' code of practice does contain measures which will undoubtedly hamper their future fund-raising efforts. For example, it recognises that substantial anonymous donations and all donations from foreign governments or rulers should be refused. However, now that the Labour party is returned to office, its proposed regulations will have a major impact on the current system, the Conservatives being the principal victims. A brief summary of its main clauses follows:

- MPs/peers with close associations to bodies which fund the governing party cannot hold a salaried government appointment.
- No honour can be given to an industrialist whose company has donated to a party in the past five years.
- The honours system is to be taken out of the hands of serving politicians.
- Fund-raising trips by ministers are no longer to be paid for by the taxpayer.
- Downing Street is not to be used for fund-raising purposes.

From: S. Foster, *Political Parties* (Sheffield, Pavic, 1994).

government to deflect the Nolan Committee from a follow-up (and potentially more damning) report into the same area. The make-up of the Select Committee reflected that of the Commons, so it was unsurprising that it eventually rejected bold reform (table 9.2).

Yet it did argue for independent auditing of party accounts, secondment of one or two civil servants to help parties with administration at

Westminster and a code of practice stating (for example) that donations do not guarantee honours and that money from foreign governments is unacceptable. To the chagrin of the main opposition parties, the majority report ruled out any need to disclose the source of donations, any curbs on gifts from abroad, any requirement for donating companies to consult shareholders beforehand and any ceilings on national campaign expenditure. Most publicised of all, though, was its conclusion that parties should not receive much more assistance from the taxpayer.

The state aid debate

For about twenty years, many reformers have seen state funding of political parties as a kind of panacea, with more recent events bolstering that opinion. Yet it is important to recognise that the state (or taxpayer) already funds the parties to a reasonable extent.

(1) Since 1918, the state has met the cost of registering electors, candidates' postal services, the hiring of schools for public meetings and the presence of returning officers on and before polling day.
(2) Since 1947, there has been free broadcasting time for parties with fifty or more candidates (the allocation of which is decided by the Committee of Party Political Broadcasting). Along with the cost of postal services, this assistance amounted to £20 million in 1997.
(3) Since 1975, monies have been paid to opposition parties at Westminster to help with their research, secretarial and administrative costs. Known as 'Short money' (after Edward Short, the Leader of the House who introduced it), it totalled about £2 million in 1996–7, with £1.6 million given to Labour and £316,000 to the Liberal Democrats – it being allocated on the basis of seats, not votes.

Academics like Ewing believe that these subsidies are too meagre when compared with those of other European democracies.[13] This belief has been upheld by the various centre parties since 1974 and, since 1980, the Labour party as well. As the main beneficiaries of the status quo, it is not a view held by the Conservatives; yet their reluctance is shared by Plaid Cymru and the SNP, who fear that state aid merely props up parties which have lost support in their respective territories.

Those who advocate more state aid claim it would:

(1) reduce the parties' financial problems and allow them more funds for policy research, thus enhancing their policies, narrowing the gap between promise and performance and improving the prospect of mass membership;
(2) equalise to some extent the resources of the major parties, producing

fairer competition at elections and giving new parties a better chance
of breaking into the party system;

(3) permit the two main parties to slacken their links with trade unions
and large companies, which in turn would have at least four benefits –

  (a) the parties could develop their ideas more freely and project them
  to a potentially wider audience (it is no coincidence that Tony Blair,
  Labour's arch moderniser, also favours more state aid);

  (b) it would diminish the 'sleaze factor', as fewer doubts would exist
  over whether policies were shaped by party financial considerations,
  and it could restore some faith in the honours system;

  (c) it could end the situation where many trade unionists and shareholders were supporting parties against their will, via subscriptions
  and investments;

  (d) it would push British politics in a modern, classless direction, for
  no longer would the main parties be tied to traditional class
  interests.

Since the mid-1970s, there have been a number of suggestions as to
how greater state aid could be introduced, notably the Houghton report
of 1976 and Hansard report of 1981. Their prescriptions are outlined in
box 9.1.

The problem of reform

Whether the system of party finance should be reformed is not a black
and white issue. It is possible, for example, to oppose further state subsidies
while accepting the need for less secrecy and (or) some constraint upon
national spending and individual donations. These 'qualified opponents' of
further state aid were represented on the Home Affairs Select Committee
by academics like Lewis Minkin, who stress that there is now a tendency
within both parties towards greater self-regulation. Following pressure from
the Charter Movement (see appendix, ch. 3), some details of Conservative
accounts have been issued by CCO since 1981, while the extension of
OMOV in the Labour party is also designed to bring greater openness to
its internal affairs (see chapter 6).

The Conservative party's view of reform is less equivocal and naturally
coloured the Select Committee's majority recommendations (see table 9.2).
This emphasises the voluntary nature of party activity in Britain: other
voluntary bodies are not expected to disclose minute details of their
accounts and the anonymity of private donors is respected. If this were
changed in respect of political parties, many donations might dry up, thus
worsening the parties' plight. Likewise, limits on spending impugn a
voluntary body's freedom of choice and would anyhow be difficult to
enforce.

Opposing state aid

Most of the opposition to reform, however, is rooted in an objection to further state aid and tends to posit the following arguments.

First, it must be remembered that state aid is a euphemism for taxpayers' money. In view of the criticism launched against the unwarranted use of shareholders' and levy payers' money, it is hypocritical to draw further upon what working people pay into the general tax pool. Voters would be subsidising to an even greater degree parties they may not support and principles they may actually loathe. An opinion poll in 1993 showed 75 per cent against further state aid.[14] Even if the amounts involved were relatively small, voters would 'not be slow to translate it in terms of extra hospital beds or nursery places'.[15] It was this type of consideration, indeed, which dissuaded the Callaghan government from introducing Houghton's recommendations in 1976.

Secondly, many of the proposed schemes for further state aid might not solve the problem of new or smaller parties being 'organised out'. Both the Hansard and Houghton schemes aimed to 'reward' parties in some way – for either votes or recruitment. But new and smaller parties might argue that they would be unable to meet such criteria without the sort of funding already enjoyed by their larger rivals: in short, a 'Catch 22' could easily emerge. Yet public support for any scheme which did not embody the 'reward' principle is even harder to envisage.

Thirdly, there is a danger that greater state aid, especially in the Houghton mode, would sustain parties that had forfeited public support and outlived their 'historic' function – at the expense, perhaps, of a party whose 'time had come'. (It has already been pointed out that, for this reason, further state aid is not supported by the nationalist parties.)

Fourthly, the Hansard scheme shows the bureaucratic complexities so often attending schemes of reform, and the possibilities for a new brand of 'sleaze' in political life. How would the state ensure, for example, that every £2 donation came from a fresh and distinctive source? Remember as well that the 'sleaze factor' is not confined to British politics. As Pinto-Duschinsky argued, 'Countries such as Italy and Germany have experienced problems relating to corrupt secret payments for election campaigns that have been far graver than anything encountered in Britain'.[16] Yet both countries have elaborate laws about the disclosure of accounts and generous state subsidies.

Finally, there is no guarantee that increased state funding would reduce, as opposed to supplement, the parties' institutional donations, nor can we be sure that it would reduce their importance. The Tories would doubtless continue to seek company funding to sustain their 'revenue lead', while companies for the same reason would continue to give it; Labour and the unions would then feel obliged to close the gap by maintaining their own financial links. So unless state funding were accompanied by a strict limitation upon institutional funding – tricky on both practical and ethical grounds – it would do little to equalise the resources of our major parties.

Conclusion: is party finance a problem?

When discussing the practicalities of reform, it is easy to lose sight of the fundamentals. To begin with, the parties' reliance upon institutional funding can be exaggerated. Pinto-Duschinsky confirms that although the Tories' central funds are dominated by company donations, their *overall* revenue tells a different story: in an average, non-election year, such donations account for only 20–30 per cent of revenue, with the bulk provided by constituency fund raising and generous levels of subscription from individual members.[17] Similarly, union affiliation fees to Labour in 1996 came to only 45 per cent of total revenue, 22 per cent less than in 1987. Labour's income has diversified markedly in recent years, with much more emphasis being placed upon constituency fund raising and financial services. Blair's leadership intensified this trend.

The extent to which parties are influenced by their donors can also be overstated. The 1974–9 Labour government was keener, *force majeure*, to appease the International Monetary Fund than the trade unions and pursued a string of policies – from wage restraint to spending cuts – which many unions bitterly opposed. (It is often forgotten that the 'winter of discontent' strikes of 1978–9 sprang from a *lack* rather than a surfeit of union power.) After 1987, the Labour leadership instigated a batch of OMOV reforms designed to weaken union influence inside the party (see chapter 6), while Blair's successful crusade against clause 4 in 1995 defied the TGWU – Labour's biggest union donor. Most union leaders, it will be recalled, accepted such changes as the price for a Labour government – a government upon which they have a limited, but not dominant, influence is preferable to one upon which they have apparently no influence at all.

After 1979, the Conservatives were also frequently at odds with those who backed them financially. Although the Confederation of British Industry itself has no financial links with the Conservatives, many of its members have, and a succession of its director generals (from Terence Beckett in the early 1980s to Howard Davies in the 1990s) were sharply critical of the government. The withdrawal of British Airways funding by Lord King in 1993 (who claimed government policy had damaged the company) and the loss of the Whitbread donation in 1995 do not suggest a government slavishly supportive of its paymasters. Even if the government wished to be so, it would be – to say the least – unwise from an electoral angle and exceedingly difficult given the obtuseness of modern economics and central decision making. As Ewing concedes, 'It would be wrong to say that the

Conservatives are pro-business simply because they are financed by business, or that Labour is pro-union because that is where the bulk of its money comes from. The relationship is much more subtle than that.'[18] The motives of those giving institutional donations seem to be a desire for the lesser evil rather than an expectation of regular and decisive influence. Conspiracy theories are simply incompatible with the parties' electoral and governmental responsibilities.

Thirdly, there is often a false impression of how shareholders' and levy payers' money actually reaches the parties and the amounts involved; the reality is not quite so scandalous as many believe. Hanson's £115,000 donation in 1994 to the Tories, for example, represents 0.008 per cent of its pre-tax profits in 1994, which, in turn, represents only 2p per 1000 shares alongside a dividend of £117; while a principle is certainly at stake, it hardly seems like a *casus belli* for Hanson's shareholders.[19] The average political levy for a trade unionist affiliated to the Labour party is only £1.80 a year, from which he or she may contract out at any time, while voting against the whole principle of a levy every ten years.

Fourthly, there is no evidence that only parties with more state funding would be able to develop brighter ideas and thereby attract new members. One of the most remarkable surges in party membership came after the formation of the SDP in 1981, when it recruited 60,000 in its first year. Yet the SDP started out with no corporate funding, few resources and only a skeletal staff during what proved its most fertile period. Its success lay in catching the public mood with a simple idea – that of 'breaking the mould' of the existing party system. Striking a chord among voters, it then attracted much media attention, which nourished interest even further. Sound party finances therefore seem an effect rather than cause of party popularity, as Labour discovered during its own renaissance under Blair. The most important cause of popularity, it seems, is novelty, imagination and raw political skill from the parties themselves – qualities which do not demand in the first instance vast sums of money.

Fifthly, it is questionable whether parties do not undertake more policy research because of financial exigencies. Parties are traditionally reluctant to 'over-prepare', as they wish to avoid giving 'hostages to fortune', raising hopes which cannot be met once in office. Opposition parties which are meticulous about their own plans also risk being put on the defensive, forfeiting one of the few advantages of not being in power – a lesson Labour learnt with its tax proposals in 1992 and which Blair was anxious to avoid repeating.

Parties normally prefer to engage in 'big ideas' – which the civil service and policy advisors can later substantiate – leaving them to concentrate on campaigning and policy. It is instructive that the two most effective post-war ministries, those of Attlee and Thatcher, came to power on significant swings with manifestos high on vision but low on detail. Throughout the

1979 election, Thatcher was asked how she would finance her own 'big idea' of lower taxation; her relentless answer was that she could not say until she reached office and 'saw the books'. Though unhelpful to journalists, this open response was evidently not a problem for enough voters. At the last general election, Blair and Brown's hopes for a 'growth harvest' were equally vague, yet sufficient to give Labour a landslide victory.

It is worth remembering that one government which did start life having done immense policy homework was Heath's in 1970. Following its U-turn of 1971–2, however, Heath's became the classic example of a government failing to deliver, ending up with policies that starkly contradicted its original aims (see chapter 3 and Conclusion). That government was floored not by a lack of preparation but by a series of unforeseen blows at home and abroad; but dealing with such blows in an *ad hoc* manner is perhaps the very essence of modern British government. It is this very un-predictability, allied to the globalisation of our economy, which leads parties to prefer the 'broad stroke' approach to policy debate.

Lastly, the parties' financial problems could be just another symptom of a more serious malaise afflicting most modern western democracies – falling party membership and a residual cynicism, on the part of voters, towards party politicians (see Conclusion). That this can be ascribed wholly, or even mainly, to the way in which parties are financed is unlikely; wider social, economic and cultural changes look a more pressing explanation. As Pinto-Duschinsky has observed, other party systems where state aid is more extensive have proved no more durable and no less unpopular than our own; state aid has merely cushioned them from the full effects of their unpopularity, acting like 'a drug that deals temporarily with the symptoms but leaves the disease itself worse'.[20]

It is interesting that in their survey of *Britain's Changing Party System* in 1994, the various authors tended to identify a recurrent problem besetting a certain aspect of party activity (organisation, ideology, candidate selection, etc.). Yet, as McConnell noted in his concluding chapter, hardly any of his co-authors thought that reform of party finance – and more state aid in particular – would make much difference. As he observed, those authors gave no more than 'the occasional passing reference' to party finance in either their diagnoses or prescriptions.[21] Finance, it would appear, is but a secondary problem affecting British political parties today.

Tony Blair came to power in 1997 having expressed strong complaints about the way in which Britain's political parties – including Labour – had been financed during Labour's long period in opposition. In September 1997, the government confirmed that reform of party finance, including the extension of state aid, was still part of its mid- to long-term agenda. In November 1997, Sir Patrick Neill, the new chairman of the Parliamentary Standards Committee, was ordered by the government to examine a range of possibilities, including a ban on foreign donations, a requirement to disclose the source of all domestic donations over £500, and an end to limitless spending on the national campaign (despite their financial problems, the Tories still spent £20 million on the 1997 campaign, compared with Labour's £13 million and the Liberal Democrats' £3 million). A green paper on the subject was expected in the spring of 1998.

It should be remembered, though, that Labour since 1993 has done much to put its own house in order. As indicated earlier, Labour's financial reliance upon trade unions has come down, while a union's influence inside the party (at conference, for example) is no longer related to the size of its donations. In 1996, Labour also abandoned the old 'Hastings Agreement' – one which allowed unions to 'sponsor' individual MPs by paying up to 80 per cent of their constituency parties' costs (all union donations now go straight to party funds).[22] Despite – or perhaps because of – these changes, Labour entered the 1997 general election in a much healthier financial position and employing three times more staff at its headquarters than in 1992.[23] Although the Conservatives may have again spent more on the campaign, there was no suggestion that Labour's campaign suffered from a shortage of funds. Indeed, Labour's campaign was widely praised for its professionalism and efficacy.

All this reinforces the idea that a party's financial strengths are, if anything, the effect rather than cause of its electoral prospects. Having come to power without the aid of legal change, it will be interesting to see how much attention ministers eventually give to the issue of party finance. At present, it does not seem to have much electoral or political mileage.

Notes

1   P. Whiteley, P. Seyd and J. Richardson, *True Blues* (Oxford, Oxford University Press, 1994), ch. 8.
2   Interview with Kelly, 3 February 1995.
3   Kelly's conversation with John Pearson, CCO Treasury Department, 27 June 1997.
4   *Sunday Telegraph*, 29 June 1997.
5   P. Seyd and P. Whiteley, *Labour's Grass Roots* (Oxford, Clarendon Press, 1992), ch. 8.
6   *Guardian*, 6 July 1995.
7   Kelly's interview with Peter Cropper (director of the Conservative Research Department), 22 February 1983.
8   *Panorama*, BBC1, 8 October 1990.
9   *Sunday Telegraph*, 29 June 1997.
10   W. Grant, *Pressure Groups, Politics and Democracy in Britain* (Hemel Hempstead, Harvester Wheatsheaf, 1989), ch. 2.
11   *Guardian*, 26 January 1994.
12   *Guardian*, 26 January 1994.
13   K. Ewing, *The Funding of Political Parties in Britain* (Cambridge, Cambridge University Press, 1987).

14　*Guardian*, 18 August 1993.
15　S. Lemieux, 'The Future Funding of Political Parties', *Talking Politics*, summer 1995.
16　*Times*, 10 October 1994.
17　M. Pinto-Duschinsky, 'The Funding of Political Parties Since 1945', in A. Seldon (ed.), *UK Political Parties Since 1945* (Hemel Hempstead, Harvester Wheatsheaf, 1990), p. 95.
18　Ewing, *Funding of Political Parties*, p. 177.
19　*Sunday Telegraph*, 7 May 1995.
20　Quoted in Lemieux, 'Funding of Political Parties'.
21　A. McConnell, 'A Concluding Thought: Should Parties be Funded by the State?', in L. Robins, H. Blackmore and R. Pyper (eds), *Britain's Changing Party System* (London, Leicester University Press, 1994).
22　P. Norris and J. Lovenduski, *Political Recruitment* (Cambridge, Cambridge University Press, 1995), p. 66; Kelly's conversation with assistant to Labour's director of finance, 27 June 1997.
23　*Sunday Telegraph*, 29 June 1996.

10

Parties and voters

No study of political parties would be complete without an analysis of the behaviour of voters. A central characteristic of liberal democracies such as Britain is that political power is granted not to those who can muster enough physical force or to those who claim a 'divine right' to govern others, but to those who receive the consent of the people through the ballot box. The result is a seemingly perpetual competition for votes. This electoral competition, of course, is now dominated by political parties. It is parties who put up candidates in each constituency, who put forward programmes of policies to the voters and who are rewarded with seats in the Commons. Likewise, with very few exceptions, it is party labels which dictate the choice of voters in the polling booths. The how and why of individual voting choices is therefore of crucial importance to the parties themselves, in addition to political commentators.

Psephology, or the study of voting behaviour, has a high profile within the academic discipline of political science. This, of course, reflects the importance of the subject matter and the considerable public interest that surrounds it. For most people, interest in politics is restricted to the party battle during election campaigns and this mass spectator sport has enabled election-night academic pundits such as David Butler, the late Robert McKenzie and – more recently – Ivor Crewe and Tony King to become minor television celebrities. Psephology also has a high profile because, unlike many other areas of political studies, it deals with a large amount of quantitative material. With the aid of – often complex – statistical techniques, psephologists can develop hypotheses which seek to explain past, and predict future, trends in electoral behaviour. Such an ability, however constrained by the unpredictability of human beings, enables students of politics to utilise the methods – and approach the predictive capacity – of natural scientists and thus claim some of the prestige which is attached to 'science' in the western world.

Models of voting behaviour

The first task for a student of voting behaviour is to discover how people voted or intend to vote. At a superficial level this is an easy task, since election results are readily available. We know, for instance, how many people voted Labour and how many Conservative in past general elections. By itself, however, this so-called aggregate-level information is not that useful. If we are to start developing theories to explain with any accuracy why people vote the way they do (the second task), we need to know how particular individuals voted and whether their vote has changed over time. Thus, psephologists make great use of surveys in which a sample of voters can be questioned about their voting habits, political opinions and social characteristics.[1] With this information, it is possible to look for patterns of behaviour which may have some explanatory validity.

There is considerable dispute among psephologists as to what motivates electoral choice. Various theories or models of voting behaviour have been put forward. At the extremes are two – the party identification model and the rational choice model.

The party identification model

This approach (often described as the 'Michigan' model because it was developed at that city's university in the 1950s[2]) was, at least until recently, the conventional wisdom in accounts of British voting behaviour.[3] The model holds that voters develop a long-term psychological attachment to political parties at an early age. This attachment is learnt through the socialisation process, initially involving parents and later reinforced by peer group influence. Voting for that party becomes a habit – an emotional response – rather than a choice based on political factors such as the party's policies or performance in office. Indeed, the party identification is used to avoid such a choice, which the voter is unwilling or incapable of making. Voters may have views on political issues but these are determined by the previously existing party identification so, if necessary, voters will change their views to fit in with their party identification. Thus, according to the theory, a Labour party identifier would become, say, a supporter of unilateral nuclear disarmament if the party adopted that position. Of course, if voters have such an attachment to parties then rapid electoral change would be difficult to account for. The model gets round this by distinguishing between short-term factors and the long-term identification. On occasions, voters may be influenced by the former to the extent that at a particular election they may vote for another party. In the long term, however, they will return to their original attachment.

The rational choice model

As the name suggests, the voters in this model are imputed with some level of rationality. Thus: 'The theory assumes that the voter recognises his own self-interest, evaluates alternative candidates on the basis of which will best serve this self-interest, and casts his vote for the candidate most favourably evaluated.'[4] The purest form of the rational choice model can be described as the issue voting model. One of the earliest versions of this was provided in the late 1950s by Anthony Downs in his book *An Economic Theory of Democracy*. For Downs, voters can be equated with consumers in the market economy buying, with their votes, a policy package which they think will provide them with the greatest satisfaction. Similarly, just as producers in a market economy are forced to make only things that consumers want to buy, political parties will offer policies which they estimate will maximise votes. As Downs explains: 'politicians in our model never seek office as a means of carrying out particular policies; their only goal is to reap the rewards of holding office *per se*'.[5] Put simply, parties will, then, adjust their policies in order to win votes.

A range of criticisms can be made of this model.[6] We will deal briefly with three here. First, the model finds it difficult to explain why so many actually bother to vote at all. A rational voter would vote only if the benefits of so doing outweighed the costs (measured in terms of finding out what the parties stand for and making the effort to vote on the day). Since most seats in Britain are safe, the chances of one vote affecting the result are minuscule and even if a marginal seat is decided in this way, the chances of that seat determining which party forms the government are also small.[7]

Secondly, the issue voting model takes the policy preferences of voters as given. This overlooks the possibility that these preferences may themselves have been 'created' by powerful forces in society, not least by the government itself.[8] This is the basis of the radical model of voting behaviour associated in particular with Dunleavy and Husbands. They note how Thatcher's governments were able to maximise support for the Conservatives, not by adjusting their policies to meet the demands of voters, but by creating an environment favourable to radical Thatcherite policies. Thus, the manipulation of news (i.e. the adjustments to the unemployment figures and the growing government advertising budget), the sale of council houses, the privatisation programme and the selling of shares have all, it is argued, produced a more pro-Thatcherite electorate. Dunleavy and Husbands argue that this 'increasingly transparent exploitation of state power for party ends, which is implicit in the new Conservative rejection of consensus' has become so all-embracing that fair and genuine competition between the parties is threatened and consequently democracy is 'at the crossroads'.[9]

The third criticism of the issue voting model is that voters just do not in reality have the sophistication that Downs wants to impute to them. Surveys have shown that the level of interest in, and information about, politics is low although – as one would expect – there is considerable variety within this broad generalisation.[10] Such evidence may come as a surprise to those – such as political activists and journalists – who take an active interest in politics, but for most people it remains a peripheral concern. Whether or not this is a desirable state of affairs is another matter.[11]

Rationality and voting behaviour

It would be wrong to reject out of hand either of these theories. For one thing, not all voters, of course, have the same motivation and therefore different theories may be required to explain different behaviour. In addition, a theory may be more applicable to one era than another. The party identification model, for instance, is far more able to deal with a period of electoral stability than one of electoral volatility. As we shall see below, for instance, the model was the orthodoxy in Britain during the 1950s and 1960s but, during the 1970s and 1980s, it went out of fashion as voting behaviour became more unpredictable. In these changed circumstances, greater emphasis was placed upon the impact of political issues and events which, it was suggested, persuaded voters to change their alignments more regularly. It should also be noted though that, even now, a large proportion of all voters choose the same party time after time and the party identification model seems best able to explain their behaviour.

The problem with the pure version of the party identification model is that it surely exaggerates the extent to which voting decisions – and particularly those which involve a switch from one party to another – involve no political judgement.[12] We can readily accept that most voters do not have the ability or inclination to behave in the sophisticated way Downs suggests, but it is possible to conceive of electoral behaviour being somehow related to what parties offer and what governments do. As Denver points out, there is a tendency for psephologists to take a very narrow view of what rational voting is – if voters are not aware of or do not have an opinion on 'transitory matters to be found in the small print of party manifestos or talked about by parties during election campaigns' then rational voting is said not to exist.[13] Yet voters may have, to a greater or lesser extent, a series of long-standing goals (equality, a free health service or whatever) and a reasonable idea of which party would further their self-interests, however defined. This may not add up to the calculating utility maximiser identified by Downs but it does involve at least some element of political choice.

Furthermore, it has been argued that elections are often about the overall competence of political parties rather than just the detail of policy. Many objectives – such as low unemployment and inflation – are widely shared and so, to judge between the parties, voters will often consider their general capacity to govern – for instance, the ability and experience of the leaders – as much as their different methods of dealing with issues such as unemployment. Thus, Miller in his analysis of the 1983 election argued that:

The issues were not inherently against Labour. Instead, disunity and incompetence in the Labour leadership destroyed Labour's credibility on its own natural issues and allowed its opponents to put their issues on the agenda ... Labour was not ready for government in 1983 and the electorate knew it.[14]

A related approach, described by Harrop and Miller as a 'helpful bridge' between the two models, is the concept of retrospective voting. Here, voters do not have to evaluate party policies but simply judge the performance of governments, thereby developing a party identification as a result of a 'running tally of retrospective evaluations rather than as an emotional attachment'.[15] Ivor Crewe suggests such an evaluation was the key explanation for the Conservative victory in 1987. If the electorate had voted according to their issue preferences, Labour would have won since the party was ahead on three of the four most salient issues (defence being the exception). What determined the result, according to Crewe, was the electorate's general feeling of prosperity – a prosperity which the Conservatives had 'created' and were trusted to maintain.[16] By contrast, one of the key reasons for Labour's landslide victory in 1997 was a retrospective evaluation of the Conservatives' handling of the economy. In this case, even though economic indicators were encouraging at the time of the election, the 'memories of the economic failure in the early nineties prevented the Tories from gaining credit' for the improvement.[17] Of particular importance was that, for the first time in many years, the Labour party was trusted far more on taxation than the Conservatives.

Britain's changing voting behaviour

It is customary to divide post-1945 British voting behaviour into two distinct periods. The first, from the end of the Second World War to the end of the 1960s, has been characterised as an era when most voters were strongly aligned with one or other of the two major parties and when social class was far and away the most important determinant of electoral choice. By contrast, the second, from the 1970s onwards, has been characterised as an era of dealignment as the strong ties which bound voters and parties together have loosened and social class has declined from its pre-eminent position as a predictor of voting behaviour.

Partisan alignment and dealignment

Following Denver, the term partisan alignment refers to 'a situation in which voters align themselves with a party by thinking of themselves as supporters of it, by having a party identification'.[18] Thus, in the era of alignment, most voters identified – with a varying degree of intensity – with one or other of the two main parties. In 1964, for instance, no less than 81 per cent of the electorate identified with Labour or the Conservatives. Of these, 51 per cent (of Labour supporters) and 48 per cent (of Conservative supporters) identified 'very strongly' with their respective parties.[19] Not surprisingly, this strong party identification produced a large degree of electoral stability. As we saw in chapter 2, the two parties dominated general elections in this period, the percentage of their combined vote never falling below the high eighties. In addition, the overall swing (a measure of the net change in the two-party vote from one election to the next) was small, averaging about 2 per cent in the six general elections between 1950 and 1966, with the highest being 3.1 per cent (in 1964) and the lowest 0.9 per cent (in 1951).

Since the 1970s, however, there has been a partisan dealignment. Fewer voters now identify with the two parties. By 1979, those identifying with either of the two parties had fallen to 74 per cent while, more significantly, the percentage of 'very strong' identifiers had dropped to 29 per cent (for Labour) and 24 per cent (for the Conservatives).[20] This fall continued in the 1980s. Between 1964 and 1970 an average of 40 per cent of the electorate regarded themselves as 'very strong' identifiers, whereas by 1997 only 17 per cent did so (rising to 19 per cent if we include all parties).[21] The result of this, as previous chapters have indicated, was a decline in the two-party share of the vote. In the seven elections between 1974 and 1997, the average two-party share was 75 per cent, with a high of about 81 per cent in 1979 and a low of 70 per cent in 1983 (see table 2.1, p. 39).

It is regularly pointed out that another consequence of partisan dealignment is increased electoral volatility – the phenomenon of rapidly changeable voter preferences. Certainly, from the 1970s onwards, there has been a tendency for greater swings in by-elections (resulting in many more defeats for the governing party) and opinion poll ratings. We saw in chapter 7, for instance, how the newly formed SDP swept to remarkably high levels before slipping back equally dramatically during and after the Falklands war. Swings between elections, too, have increased. Those recorded in 1970, 1979 and 1983 (4.7 per cent, 5.2 per cent and 4.2 per cent, respectively) were high by post-war standards but even these were dwarfed by the 10 per cent swing to Labour recorded in 1997. We need, however, to treat these statistics with care. They all deal with the net movement in the vote – the combined result of all vote switching. What is more important is the overall movement – the measure of the actual proportion of voters who switch from one party to another. Although net volatility increased during the 1970s and early 1980s, studies of the British electorate have concluded that overall volatility has not substantially increased. It still remains the case that, as panel surveys (which involve the same group

Table 10.1. *Rates of individual constancy and change between each pair of consecutive elections from 1959 to 1979 and from 1992 to 1997*

	1959–64	1964–6	1966–70	1970–Feb. '74	Feb.–Oct. 1974	Oct. 1974–9	1992–7
% constant	64	74	66	58	69	62	77
% changing	36	26	34	42	31	38	23

Sources: B. Sarlvik and I. Crewe, *Decade of Dealignment* (Cambridge, Cambridge University Press, 1983), p. 62; A. Heath *et al.*, 'Partisan Dealignment Revisited', in D. Denver and G. Hands (eds), *Issues and Controversies in British Electoral Behaviour* (Hemel Hempstead, Harvester Whetsheaf, 1992), pp. 166–7.

of voters over a series of elections) have shown, about two-thirds of the electorate vote for the same party, or abstain, from one election to the next.[22] As table 10.1 shows, there was no significant drop in the percentage of those voting for the same party across two elections between 1959 and the supposedly volatile 1970s and 1980s.

The discrepancy, between the level of net and overall movement, is caused partly by the fact that, as Moran points out, voters are now more likely to switch from a major party to a minor one rather than – as before – between the two major parties. The latter produced a small net swing (because vote switching tended to cancel itself out) at the same time disguising the extent of the overall movement, which was comparable with the period of dealignment.[23] In addition, electoral change is not just produced by voters switching from one party to another. It is also a consequence of changes in the electorate itself, caused by deaths, young voters registering for the first time, immigration and emigration. Thus, for example, fully 20 per cent of the Conservative vote at the 1997 election was made up of first-time voters too young to vote in 1992.[24]

Class alignment and dealignment

During the era of alignment, by far the most important factor in determining how individuals voted was their social class. There was, then, a class alignment. In a much-quoted passage, P. G. Pulzer wrote during this period that: 'Class is the basis of British party politics; all else is embellishment and detail.'[25] Thus, if you knew a person's class, there was a good chance that you could predict how he/she was going to vote. The working class tended to vote Labour and the middle class tended to vote Conservative. Of course, this was never a perfect correlation. Since the working class has traditionally formed a majority of the electorate, such a correlation would have produced permanent Labour governments. Instead, a substantial proportion of the working class (usually about 30 per cent) voted Conservative and, although (in the past at least) far less important in numerical terms, a slightly smaller proportion of the middle class (about 20 per cent) voted Labour. Nevertheless, so clear and stable was this pattern of voting that psephologists spent a great deal of time and effort in trying to explain the behaviour of the so-called 'deviant' voters – those who voted differently from the majority of their class.[26]

Before providing some statistical evidence of the class alignment, it is necessary to define what is meant by 'class'. Such an exercise is notoriously difficult and, as we shall see below, has recently been the subject of intense debate between psephologists. One definition of class is the classical Marxist account, but Marx's distinction between the bourgeoisie (the owners of the means of production – the mines, factories, etc.) and the proletariat (those who sell their labour to earn a living) takes too little account of the complexities of the modern social structure to be of much use to students of voting behaviour. Various more discriminating factors could be taken into account, such as income or status, but the criterion usually adopted is that of occupation. Here, it is common to divide occupations into groups represented by different letters, as illustrated by table 10.2, with A, B, C1 regarded as the non-manual middle class and C2, D, E regarded as the manual working class.

Table 10.3 demonstrates the strength of the class alignment from 1945 to 1970. It can be illustrated in three ways. First is by the overall share of the vote gained by each party in the middle- and working-class occupational groups. Here, Labour's support in the working class and the Conservatives' support in the middle class did not fall below 60 per cent during this period and was often higher. Secondly, by using the so-called Alford index (named after the political scientist who invented it), a class 'index' or 'score' for Labour voting can be calculated. This works by comparing the proportions of each class that supports the Labour party.[27]

Table 10.2. *Occupational class categories*

Class category	Occupations
A	Higher managerial, administrative or professional
B	Intermediate managerial, administrative or professional
C1	Supervisory, clerical; junior managerial, administrative or professional
C2	Skilled manual workers
D	Semi-skilled and unskilled manual workers
E	State pensioners, casual workers

Source: P. G. Pulzer, *Political Representation and Elections in Britain* (London, Allen and Unwin, 1975), p. 104.

Table 10.3. *Measures of class voting, 1959–97 (%)*

	1945– 70	1970	Feb. 1974	Oct. 1974	1979	1983	1987	1992	1997
Conservative									
manual	30	33	24	24	35	35	34	36	23
non-manual	65	64	53	51	60	55	54	56	34
Labour									
manual	62	58	57	57	50	42	45	51	58
non-manual	24	25	22	25	23	17	20	24	39
Liberal[a]									
manual	8	9	19	20	15	22	21	14	19
non-manual	10	11	25	24	17	28	27	21	27
Alford index[b]	38	33	35	32	27	25	25	23	19
Absolute class voting[c]	63	60	55	54	55	48	49	50	46

[a]In 1983 and 1987 the Liberals fought with the SDP as the Alliance, and became the Liberal Democrats thereafter.
[b]The Alford index is calculated by subtracting Labour's share of the non-manual vote from its share of the vote among manual workers.
[c]Absolute class voting is the proportion of voters supporting their 'natural' class party.

Sources: D. Denver, *Elections and Voting Behaviour in Britain* (Hemel Hempstead, Harvester Wheatsheaf, 1989), pp. 54–5; B. Sarlvik and I. Crewe, *Decade of Dealignment* (Cambridge, Cambridge University Press, 1983), p. 87; *Sunday Times*, 12 April 1992; *Sunday Times*, 4 May 1997.

The higher the percentage score, the stronger is the class alignment, and vice versa. Thus, up to 1970, the average Alford index remained around 40 per cent. Thirdly, we can calculate a score for absolute class voting – the proportion of all voters who choose their 'natural' class party. Here again, we find that manual Labour voters and non-manual Conservative voters made up about two-thirds of those who voted.

The dominating role of class was such that other social characteristics played a minor role in explaining voting behaviour. In terms of age and gender, there was a slight tendency for older voters and female voters to prefer the Conservatives. The age discrepancy has remained and intensified. Thus, in the 1997 election the Conservatives led Labour among those aged over sixty-five, with 44 per cent compared with 34 per cent, while among voters under thirty, the Labour lead was 35 per cent (57 per cent to 22 per cent). The so-called 'gender gap', where women are more likely to vote Conservative than Labour, largely disappeared in the 1980s, although it made a comeback in the 1987 election and intensified five years later, before disappearing once again in 1997. Similarly, religion (although a crucial characteristic in the nineteenth century) is now so peripheral (except of course in Northern Ireland) that it is not usually included in survey questions. Ethnic origin is a strong determinant of voting, with the majority of Asians and West Indians voting Labour, but this is significant numerically in only a handful of constituencies. In terms of region, there was always a slight variation, partly accounted for by the simple fact that there have always been more working-class voters in the north of England and Scotland. What was significant in the period of alignment, though, was that swings at general elections were remarkably uniform across the country, thus enabling psephologists to predict an election outcome on the basis of a few constituency results.[28]

It is important to recognise that the class–party link is only a pattern of voting behaviour and, as such, does not tell us why there should be such a link. Indeed, the class pattern of voting can be 'explained' by both the models of voting behaviour we discussed earlier. According to the party identification model, from an early age individuals inherit voting patterns from their parents and these are reinforced by peer groups. Since this socialisation takes place within a class context, it is not surprising that voting takes on a class character. As Dunleavy and Husbands point out, occupational class positions are a good guide to how people vote: 'not because class is an "issue" or a "problem" that is consciously perceived by voters, but because knowing someone's occupational class is the best summary index that we have of the kind of contexts in which he or she passes his or her daily life'.[29] For adherents of a more 'rationally' based model of voting behaviour, a class pattern exists because the vast majority of voters tend to define themselves in class terms and are inclined to view their personal interests – in the social and economic sense – as synonymous with those of a particular class. In political terms, this class consciousness is translated into support for either of the two class-based parties (whose clear class origins and historical perspectives have been documented in previous chapters).

Clearly, both perspectives are based upon the existence of a homogenous working class. The causes of this phenomenon relate to the nature of the British economy, which for most of this century was dominated by 'heavy' industry (coal, steel, shipbuilding, manufacturing, etc.) and units dealing in the mass production of goods. Marxists now often refer to this period as the 'Fordist era', taking their cue from Gramsci's observation that modern capitalism reflected the 'mode' of production pioneered by the Henry Ford motor company – one involving a series of standardised factories, engaged in standardised production on a huge scale and employing a large unskilled and semi-skilled workforce with similar jobs, wages and conditions.[30]

The consequences for the British workforce and, *inter alia*, British politics, were profound. The bulk of the electorate after 1918 (when the Representation of the People Act finally removed the property franchise) were employed in these industries as manual workers, and thereby had similar incomes and 'lifestyles' – reinforced by the fact that most of them lived in the same, tightly knit, urbanised communities. These factors produced a strong sense of class consciousness among manual workers and a sense of being socially, economically and culturally different from those who did not share their living and working conditions. This class division was to prove far more potent than any regional division and was generally accepted and echoed by those in non-manual or middle-class occupations. Put simply, the attitudes and socio-economic interests of a working-class voter in Manchester would have much less in common with a middle-class voter in Manchester than with a working-class voter in Southampton.

Since 1970, as table 10.3 illustrates, it has become gradually more difficult to predict people's voting intentions from their occupational class. It is important to recognise that the 1997 election confirmed this trend. Between 1979 and 1992, the most striking feature of voting behaviour was the working-class desertion of Labour. Thus, in 1966, 69 per cent of manual workers voted Labour but by 1987 only 45 per cent did so (rising to only 46 per cent in 1992). The severest decline occurred in the C2 category of skilled manual workers where, by 1987, Labour's share had fallen to 34 per cent (compared with an average of 60 per cent between 1945 and the late 1950s) rising to only 40 per cent in 1992. On the basis of these figures, Ivor Crewe could state in 1987 that 'Labour's claim to be the party of the working class' was 'sociologically, if not ideologically, threadbare'.[31]

Since the decline of class voting in the 1980s was accompanied by Labour's poor electoral showing, it might be thought that Labour's overwhelming victory in the 1997 election marks the return of class voting. We should not, however, confuse Labour's decline with the decline of class voting. Indeed, as table 10.3 shows, only 46 per cent of voters supported their 'natural' class party in 1997, compared with 50 per cent in 1992 and 49 per cent in 1987. Even though 1997 was an exceptionally good election year for Labour, the party's support among working-class voters (58 per cent) was still not as high as it had been between 1945 and 1970. Likewise, the Conservative share of the working-class vote in 1997 (23 per cent) was only slightly lower than it had been in the period 1945–70, a remarkable fact if we compare the scale of the party's defeat in 1997 with its three successive victories in the 1950s.

The direction of the middle-class vote has also become much more difficult to predict in the era of dealignment. In elections between 1970 and 1992, the Conservative share of the non-manual vote declined, even in a period when the party was winning elections. Only just over half the A, B, and C1 voters supported the Conservatives in 1983, 1987 and 1992. The Conservatives more than made up for the loss of middle-class support in the 1980s by capturing working-class votes from Labour. Thus, in 1987, fully 43 per cent of C2 voters chose to vote for Thatcher's party and the Conservative vote among manual workers as a whole remained remarkably consistent between 1979 and 1992, at a level higher than in the 1960s and 1970s.[32] In addition, it was the Alliance – and not Labour – in these elections who were the main beneficiaries of the decline in the Conservatives' vote share among non-manual workers.

The position pertaining in the 1980s was radically transformed in 1997 but not in a way which restored class voting. Labour's success was based partly upon increasing their share of the working-class vote to a level which was broadly compatible with that in the era of alignment. Crucially, though, the election was won and lost in the battle for the votes of non-manual workers, a social grouping which has become much more numerous as a consequence of social and economic change (discussed further below). Labour's landslide victory can be explained by the quite astonishing support they received from this group of voters. For the first time in the post-war period, a greater proportion of the non-manual electorate voted Labour (39 per cent) than Conservative (34 per cent). To put this into context, even when Labour won a comfortable victory in 1966, 60 per cent of non-manual workers still voted Conservative and only 26 per cent Labour. The biggest shift in 1997 occurred among the electorally significant C1 voters, where Labour increased its share from the 1992 election by 19 per cent and the Conservative share fell by a massive 22 per cent. As a result, nine of the twenty-five most middle-class constituencies in Britain – including Bristol West and Wimbledon – elected Labour MPs.[33] Labour had captured 'Middle England' and with it the keys to 10 Downing Street.

Heath, Jowell, Curtice and class voting

Three well known psephologists, Andrew Heath, Roger Jowell and John Curtice, dispute the conventional assertion that class has declined in importance as a determinant of voting behaviour.[34] Their arguments largely depend upon the validity of complex statistical techniques, which makes it difficult for lay people to assess their contribution. What is offered here is a simplified (albeit useful, we hope) account of their case.[35]

Heath and his colleagues base their revisionist claim that class voting has not declined on two main grounds. First, they argue that the conventional A–E occupational scale is inadequate, since it fails to take into account the real class interests of voters. Three main changes are made. First, married women are assigned to a class according to their own occupation (if they have one) rather than, as is traditionally the case, their husband's. This has the effect of removing from the working class the many women, married to manual workers, who themselves have non-manual

Table 10.4. *Heath, Jowell and Curtice's class categories and voting behaviour*

	% of electorate	Conservative (%)			Labour (%)			Alliance (%)		
		1983	1987	1992	1983	1987	1992	1983	1987	1992
Petit bourgeoisie	8	71	65	66	12	16	17	17	20	18
Salariat	27	54	56	56	14	15	20	31	29	25
Foremen/technicians	7	48	39	41	26	36	45	25	24	15
Routine non-manual	24	46	52	53	25	26	30	27	23	17
Working class	34	30	31	32	49	48	56	20	21	12

Sources A. Heath, R. Jowell and J. Curtice, *How Britain Votes* (Oxford, Clarendon Press, 1985), p. 33; A. Heath, R. Jowell and J. Curtice, *Understanding Political Change* (Oxford, Clarendon Press, 1991), p. 69; D. Denver, *Elections and Voting Behaviour in Britain*, 2nd edn (Hemel Hempstead, Harvester Wheatsheaf, 1994), p. 73.

occupations. Secondly, the authors distinguish between levels of responsibility in the workplace, removing from the working class all those with supervisory functions in their employment. Third, self-employed manual workers are removed from the working class and allocated to a new 'petit bourgeoisie' group.

Table 10.4 shows the rearranged class categories and how they voted in the three elections between 1983 and 1992.[36] Sharper voting patterns than those produced by the traditional occupational scale emerge. Almost a majority of the working class voted Labour in 1987 and more than 50 per cent in 1992. In addition, a very strong pattern of Conservative voting, particularly in 1983, occurs among the petit bourgeoisie and, to a lesser extent, in the salariat. The newly defined working class is smaller than that traditionally defined, and has declined, shrinking from 47 per cent of the electorate in 1964 to 34 per cent in 1983. The conclusion drawn from this (before Labour's landslide victory in 1997) is that Labour's problems stem not so much from a weakening of class loyalties as a contraction in the numbers of working-class voters. This, they argue, accounts for about half of Labour's lost support since 1964.

The second major argument put forward by Heath, Jowell and Curtice is that psephologists have confused Labour's poor electoral performance in the 1980s – caused partly, as we have seen, by a shrinking working class and also by an ineffective political performance, particularly between 1979 and 1983 – with a decline in class voting. This confusion comes about, it is argued, because an incorrect measure of class voting is utilised. Thus, what is important is not the absolute measure of class voting (the proportion voting for their 'natural' class party) but the relative level of class voting (the difference between the parties' share of the vote from the middle class and the working class). What matters, therefore, is whether Labour's support in the working class has changed relative to its support from other classes. If one uses this method then it becomes apparent that Labour's support had declined across the board in all of the authors' class categories. The Conservatives did become more popular among working-class voters between 1979 and 1983 but this was because of short-term factors – Labour's divisions, poor campaign, unpopular leader and so on – rather than any long-term decline in class voting. The implication, then, is that in a more 'normal' election, the working-class voters who deserted Labour in 1983 would return and, as a consequence, class voting would be stronger.

Heath, Jowell and Curtice provide an interesting challenge to the conventional view but, as Denver points out, it 'emerges relatively unscathed' from their assault.[37] Their redrawing of class categories has been criticised, particularly because it has the effect of 'minoritising' the working class. Given the fact that 60 per cent of the electorate in 1983 regarded themselves as working class it is a little strange that many of them are excluded from the working class described by Heath *et al.*[38] It is as though they have artificially contracted the working class in order to recreate a class alignment that was declining because the working class was fragmenting.[39] Furthermore, barely half of this smaller working class voted Labour in 1983 and in 1987, and 1992, when many of the short-term problems faced by Labour had disappeared, the party's support among working-class voters was only marginally over 50 per cent.

It might be thought that Labour's victory in 1997 confirms the Heath, Jowell and Curtice analysis. It is true that Labour's support among working-class voters, whether defined in the traditional or revisionist way, returned to more or less what it had been during the period of class alignment. However, as we pointed out above, Labour's share of the vote among the other classes identified by Heath, Jowell and Curtice rose too, so that the ratio between Labour's support in the working class and the middle class has declined. Although not as extensive as the dealignment produced by absolute levels of class voting, this is quite consistent with class dealignment.[40]

Explaining dealignment

It is a much easier task to describe dealignment than to explain why it has taken place. Although a partisan alignment can exist independently of a class alignment, in the British context the two are obviously related. Nevertheless, for the sake of simplicity, it is probably wise to consider partisan and class dealignment separately.

Explaining partisan dealignment

A simple explanation for partisan dealignment, or the weakening attachment of voters to the two major parties, is that voters feel less reason to be attached to them. Part of the explanation for this derives from a disillusionment with their governing record in the 1970s. An additional factor was the breakdown of the social democratic consensus and the polarisation of the two major parties, which proved unpopular with many voters who occupy the 'middle ground'. This vacation of the centre ground, therefore, created a space which the centre parties were able to exploit.[41] This simple 'unpopularity' theory is backed up by Crewe, who discovered that over the past twenty years or so there have been significant changes in issue preferences. This was particularly bad news for Labour, since Crewe's analysis revealed: 'a quite exceptional movement of opinion away from Labour's traditional positions amongst Labour supporters.... There has been a spectacular decline in support for the "collectivist trinity" of public ownership, trade union power and social welfare.'[42] Given that Conservative policies remained relatively popular, this would seem to explain why Labour suffered more (up to 1997) than the Conservatives from dealignment.

A related change here is the argument that voters have become increasingly sophisticated. Thus, they no longer choose between parties on the basis of a long-standing identification but are far more instrumental, examining party policies and records in office. This growing sophistication is itself put down to the impact of greater educational opportunities and the massive increase in television coverage of politics over the last twenty years or so. This has enabled ordinary voters to become more informed about and interested in politics.[43] Evidence for this is provided by Mark Franklin, among others. Franklin stresses the growth of issue voting, which, he argues, increased substantially between 1964 and 1983. Many voters, he suggests, no longer blindly identified with a particular party and their issue preferences became independent variables determining the choice of party.[44] The problem here is that, as Franklin himself admits, party identification still accounts for the choice of most voters, whose knowledge of political issues is slight. In addition, it is very difficult to prove that issue preferences determine party choice since the direction of causation is problematic. It could be that party identification determines issue preferences so, for example, falling support for a particular party's policies could be the result of falling party identification rather than the other way round.[45]

Explaining class dealignment

Class dealignment would seem to be a political reflection of the vast amount of social and economic change that has occurred in recent years. Of particular significance is that social mobility has increased markedly over the past thirty years. This is a product of the rise in non-manual occupations (60 per cent of the voters were non-manual workers in 1997, only 35 per cent were in 1959). Many of those who belong to the new enlarged middle class have working-class backgrounds and may retain their Labour voting habits. Linked to this is the fact that the growth of the middle class since 1945 mirrors to a large extent the growth of the public sector of the economy, encouraging a wide range of new white-collar employment in state education, the civil service, the National Health Service, the nationalised industries and local authorities. The ideals underpinning these new areas of employment (emphasising social need and state-led provision rather than commercial gain) served, it is suggested, to foster a centre-left outlook among public sector workers which was rather at odds with traditional middle-class attitudes to politics and society. This is illustrated in table 10.5, which demonstrates that in the 1987 and 1992 elections Conservative support was far weaker in the public sector middle class than in the private sector middle class.

Table 10.5. *Voting patterns among the public and private sector middle class (%)*

| | Public sector | | Private sector | |
	1987	1992	1987	1992
Conservative	44	45	65	61
Labour	24	30	13	19
Alliance/Liberal Democrats	32	22	22	19

Source: I. Crewe, 'A New Class of Politics', *Guardian*, 15 June 1987; D. Denver, *Elections and Voting Behaviour in Britain*, 2nd edn (Hemel Hempstead, Harvester Wheatsheaf, 1994), p. 168.

The manual working class has changed even more fundamentally. Over the past twenty years or so, the previously homogenous working class has fragmented. This has been a product of the changing nature of the British economy. The dominance of heavy 'Fordist' industry, so vital to the development of class consciousness, has gradually given way to new forms of economic production, characterised by smaller units employing a smaller, more diverse, more skilled workforce where trade union membership, for example, seems less relevant (union membership has fallen by about three million since 1979 alone and now represents only 23 per cent of the British electorate).

This development has had a crucial effect upon the class consciousness of the workforce and therefore the character of the British electorate. As units of production have become more diverse, so have the wages and conditions of manual workers (reflected in the growing divisions within the trade union movement, as shown by the fragmentation of the National Union of Mineworkers after 1984 and the expulsion of the Electricians Union from the Trade Union Congress in 1988). The living standards of some manual workers have changed to the extent that they have taken on the trappings of the traditional middle-class lifestyle, a change often referred to as *embourgeoisement*. A growing number are home owners (70 per cent in 1997, 20 per cent in 1959), live in suburban areas (46 per cent in 1997, 20 per cent in 1959), own shares (20 per cent in 1997, 6 per cent in 1979) and take foreign holidays. Thus, the homogeneity of income and lifestyle which formed the basis of class consciousness among manual workers has been corroded, with the result that divisions within the working class are, perhaps, now more revealing than those between manual and non-manual workers.[46]

These new divisions within the working class were powerfully reflected in voting behaviour in the 1980s and early 1990s. As table 10.6 shows, it was in this era possible to divide the working class into two distinct groups. The 'old' or traditional working class tended to remain strongly Labour but the 'new', more affluent, working class veered towards the

Table 10.6. *The fragmentation of working-class voting behaviour (%)*

	Conservative	Labour	Alliance[a]
The new working class			
Lives in south			
1987	46	28	26
1992	38	36	22
Owner occupier			
1987	44	32	24
1992	40	39	18
Non-union			
1987	40	38	22
1992	34	43	16
Works in private sector			
1987	38	39	23
1992	31	50	18
The traditional working class			
Lives in Scotland/north			
1987	29	57	15
1992	29	56	13
Council tenant			
1987	25	57	18
1992	24	58	12
Union member			
1987	30	48	22
1992	23	45	16
Works in public sector			
1987	32	49	19
1992	35	47	16

[a]1992 figures refer to the Liberal Democrats.
Sources: I. Crewe, 'A New Class of Politics', *Guardian*, 15 June 1987; *Sunday Times*, 12 April 1992.

Conservatives. In the 1987 election, the Conservatives had substantial leads over Labour among working-class voters living in the south, owning their own homes and not belonging to a union, and were only narrowly behind Labour among working-class voters employed in the private sector. In 1992, Labour narrowed the gap among southern and owner-occupier working-class voters but a significant difference between the voting behaviour of the new and traditional working class remained. A fundamental factor underlying Labour's success in the 1997 election was the extent to which the party was able to win back the support of a sufficient numbers of the new working class (see below). As an indicator of this, support for Labour among the vital sector of skilled manual workers, many of whom can be classified as part of the new working class, increased by 15 per cent, with an equivalent decrease in the proportion voting Conservative.

Dealignment or realignment?

Since class has declined as a key determinant of voting behaviour, psephologists have sought to identify a replacement. If a new cleavage – or cleavages – emerges which has the same force as class used to have, we can usefully talk about a realignment.

Sectoral cleavages

One view is that a cleavage based on occupational class has been replaced by one based on sectors of employment and consumption.[47] Here, it is argued that the growth of the state since 1945 has created new divisions in society which cut across occupational class. Thus, those who are employed in the public sector and who are reliant upon publicly provided services (housing, transport, state benefits) tend to vote Labour whatever their class, whereas those who work in the private sector and provide for themselves in areas such as housing and transport are more likely to vote Conservative whatever their class. This is backed up, to a certain extent, by the figures from the 1987 and 1992 elections illustrated in tables 10.5 and 10.6. Labour received much more support from council tenants than from owner occupiers within the working class while the Conservatives were much stronger among middle-class voters who work in the private sector as opposed to those who work in the public sector. Likewise, in the 1997 election, Labour's lead among council tenants was a massive 52 per cent (65 per cent to 13 per cent) whereas the party's lead among home owners was only 6 per cent (41 per cent to 35 per cent).

Two cautionary remarks should be made though. First, the correlation is not that strong (with the exception of housing, which is now at least as good a predictor of voting behaviour as occupational class[48]). For example, in patterns of employment, class, rather than sector, was still more important. Labour still led in the private sector working class (narrowly in 1987 and by a margin of 19 per cent in 1992) as did the Conservatives in the public sector middle class. Moreover, in the 1992 election, Labour's share of the vote among the private sector working class was higher than their vote share among the public sector working class. As Crewe explains, this was probably a consequence of the nature of the recession at the end of the 1980s. Whereas the recession of the early 1980s hit the traditional heavy industry areas of the north and Scotland and the public sector generally, the later recession damaged the service and high-technology private sectors of the south and did not have such a big impact on the public sector.[49]

Secondly, it is by no means certain that sectoral cleavages actually explain the way people vote. For instance, does working in the public sector cause middle-class voters to be more likely to vote Labour or are Labour-inclined middle-class voters more likely to work in the public sector? Similarly, do working-class home owners tend to vote Conservative because they perceive that party as more likely to further the interests of owner occupiers or because they are affluent and live in the south?[50]

Regional voting

Regional variations in voting behaviour have been apparent for a considerable time but they have intensified in recent years with both a north–south and an urban–suburban divide becoming increasingly apparent. In 1987, for instance, there was a national swing to Labour of just over 1 per cent. In the north of England and Wales, however, there was a 4.5 per cent swing to Labour, in Scotland the swing was 6 per cent to Labour but in the south-east there was a small swing to the Conservatives. The Conservative share of the two-party vote was nearly 20 per cent below what it would have been if Scotland had moved in line with Britain as a whole in the period 1955 to 1987.[51]

In 1992, similarly, Labour won twice as many seats from the Tories as they would have done if the average swing had been uniform across the whole country because the party tended to perform better (although not well enough) in their key target seats. In 1997, Labour's support was tactically employed to greater effect so that on a national vote share of 43 per cent the party won 63 per cent of the seats. By contrast, the Conservatives, because their share of the vote was more evenly spread, were seriously disadvantaged under the first-past-the-post election system, winning 31 per cent of the vote but only 25 per cent of the seats. The regional swings, however, were less marked in 1997, ranging from 7 per cent to Labour in Wales and Scotland to 12 per cent in the south-east and 13 per cent in Greater London. These swings reflected Labour's success in winning back seats lost in the 1980s. Whether or not it will be followed by the return of a more uniform national swing remains to be seen.

The regional pattern of voting which has emerged in recent years has also, of course, affected parliamentary representation. As table 10.7 reveals, the Conservatives held thirty-six seats in Scotland and seventy-five seats in the north of England after the 1955 election but by 1992 the figures were eleven and forty-seven, respectively. Similarly, Labour held forty-two seats in the south of England (including East Anglia) after the 1955 election whereas in 1992 they held only ten, itself a major improvement on the three seats the party had when the election was called. In 1997, Labour regained much of the ground lost in the 1980s and can lay claim to being a genuinely national party. After their decimation in 1997, the Conservatives can make no such claim (see also table 10.8). They now have no seats in the major British cities outside London, and no seats in Scotland or Wales (down from eleven and six, respectively, since 1992).

Table 10.7. *Geographical distribution of parties' seats in selected elections*

	Conservative	Labour	Liberals[a]	Nationalists[b]
1955				
London	15	27	–	n/a
Southern England[c]	163	42	–	n/a
Midlands	39	57	–	n/a
Northern England	75	90	2	n/a
Wales	6	27	3	–
Scotland	36	34	1	–
1970				
London	9	33	–	n/a
Southern England	169	34	2	n/a
Midlands	51	45	–	n/a
Northern England	63	104	–	n/a
Wales	7	27	1	1
Scotland	23	44	3	1
October 1974				
London	41	51	–	n/a
Southern England	128	29	5	n/a
Midlands	40	58	–	n/a
Northern England	44	117	3	n/a
Wales	8	23	2	3
Scotland	16	41	3	11
1987				
London	58	23	3	n/a
Southern England	170	3	3	n/a
Midlands	67	33	–	n/a
Northern England	55	68	3	n/a
Wales	8	24	3	3
Scotland	10	48	9	3
1992				
London	48	35	1	n/a
Southern England	161	10	6	n/a
Midlands	57	43	–	n/a
Northern England	47	77	2	n/a
Wales	6	27	1	4
Scotland	11	49	9	3
1997				
London	41	57	6	n/a
Southern England	109	59	22	n/a
Midlands	28	75	1	n/a
Northern England	17	138	4	n/a
Wales	–	34	2	4
Scotland	–	56	10	6

[a]The Liberal total of seats becomes that of the Liberal–SDP Alliance in 1983 and 1987 and the Liberal Democrats in 1992 and 1997.
[b]Nationalist usually denotes the SNP in Scotland and Plaid Cymru in Wales.
[c]The figures for southern England include East Anglia.

Table 10.8. *Parties' share of votes by region, 1997*

	Conservative	Labour	Liberal Democrats	Nationalists
North	22%	61%	15%	–
North-west	27%	54%	14%	–
West Midlands	34%	48%	14%	–
Wales	20%	55%	12%	10%
South-west	37%	26%	31%	–
South-east	41%	32%	21%	–
Scotland	18%	46%	13%	22%
Yorkshire/Humberside	28%	52%	16%	–
East Midlands	34%	48%	13%	–
East Anglia	39%	38%	18%	–
Greater London	31%	49%	15%	–

It is by no means clear why these regional patterns have emerged. Certainly, territorial loyalties (seen, in particular, in support for the nationalist parties in Scotland and Wales) play only a small role. Another theory is that of the 'neighbourhood factor'. Here, there is a tendency for individuals to vote for the party which dominates in the area in which they live. Thus, middle-class voters in working-class dominated Labour strongholds are more likely to vote Labour than in middle-class Conservative seats, and vice versa. Why this occurs is not known, although there is some evidence for a 'contagion' effect whereby voters take on board the traits of the dominant class.[52] A more likely explanation for regional voting patterns is that social and economic trends have affected regions differently. Crucially important in explaining Labour's decline in the 1980s is that the 'new', more prosperous, working class tends to be heavily concentrated in the south while the 'traditional' working class employed in the remaining heavy manufacturing industries and living in council houses tends to be concentrated in the north. To the latter, Labour remained popular throughout the period since 1979 while, until 1997, support for the party from the former was drifting away.[53]

Voting behaviour and Labour's fall and rise

After the 1992 election, Labour appeared to be in deep trouble. The party had not won an election for almost twenty years and it had been more than twenty years since it had gained over 40 per cent of the vote in a British general election, whereas between 1945 and 1970 the party did not once fail to achieve this level of support. In 1983, Labour's share of the vote was their lowest since 1918 and even though the 34.4 per cent gained in the 1992 election represented an improvement (on both 1983 and 1987) it still ranked as the seventh worst result for the party in the twenty-one elections fought since 1918.

The 1992 defeat seemed even more ominous for Labour than the previous two. The party could comfort itself in 1983 and 1987 with the thought that defeat could be explained by a variety of short-term factors – a poor leader, disunity and extreme policies in 1983; unilateralism and an economic boom in 1987 – which would not recur. In 1992, however, Labour went into the election with a cautious programme of policies, with an experienced leader and in the midst of a steep recession which many blamed on the government. Yet despite all this, Labour received only 34 per cent of the vote, a mere 3 per cent or so increase on 1987 and still over 7 per cent behind the Conservatives.

It was in this context that many political commentators began to express real doubts about Labour's prospects of ever winning a general election again, at least without some form of electoral pact with the Liberal Democrats. The analyses offered from a variety of quarters were remarkably uniform.[54] They centred on the view that social and economic change had put too many voters permanently beyond Labour's grasp. More specifically, the changes had produced an electorate to which Labour's collectivist and egalitarian philosophy (which finds its practical expression in state-led social provision funded by redistributive taxation) no longer held sufficient appeal. Instead, voters in the 'New England' – detached from traditional working-class communities where solidarity, collectivism and Labour voting once went hand in hand – had become imbued with individualistic values and the desire to succeed through personal initiative and effort rather than reliance on the state.

It was this new culture, of course, which Margaret Thatcher (through allowing ordinary people to buy their council houses, buy into privatised industries and, at least rhetorically, keep more of their earned income) was able to promote. By contrast, Labour, it was argued, was regarded with suspicion by this new culture, as the party which threatened individual achievements and sought – in the words of Bryan Gould – to 'cap the aspirations' of those who sought to better themselves (hence the un-popularity of Labour's tax proposals in 1992 which, although hitting only those who earn over £22,000 a year, were seen as a disincentive to those who aspired to earn that amount). As Vernon Bogdanor pointed out after the 1992 election:

> For voters in the new England, a Labour vote reflects the background from which they have come, a background of organised trade unionism and collective provision. A Conservative vote, by contrast, expresses an aspiration, an aspiration to a world in which they can make decisions for themselves, free from the paternalism of trade union leaders or local councillors.[55]

The roots of Labour's decline, it was suggested, lay in the changing nature of British society. The fragmentation of the working class, described above, produced an expanding 'new', more affluent, group of manual workers who were increasingly turning their back on Labour. Secondly, the manual working class as a whole has been declining as the proportion of the electorate employed in non-manual occupations increases. Put simply, Labour in the 1980s was receiving a declining share of a declining class.[56] The party's malaise was summed up by Crewe after the 1987 election. Labour, he wrote, had:

> come to represent a declining segment of the working class – the traditional working class of the council estates, the public sector, industrial Scotland and the North, and the old industrial unions – while failing to attract the affluent and expanding working class of the new estates and new service economy of the South.[57]

The thesis about Labour's decline described above makes Labour's landslide victory in 1997 all the more surprising. Does this mean, we need to ask, that some psephologists got it badly wrong? To some degree, the answer to this question must be yes. In particular, it might be argued that political commentators underestimated the progress Labour made in 1992 which made it plausible to conclude that 'one more heave' would see the party back in office. To win the 1992 election, Labour had to achieve an unprecedented 8 per cent swing to secure the barest of overall majorities. As it was, the party made a net gain of forty-two seats, the highest since 1966. In addition, Labour 'saw off' the challenge of the centre party. Whereas the Alliance was second in 261 seats after the 1987 election, the Liberal Democrats finished second in only 154 in 1992. In addition, Labour recovered ground in the south, winning more seats than at any time since 1974 and after the election there were seventeen seats where the Conservative lead over Labour was less than a thousand votes. Finally, the gap of 8 per cent between the two major parties was misleadingly high in the sense that, because the swing to Labour was greater in their target seats than it was overall, the party was relatively close to depriving the Tories of an overall majority. Indeed, had just 3,899 people in twelve constituencies voted in a different way in 1992, a hung parliament would have been the outcome.[58]

Moreover, it is clearly an exaggeration to suggest that social and economic change has produced widespread support for Thatcherite individualistic values, and widespread resistance to collectivism. A majority of voters, for instance, said in the 1980s they would prefer increased spending on public services rather than tax cuts and even in 1992 an exit poll by MORI revealed that fully 60 per cent favoured the distribution of income from the better off to the less well off.[59] Thatcher's demise was itself, it should be remembered, the product of Labour's large lead in the opinion polls, which seemed to demonstrate the popularity of a moderate social democratic party in British politics. In this context, John Curtice's analysis of the 1992 result now seems particularly pertinent. Labour's defeat, he argued, was not inevitable but was the 'product of political difficulties and mistakes at least as much as sociological or economic determinism'.[60] For Curtice, the key factor was not so much that Labour's tax policies frightened voters but that the Conservatives managed to persuade enough of the electorate that they were more competent managers of the economy than Labour and as such offered the prospect of both lower levels of taxation (or at least a more effective use of existing tax revenues) *and* higher public spending.[61]

We should not, on the other hand, belittle the importance of the problems Labour has faced in the past twenty years or so and the social and economic changes, in particular, which have reduced the party's natural constituency of voters. It can be readily agreed that society has changed and that a state-dominated collectivism which seeks uniformly to protect, control and direct people – through the use of a heavily redistributive tax system – is no longer able to attract a large enough coalition of electoral support. Labour, though, was already, by 1992, moving a long way from this post-war ideal and under Blair the party has adapted itself even further to a society with a larger non-manual middle class and a more mobile and affluent working class.

The 1997 result, then, was not a victory for Labour's traditional ideals but was a comment on the party's ability to adapt to a much changed social, political and economic environment. Because of this, the Conservatives may have lost anyway, but the scale of their defeat was ensured by the failure of Major's government to counter the widespread image of division and incompetence and, more importantly, the damage that was inflicted on those sections of the electorate whose prosperity had been promoted by Conservative governments since 1979. Taxpayers, home owners and consumers all suffered through higher taxes and more expensive mortgages paid, by many, for houses now worth less than the purchase price.[62] This combination of factors will probably keep Labour in power for a generation.

Conclusion

The period since 1970 has witnessed profound changes in voting behaviour which in turn have had equally profound consequences for the character of British political parties. A much more dealigned electorate, no longer rooted in automatic voting habits based upon social class, makes predicting election outcomes much more difficult. Support for political parties, as both major parties have found, is much more conditional. Social class still remains the single most important indicator of voting choice in Britain, but knowing an individual's class is nowhere near as effective a predictor of voting behaviour as it was in the 1950s and 1960s. Today we need more information, such as region, sector of employment, and housing tenure. Social and economic change has produced not only a different kind of working-class voter but has also decreased the number of manual workers. As a consequence, Labour's return to power depended upon its ability to break out of its heartlands, which no longer provided an election-winning coalition of support. The party's success in achieving this leads us to the, rather sanguine, conclusion that, ultimately, parties are led by the people. That is how it should be.

Notes

1   D. Denver, *Elections and Voting Behaviour in Britain* (Hemel Hempstead, Harvester Wheatsheaf, 1989), pp. 4–5.
2   A. Campbell, P. Converse, W. Miller and D. Stokes, *The American Voter* (New York, Wiley, 1960).
3   The classic account of its application to British politics is D. Butler and D. Stokes, *Political Change in Britain* (London, Macmillan, 1974).
4   M. Harrop and W. L. Miller, *Elections* (Basingstoke, Macmillan, 1987), p. 145.
5   A. Downs, *Economic Theory of Democracy* (New York, Harper Row, 1957), p. 28. For a modern application of this theory to British politics see H. T. Himmelweit, P. Humphreys and M. Jaeger, *How Voters Decide* (Milton Keynes, Open University Press, 1981).
6   For a full assessment see B. Barry, *Sociologists, Economists and Democracy* (London, Macmillan, 1970).
7   For further discussion of this point see I. McLean, *Elections* (London, Longman, 1980), pp. 37–8.
8   P. Dunleavy and H. Ward, 'Exogenous Voter Preferences and Parties with State Power: Some Internal Problems of Economic Theories of Party Competition', *British Journal of Political Science*, January 1981, pp. 351–79.
9   P. Dunleavy and C. T. Husbands, *British Democracy at the Crossroads* (London, Allen and Unwin, 1985), p. 215. For an assessment see W. Miller, 'Voting and the Electorate', in P. Dunleavy, A. Gamble and G. Peele (eds), *Developments in British Politics 3* (London, Macmillan, 1990), pp. 55–61.
10   Harrop and Miller, *Elections*, ch. 5.
11   W. H. Morris Jones, 'In Defence of Apathy', *Political Studies*, March 1954, pp. 25–37.
12   Note that, as Harrop and Miller, *Elections*, p. 161, point out: 'Most advocates of the party identification model now accept that party identification reflects as well as shapes voting choices'. In what proportions we are not told!
13   Denver, *Elections and Voting Behaviour*, p. 86.
14   Quoted in M. Harrop, 'Voting and the Electorate', in H. Drucker *et al.*, *Developments in British Politics 2* (London, Macmillan, 1986), p. 52.
15   Harrop and Miller, *Elections*, pp. 148–9.
16   I. Crewe, 'Tories Prosper from a Paradox', *Guardian*, 16 June 1987.

17 P. Kellner, 'Boom that Backfired on the Tories', *Observer*, 4 May 1997.
18 Denver, *Elections and Voting Behaviour*, p. 29.
19 B. Sarlvik and I. Crewe, *Decade of Dealignment* (Cambridge, Cambridge University Press, 1983), pp. 333–8.
20 Sarlvik and Crewe, *Decade*, p. 337.
21 Denver, *Elections and Voting Behaviour*, p. 47; *Observer*, 4 May 1997.
22 Harrop, 'Voting and the Electorate', pp. 34–5; see also A. Heath, R. Jowell and J. Curtice, *Understanding Political Change* (Oxford, Clarendon Press, 1991), pp. 10–31.
23 M. Moran, *Politics and Society in Britain* (London, Macmillan, 1985), pp. 74–5.
24 NOP–BBC exit poll 1997.
25 P. G. Pulzer, *Political Representation and Elections in Britain* (London, Allen and Unwin, 1975), p. 102.
26 See Denver, *Elections and Voting Behaviour*, pp. 39–43.
27 See D. Robertson, *Class and the British Electorate* (Oxford, Clarendon Press, 1984), pp. 18–29.
28 Denver, *Elections and Voting Behaviour*, pp. 33–5, 65–6.
29 Dunleavy and Husbands, *British Democracy*, p. 4.
30 See S. Hall and M. Jacques, *New Times: The Changing Face of Politics in the 1990s* (London, Lawrence and Wishart, 1989).
31 I. Crewe, 'A New Class of Politics', *Guardian*, 15 June 1987.
32 Crewe, 'New Class'.
33 C. Rallings and M. Thrasher, 'This Avalanche Changes the Laws of Elections', *Sunday Times*, 4 May 1997.
34 A. Heath, R. Jowell and J. Curtice, *How Britain Votes* (Oxford, Clarendon Press, 1985); Heath *et al.*, *Political Change*, pp. 62–84.
35 See D. Denver and G. Hands (eds), *Issues and Controversies in British Electoral Behaviour* (Hemel Hempstead, Harvester Wheatsheaf, 1992), pp. 51–126, which reproduces a number of key articles in the debate.
36 At the time of writing, the equivalent figures for the 1997 election were not available.
37 Denver, *Elections and Voting Behaviour*, p. 65.
38 Denver, *Elections and Voting Behaviour*, p. 63.
39 I. Crewe, 'On the Death and Resurrection of Class Voting: Some Comments on *How Britain Votes*', in Denver and Hands, *British Electoral Behaviour*, pp. 85–96.
40 Harrop, 'Voting and the Electorate', p. 40.
41 Dunleavy and Husbands, *British Democracy*, p. 17.
42 Quoted in Harrop, 'Voting and the Electorate', p. 51.
43 Denver, *Elections and Voting Behaviour*, pp. 49–50.
44 M. Franklin, *The Decline of Class Voting in Britain* (Oxford, Clarendon Press, 1985).
45 Denver, *Elections and Voting Behaviour*, p. 76.
46 G. Marshall, 'What is Happening to the Working Class?', *Social Studies Review*, January 1987, pp. 37–40. For a full statistical analysis of social change and its relationship to voting behaviour see M. Harrop and A. Shaw, *Can Labour Win?*, pp. 113–39.
47 Dunleavy and Husbands, *British Democracy*.
48 Harrop and Miller, *Elections*, pp. 195–7.
49 I. Crewe, 'Why Did Labour Lose (Yet Again)?', *Politics Review*, September 1992, p. 6.
50 Harrop, 'Voting and the Electorate', pp. 44–5.

51 D. Butler and D. Kavanagh, *The British General Election of 1987* (London, Macmillan, 1988), p. 331.

52 Harrop and Miller, *Elections*, pp. 207–9.

53 See R. J. Johnston and C. J. Pattie, 'The Changing Electoral Geography of Great Britain', in Denver and Hands, *British Electoral Behaviour*, pp. 316–21.

54 See V. Bogdanor, 'Britain's Quiet Revolution', *Sunday Independent*, 12 April 1992; M. Ignatieff, 'How the Glitz turned to Ashes', *Observer*, 12 April 1992; B. Crick, 'In Defence of Compromise', *Guardian*, 13 April 1992; M. Jacques, 'The Party that Nobody Wants', *Guardian*, 20 June 1992; G. Mackenzie, 'Fatal Flaws in the Machine', *Times Higher Education Supplement*, 31 July 1992.

55 Bogdanor, 'Quiet Revolution'.

56 I. Crewe, 'Can Labour Rise Again?', *Social Studies Review*, September 1985, pp. 13–19.

57 Crewe, 'New Class'.

58 *Sunday Times*, 12 April 1992.

59 *Guardian*, 13 April 1992.

60 J. Curtice, 'Labour's Slide to Defeat', *Guardian*, 13 April 1992.

61 See A. Heath, R. Jowell and J. Curtice, *Labour's Last Chance? The 1992 Election and Beyond* (Aldershot, Dartmouth, 1994).

62 See W. Hutton, 'When a House is Not a Home', *Guardian*, 27 January 1995.

Conclusion: are parties making a difference?

In the introduction to this study we examined the functions of political parties in a modern liberal democracy. In this concluding chapter, we shall re-examine some of those functions more critically and consider the extent to which they are realised in Britain today.

It will be recalled that the defining feature of political parties is their quest for governmental power, either immediately or in a more long-term fashion, as with the SNP. It will also be recalled that parties do this by condensing and articulating various public interests so that the electorate has a clear, packaged choice of policies at a general election.

The view that parties allow such a choice, however, rests heavily on two conditions. First, there must be a clear and substantial contrast between the parties which contend seriously for government, something plainly undermined if their policies are strikingly similar. Secondly, there must be general confidence that a party elected on a specific programme – especially a radical programme – will be able to implement it in government. If it is evident that parties in office cannot translate their election promises into reality, then the notion that they offer voters a chance to change society becomes meaningless.

Party membership and the parties' reputation for allowing popular involvement in politics are also likely to crumble if parties in government are unable (or unwilling) to effect changes that would not simply have occurred anyhow; it is true that party membership was relatively high in the 'consensual' 1950s, but this was largely a product of class alignment – a phenomenon which has since largely disappeared (see chapters 2 and 10). Research indicates that the social attractions of political parties are diminishing and that the new generation of members is not just smaller but also more motivated by specific policy concerns.[1] Modern party members, in other words, expect clear and effective action from their party when it reaches government. The parties' capacity to make parliamentary government more efficient is much less impressive – to activists and voters

246

alike – if it is felt that parties with a Commons majority seldom use it to radical effect.

In short, the credibility of British political parties owes much to a perception that they can make a difference in office. But does that perception really exist and, if so, is it misplaced?

Too much of a difference?

In recent years, there has been in Britain a growing interest in electoral reform. Much of the criticism aimed at the present electoral system naturally stems from its disproportionate effects; in 1997, for instance, the Liberal Democrats won 17 per cent of the votes yet only 8 per cent of seats in the House of Commons. Yet support for reform also comes from a belief that perpetually hung parliaments and coalition governments (the most likely outcome of reform) would provide greater continuity in policy, releasing Britain from the adversarial nature of party politics (see chapter 1). This argument was put cogently in S. E. Finer's study of 1975, *Adversary Politics and Electoral Reform*. This claimed that alternating single-party governments, as allowed by the present electoral system, encouraged ruptures in government policy that were inimical to the national interest. West Germany and many of the Scandinavian democracies were used to substantiate the idea that alternative electoral systems (particularly pro-portional representation) led to superior economic achievement.[2] This argument was endorsed by the Hansard Society's report of 1979, *Politics and Industry: The Great Mismatch*, which claimed that the first-past-the-post system precluded the sort of long-term planning required by industrialists, who were concerned lest the next election produce another sudden and drastic change of policy – what Roy Jenkins termed 'the ideological big dipper'.[3] Some examples cited in support of this thesis were the fate of the iron and steel industry (nationalised, denationalised and renationalised between 1949 and 1965), incomes policies (established, dismantled and resumed between 1961 and 1979), and the legal status of the trade unions (enhanced, diminished and fortified between 1946 and 1976). This discontinuity, Hansard argued, was bad enough, but when caused by governments without majority support was nothing short of scandalous. All this implies, of course, that parties in government have not only the capacity to make an impact, but *too much* of a capacity, which needs to be curbed by electoral reform.

Politics in the 1980s: a vindication of party power?

Complaints about the effects of alternating, single-party governments naturally receded after 1979, when Britain went on to experience a prolonged period of rule by one party. Indeed, electoral reformers on the centre-left (where most reformers are) became worried that first past the post now gave too much continuity, in that it favoured overwhelmingly the Tories.[4] Yet the 1980s did much to strengthen the idea that parties in government could engineer major socio-economic change. This belief is borne out by a string of academic works which appeared during the latter part of the decade – the very titles of which are revealing: *Mrs. Thatcher's Revolution* by Peter Jenkins, *The Thatcher Years: A Decade of Revolution in British Politics* by John Cole, *Thatcherism and British Politics: The End of Consensus?* by Dennis Kavanagh, and *The Thatcher Phenomenon* by Hugo Young and Ann Sloman.[5]

Kavanagh's study maintained that the Thatcher governments proved beyond doubt what a sufficiently determined and programmatic government could achieve. He recalled an essay, written in 1978 by Tory MP Rhodes Boyson, which pointed to six key reforms that would need to be effected if Britain were to be transformed in the way most Tories wanted. These were: the reduction of income tax and a top rate of 60 per cent, a substantial increase in police numbers and pay, the ending of exchange controls and the statutory monopoly of nationalised industries, a 5 per cent cut in annual government spending and the replacement of state welfare with a voucher scheme. Kavanagh argued that all but the last two objectives had been fulfilled by 1985 – an extraordinary achievement given their ambitious nature.[6] He argued further that there had been 'significant discontinuities' of policy in many other areas, such as trade union reform, the rejection of incomes policies and 'tripartite' decision making, the toleration of rising unemployment and the reversal of long-standing arrangements in local government. Andrew Gamble agreed that the Thatcher governments had changed the terrain of British politics and society, claiming that 'the traditional post-war argument about different kinds of state intervention' had been replaced by a much broader debate.[7]

Riddell's survey of *The Thatcher Decade* (another revealing title) offers further support, noting that the 'political agenda has changed. The focus has shifted from the problems of producers and trade union obstruction to the freeing of markets and the extension of consumer choice.'[8] For Riddell, the key factor in the 1980s was the type of party leadership shown by Thatcher:

> Mrs. Thatcher's distinctive contribution has probably been to ensure that critical events – the 1981 Budget, the Falklands War in 1982 and the miners' strike of 1984–5 – that might have fatally weakened her government were overcome. She has forced the pace of change and extended her free-market counter-revolution further than alternative Tory leaders might have done.[9]

Hugo Young endorses the view that her determination not to reflate the economy in July 1981 was vital to the government's radical thrust. This required, Young asserts, 'extraordinary political will' in the face of contrary advice from large sections of the cabinet and numerous 'experts'.[10] John Vincent agrees that 1981 was 'the pivotal year' of Thatcherism and marked a 'new determination by government to govern'.[11] This willingness to defy the pressures for consensus from both internal and external sources was saluted not just by the radical right: left-wingers like Tony Benn contested that Thatcherism hinted at what could be achieved by a Labour government which was 'prepared to pursue doggedly its own brand of class politics'.[12]

For many on the left, the Thatcher years also had echoes of a particularly effective period of Labour government – that of Clement Attlee's (1945–51) – which, through its nationalisation and welfare policies, established the parameters of political debate in Britain for the next quarter of a century.[13] But in one important respect the Thatcher years still offered a more bracing impression that political parties mattered. For most of the Attlee years, there was already in place a new, social democratic consensus – the Tories having moved quickly to adopt the popular aspects of Labour's 1945 agenda. By contrast, Labour reacted to Thatcher's victory in 1979 by adopting its own alternative brand of radicalism, providing voters not just with affirmation that a party in government was indeed having a big effect, but the chance of heading off in a dramatically different direction. At the time of the 1983 general election, the claim that parties could make little difference, and that there was little difference between them, was not easily borne out.

Politics in the 1980s: a revisionist view

Although the 1983 and, to a lesser extent, 1987 general elections showed a clear divergence between the two main parties, it is not clear that voters were therefore offered a plausible choice. The fact that Labour's popular vote plunged to 28 per cent and 31 per cent in those elections suggests that Labour's own prospectus was *implausible* to the bulk of voters and that Labour did not offer the more 'sensible' (*ergo* less radical) alternative they actually wanted.

This analysis, which argues that for Labour to have won in 1983 or 1987 it needed to be closer to the policies of the government (a view implicitly accepted by Labour's last three leaders), ties in with the main 'revisionist' charge concerning the Thatcher governments: that many of the changes which occurred in the 1980s would have occurred regardless of her three election victories. That Labour failed to understand these changes is, allegedly, the main reason for its electoral failure; yet even if, by fluke, Labour had won on its 1983 and 1987 manifestos, the argument runs that it could still not have reversed most of the changes which pass – erroneously – for 'Thatcherism'.

Ben Pimlott observed in 1989 that 'Britain is very different now from what it was in 1979; but it was also very different in 1959 from what it was in 1949 after a decade of consensus politics', his point being that any ten-year period is bound to witness huge changes.[14] Pimlott asserts that the Thatcher governments only sailed with the tides which were already altering politics and society. Thatcher's task of revoking the social democratic consensus was made much easier by the fact that it was already discredited by events in the 1970s; this was arguably why she won the 1979 election. As Vincent concedes, 'Many of the decisions that shaped government in the 1980s had already been made under Labour' – prime examples being the introduction of monetary discipline after 1976, and a recognition that nationalised industry was not working (as reported by the National Economic Development Council in the *Future of Nationalized Industries*, in 1976).[15]

It is undeniable that the growth of a white-collar society in the 1980s was as influenced by the long-term decline of heavy industry (and the corresponding shift towards a service-based economy) as by the policies of the Conservatives, which were after all merely a response to such changes. Peter Riddell has even suggested that the growth of home and share ownership – often claimed by Thatcherites to be their greatest triumph – may have occurred anyway:

> By far the greatest influence has been the death of that generation of first-time homeowners from the 1950s and 1960s. Their homes have been inherited by children in their thirties and forties, often already owning their own homes and who therefore receive a big increase in available capital. The sale of council houses, cuts in income and capital taxes and the inducements to buy shares in the main privatisation flotations have ... extended an existing trend rather than created a new one.[16]

In a similar vein, John Kelly's survey of trade unions in the 1980s concludes that, although the Acts of 1980, 1982, 1984 and 1988 did weaken union power, there were much more pressing factors behind the unions' decline as a political force – without which the Tories' own legal reforms might not have been possible. Chief among these was the relentless rise in blue-collar unemployment and the inevitable demise of those industries upon which union strength was based.[17] Kelly therefore doubts that union power (insofar as it ever existed) could have survived the 1980s, irrespective of which party was in office.

Hugo Young has also accepted that the anti-Keynesian posture of the Thatcher governments was scarcely unique in democratic western states.[18] During the 1980s there was a shift towards such policies in West Germany, the USA, Canada, the Netherlands, Belgium, Japan, Sweden, Denmark and Norway. Even more significant was the adoption of a monetarist programme in France, after the same socialist government swept to power promising the opposite.[19]

Was Rose right?

All this appears to lend weight to a thesis first expounded in 1980 by Professor Richard Rose in his book *Do Parties Make a Difference?*.[20] Rose made three central points which have particular relevance to this chapter: first, that parties are largely reactive rather than proactive *vis-à-vis* public opinion; second, that rival party programmes have more in common than their advocates care to admit; third, that policy developed by the parties via their own machinery has surprisingly little influence upon the actions of a government.

A large chunk of this book has already given support to two of Rose's points by accepting that, for much of the post-war era, there was a strong consensus between the two parties (see chapter 1). As Cook and McKie wrote of the 1964 election, the contest was 'less between competing philosophies, much more about which set of managers was likely to get the better set of results'.[21] Given that much the same could be said of the 1992 and 1997 general elections, British politics seems to have come full circle in this respect, with the deep divisions of the 1980s being very much an aberration.

For Rose (echoing the analysis of Anthony Downs[22] twenty-three years earlier), this tendency towards consensus was a product of how serious parties really worked in a modern democracy. Parties, as pointed out in the Introduction, are primarily interested in attaining office which, for Rose, means *reflecting* (and not, as some radicals recommend, *changing*) the views of non-aligned voters. Rose implies that these non-aligned voters are, by definition, 'middle of the road', which tends to draw both major parties to the same centre ground. If there are substantial differences between the parties, as there were in 1983 and 1987, this normally means that one party (Labour in this case) has either ignored or hopelessly misread the opinion of floating voters, thus securing an emphatic victory for its rival. Rose believes it is no coincidence that during the 1945–79 period, when each party governed for roughly seventeen years apiece, the policy differences between those parties were marginal, whereas a period of prolonged government by one party (as after 1979) usually points to a period of polarisation. Put simply, if there is to be more than one party of government, then the parameters of policy debate cannot be too wide.

Rose did not dispute the existence of adversary politics (see chapter 2). But he did insist that, in a period of 'normality' (unlike the 1980s), the bulk of manifesto pledges would have a bipartisan flavour – like 'we attach importance to the maintenance of law and order', 'we shall improve the quality of life for the elderly', 'we are concerned about opportunities for school leavers' and so on.[23] Many of the differences between party manifestos stemmed from what Rose called 'talking past' each other, one party promising to build more council houses than the other (as in 1951) being an illustration. In other words, Rose claims that manifesto clashes are deliberately exaggerated by their proponents, with differences arising from details and points of emphasis rather than grand principles.

In developing this argument, Rose was not drifting into uncharted waters. Robert McKenzie had argued that the 'oligarchic' structure of both main parties was necessary to ensure that they did not stray as far from the middle ground as activists might wish.[24] If a party does seem to have 'gone radical', this is often because it has sensed a similar change of mood among the electorate; parties thus respond to change rather than instigate it. As Peter Hennessy wrote, the 'radicalism' of the Attlee government needs to be put in historical context:

> A huge advantage [for the government] was the highly disciplined condition of the British people. Almost six years of total war had left almost no citizen untouched by its rigours, whether in the form of a siege economy on the home front or by military service abroad. The population was used to receiving orders and to strict regulation [which] helped create an atmosphere in which centrally directed schemes of national improvement became a norm and not a pipedream.[25]

Sarlvik and Crewe have also contested that the Thatcher 'revolution' was assisted by a change of public attitudes during the 1970s, when there was a growing hostility to trade unions and nationalised industries and a growing interest in lower taxation, greater individual choice and a sterner approach to law and order.[26] Likewise, the Conservative failure to reduce public spending in the bold way it initially suggested (as a share of gross domestic product it never fell below 1979 levels) owed much to a lack of political courage which, in turn, stemmed from its failure to alter public thinking on welfare policy. The Thatcher governments had hoped to promote a 'cultural revolution' in which the 'dependency culture would be replaced by the enterprise culture', yet surveys conducted by the end of the 1980s indicated that this 'crusade' had failed. The public was seen to favour the extension of public services over further tax cuts, more public ownership over further privatisation and a country 'which emphasised the social and collective provision of welfare' over one in which individuals are encouraged to look after themselves.[27]

Such data seem to confirm Rose's thesis that the parties have a limited ability to fashion public opinion. What he could not foresee in 1980, however, was that governments apparently at odds with public opinion over most key issues (as were the Thatcher governments) could still get

re-elected given a certain and highly peculiar combination of circumstances – such as a weak and divided opposition, qualified economic
optimism and perverse good luck (as provided, for example, by the Falklands
war). It is also quite likely that the Thatcher governments' electoral success,
in defiance of much popular opinion, may encourage future governments
to be more single-minded and less sensitive to public mood than Rose ever
imagined possible.

Office without power?

The Thatcher governments, however, could not detract from what is arguably
the central fact about post-war British politics, one which is still overlooked
by many textbooks. That fact is the interdependence of the British economy
and the limited control exercised by British politicians over Britain's economic
destiny. Furthermore, so much of their control over other aspects of public
policy flows from economic security – in which case it may be argued that
British political parties, and the British political process in general, are
much less decisive than we care to imagine. As one observer of the post-
war scene commented:

> The major source of Britain's difficulties is to be located among the non-
> state actors.... Politicians in power prate and posture, taking the credit and
> the blame for the interplay of international market forces, without usually
> being responsible for either the good or bad results.[28]

This analysis complements Rose's research which established that the
implementation of manifesto promises normally accounts for less than a
fifth of what governments get up to – most of their work being *ad hoc*
responses to unforeseen events.[29] David Butler agreed that the major
landmarks in post-war British history 'would have occurred whichever
party was in power and would have evoked a broadly similar reaction',
citing these landmarks as the sterling crises of 1947 and 1949, the Suez
crisis of 1956, devaluation in 1967, the oil crisis of 1973 and the
International Monetary Fund's intervention in 1976 – to which we might
add the devaluation of 1992.[30] The Labour governments of the 1960s and
1970s are always invoked to support this sort of argument, simply because
it was felt by many of those involved that there was a marked gap between
promise and performance. There is a vast literature concerning these
governments and many of the book titles (*Labour in Power?, Office Without
Power, Breach of Promise*) are themselves revealing about the feeling they
created.[31] A favourite test case in such studies is the record of the
Department of Economic Affairs, set up in 1964 with the intention of
bringing about a 25 per cent increase in gross domestic product by 1970;

the actual increase was only 14 per cent and the Department was effectively shut down after two years. The next Labour government came to power in 1974 promising a 'fundamental and irreversible shift of power and wealth', yet ended up pursuing an early form of monetarism and severe wage restraint. The claim that these governments failed on their own terms is therefore not without justification, and to put the blame on individuals seems inadequate; with Wilson, Healey, Jenkins, Castle, Crosland, Crossman, Shore, Williams *et al.*, these governments were blessed with the intelligentsia of British social democracy. A more compelling explanation is provided by another such luminary, Harold Lever:

> These governments overestimated their ability to shape and manage the complex drives of a mature economy. They wrongly assumed that governments could produce remedies for all its problems.... The real world obstinately refused to conform to the principles of a party manifesto.[32]

Tony Benn's analysis is broader, embracing not just the restraints of international finance/capitalism, but the institutional restraints within Britain – notably Whitehall, the City, the security forces, the military chiefs and the mass media, all of whom conspire against fundamental change.[33] Benn, however, is no fatalist and argued after 1979 that Labour in office could make a radical difference if it were sufficiently prepared and determined; this would require above all a parliamentary leadership more accountable to the party rank and file (see chapter 6).

Yet it is not only Labour governments which exemplify the difference between promise and performance. The government of Edward Heath came to power in 1970 promising nothing less than 'a quiet revolution', overturning Keynesian social democracy in favour of a more bracing, market-led society. There would be less state intervention in industry, a rejection of the prices and incomes policies practised in the 1960s, less public expenditure and reform of the trade unions. Neither was the Tory party ill-prepared for office, having devoted an extraordinary amount of time in opposition to policy research.[34] Indeed, central to the Tory campaign in 1970 was a pledge to 'close the gap' between the rhetoric and achievements of party politicians – a barbed reference to the contemporary view of Wilson's government.

Heath's government did not foresee the problems that would engulf it within two years of office and its U-turn of 1971–2 was a fevered response to rising unemployment, public hostility and the threat of electoral disaster. Nevertheless, the record of Heath's government after 1972 was a startling contradiction of its original aims. The economy was reflated, public expenditure was increased and there were much sterner prices and incomes policies than anything witnessed in the 1960s. Indeed, Heath's government – having promised *laissez-faire* in industry – turned out to be one of the most interventionist since the war. As a result, Heath's government vainly sought re-election in 1974 'in defence of policies it had explicitly repudiated three and a half years earlier'.[35]

Despite Kavanagh's admiration for the programmatic success of the Thatcher governments (see above), they too are not immune to the charge that governments are hidebound by internal and external restraints and therefore ill-equipped to fulfil their initial aims. Of particular interest here is the Thatcher government's early stress upon monetary discipline. Yet between 1981 and 1984, the money supply (control of which was supposedly essential to the government's anti-inflationary strategy) rose by 50 per cent against a target of 16–30 per cent and continued to rise at around 20 per cent a year.[36] By early 1986, the government was considered guilty by many of its ideological advisers of a 'potentially reckless monetary binge and a reflationary feast of backdoor Keynesianism', and it was notable that the approach to inflation in the late 1980s was the traditional Keynesian panacea of high interest rates rather than monetary stringency.[37]

Thus, the Tory claim that economic policy in the 1980s embodied 'the resolute approach' from a 'lady who wasn't for turning' merits stern qualification, as does any claim that there was an 'economic miracle'; although economic growth rose significantly after 1979, by 1989 it had reverted to the rates of 1969, when Britain was already derided as 'the sick man of Europe'.

On another plain, no account of the final Thatcher government can overlook the fate of the poll tax, which Thatcher billed 'the flagship' of her third administration. After almost unprecedented levels of public opposition, it was watered down to almost a travesty of its original purpose before finally being scrapped – representing what certain authors consider 'a supreme example' of 'failure in British government'.[38] It is telling that this failure should be associated with the most dogmatic and determined of post-war ministries.

Parties in the 1990s: a deepening crisis

For students of British political parties, the Thatcher era may come to represent an Indian summer, in which the parties' reputation for effective action was revived. The fall of Thatcher in 1990 marked not only a more sober style of government, but also a more sober assessment of the parties' potential.

Post-war party politics in Britain has rested heavily on three assumptions which play no small part in our own particular study. All three of these assumptions came under further strain during the 1990s.

The first of these was class alignment. For much of this century, Britain has had a society which divides fairly neatly along class lines, with most voters defining their own interests in class terms. As chapter 2 explained, this formed the basis of Britain's stable party system in the 1950s and 1960s, providing each of the two class-based parties with a solid membership and reliable source of income. As chapter 10 pointed out, class alignment has dwindled steadily during the last quarter century, with serious consequences for the parties' electoral support, grass-roots strength and financial survival. During the 1990s, with society becoming more and more individualistic, there was little sign that this problem had abated for the main parties.

The second assumption has been that the parties are ideologically distinctive. Both Labour and Conservative members were attached, with varying degrees of intensity, to a body of beliefs which formed the embryo of voter choice. Between 1945 and 1975, these beliefs were fine tuned by party leaders to meet the demands of floating voters, resulting in a strong measure of consensus (see chapter 1). Yet within each party, there did seem to be clear and alternative 'world views' which filtered into mainstream political debate. The bulk of the Labour party was convinced that capitalism did not represent the 'end of history' and that a superior alternative could be found, one that would produce a more just and harmonious society. The mass of Conservative members, by contrast, had a firm belief in market economics *plus* faith in traditional Tory values like national unity, national self-determination, conventional family structures and a thriving system of local government – unaware, perhaps, that all these things could prove contradictory.

During the 1990s, research pointed to a decline of ideological self-confidence in both the main parties, with there no longer being such a gap between the certainties of party members and the customary ambivalence of voters.[39] Electoral defeat and the end of the cold war forced Labour members into an acceptance of the existing economic system, which duly made their other ambitions more cautious as well. Rifts within the government (from the mid-1980s onwards) also made many Tories question the compatibility of their beliefs. The government's stress upon individualism and equality of opportunity, for example, fuelled feminist arguments (even inside the Conservative Women's Organisation) and sat ill alongside party support for traditional family life. Similarly, its support for an ultra-competitive, consumer-led society clashed with its paternalistic, 'one nation' elements (see chapter 3), while its faith in an increasingly international free market conflicted with the old Tory shibboleth of national sovereignty. In short, developments in the late 1980s and 1990s left both parties doctrinally confused and unsure of their future direction.

The point about national sovereignty ties in with the third assumption of party politics for much of this century, namely, that parties seeking power could expect to find it by winning national elections. As indicated earlier, this assumption had been questioned long before the 1990s. But scepticism became much more acute following Thatcher's departure from office in 1990 and, as Neil Acherson wrote in 1994, 'we are watching the slow but terminal decline of the nation state'.[40] In Britain, two related factors have contributed to this view.

First, there is what Andrew Marr calls 'the big story of our times', which is that 'power has blown away from the traditional nation state to the international markets and the big companies which ride them'. Marxists have always argued that those who have economic power dictate the agenda of national governments. But the internationalisation of capital has made that power all the more dynamic and politically unaccountable. The global market, Marr observes, has 'the power to impose economic pain in order to limit national policies to the market's own views of financial orthodoxy'.[41]

Politicians are not by nature fatalistic and political science is seldom diagnostic without also being prescriptive. Marxists used to argue that the impotence of politics *vis-à-vis* economics could be ended by revolution and a new mode of production. During the 1990s, it became more common to argue that the solution now involved matching the internationalisation of capital with the internationalisation of government. This leads to the second drain upon the authority of national party governments – the movement towards an integrated European state.[42]

Again, an awareness that British politicians are constrained by membership of the European Union (*née* Community) predates the 1990s. It existed in the years leading to Britain's entry in 1973, during the referendum on continued membership in 1975, and led to a rupture inside the Labour party in 1981 (see chapter 7).

As a result of the European Communities Act 1972, British governments accept that laws emanating from (what is now) the European Union's institutions take precedence over those passed at Westminster and that, in the event of conflict between the British parliament and the European Union (EU), the final verdict rests with the European Court of Justice. The British government, through the European Council of Ministers, naturally contributes to the formulation of EU policy and has the power of veto in many cases. Yet, as Nugent points out, this veto is not easy to exercise in practice, owing to 'the combined effect of increased majority voting' and 'political pressure to concede and compromise so as to allow progress to be made'.

The limitation placed upon governing parties at Westminster increased from the mid-1980s, when there was a steady increase in Europe's policy responsibilities. (The involvement of British parties in the European parliament is discussed briefly under 'Rescuing party politics', below.) In areas such as control over company mergers and state aid to industry, this took the form of strengthened authority, while with anti-terrorism and consumer protection it involved invading areas previously the prerogative of national governments. As Nugent explained, 'There are now few policy areas in which European policy is not involved in at least some way'.[43]

The 1986 Single European Act was particularly important in this respect, for it allowed much greater use of majority voting in the Council of Ministers as part of the drive towards the 1992 single market, thus circumscribing further the value of national veto. The rules of majority voting also prevent a member state from blocking a European Commission proposal without the support of at least two other states. This was shown vividly during the crisis of 1996 over bovine spongiform encephalopathy, when Britain was forced to accept a ban on the export of British cattle after being outvoted in the Council. The past decade has therefore witnessed a steady flow of authority from national to European level which, by implication, undercuts the autonomy of Britain's governing parties.[44]

Britain's entry into the European exchange rate mechanism in October 1990 was seen as a vital step on the road to a federal Europe. Although it was Thatcher's government which took this decision, her inability to accept its implications caused her downfall only a few weeks later.[45] For Euro-federalists, the Maastricht treaty of 1991, ratified by Westminster in 1993, was another welcome milestone. Despite securing an 'opt out', Major's government – by signing the treaty – still legitimised the aim of a single European currency by 1999, accompanied by a European central bank controlling member states' interest and inflation rates, public spending and national debt.[46] For Conservative economist Tim Congdon, the implication was clear: the end of independent, sovereign states, with Tory governments in London 'reduced to the status of a charge-capped borough council'.[47] Neither were such fears confined to the right. Bryan Gould's decision to quit British politics in 1994 arose from his belief that European monetary union would preclude any Keynesian-style dash for full employment by a future Labour government.[48]

After the 1997 election, the British government retained its ambivalence towards a single currency. Yet this is said to be regarded by other EU members as nothing more than a short-term political ruse: in the long term, many believe that Britain's exclusion from the single currency is incompatible with it remaining an effective member state.[49] The financial incentives to join are already considerable for, under article 28 of the Maastricht treaty, Britain is still obliged to pay in 1999 £700 million towards the establishment of the European central bank.

Party-free politics?

If the governing parties' loss of power is sensed by voters, this offers an obvious reason for their loss of interest in party activity. Those on the left, for example, are in no doubt that 'parties lose members as soon as they seem unable to change anything'.[50] Throughout the western world, in fact, there is evidence of diminished interest among voters. The 1993 *International*

Social Attitudes survey found that, among advanced industrial societies, only Australia had a majority who were 'very' or 'fairly' interested in politics.[51] In Britain the figure was 41 per cent, with 34 per cent 'not very' or 'not at all' interested, while a Gallup poll in the same year found that most British voters thought their politicians were liars.[52] This disenchantment seems particularly marked among the young. According to a *Demos* report in 1995, only 43 per cent of potential first-time voters actually used their vote in the 1992 general election, while Seyd *et al.* found that the average age of Labour and Tory members was forty-eight and sixty-two, respectively.[53]

Yet this disinterest should not be confused with attitudes towards politics generally. The explosion of organised protest against the poll tax (1989–90), the Child Support Agency (1993–4), the live export of veal (1994–5), the Brent Spar oil platform (1995) and the second runway at Manchester Airport (1996–7) all point to a vital development: the politically aware are turning from an 'old' (party-based) model of activity to a new, group-based approach. These cases also indicate that faith in group activity is not confined to those with leftish tendencies – the veal protests, for example, attracted support from 'old ladies in tweeds as well as students in donkey jackets'.[54]

Even within the parties themselves, there appears to have been a loss of confidence in party politics and a curious flirtation with unelected 'experts'. Between 1992 and 1997, for instance, it may have seemed strange to hear leftish politicians argue that the wishes of bankers (at the proposed European central bank) and judges (at the European Court of Human Rights) should prevail over those of elective governments; indeed, one of the new government's first acts in 1997 was to free the Bank of England from the operational control of ministers.

This anti-party culture was again demonstrated by the willingness of British judges to challenge openly the political judgement of ministers – as when the Lord Chief Justice rebuffed Michael Howard's call for more custodial sentencing in 1995. Encouraged by the 'sleaze' which engulfed Major's government in 1994, it became quite fashionable to argue, by the late 1990s, that a more 'objective' approach to politics was now required. This argument (closely linked to support for constitutional reform) asserted that various 'binding principles' should be defined for politicians by those who were somehow 'above' politics – be they bankers in Bonn, bureaucrats in Brussels or judges in the Hague.

At the same time, there seemed to be growing support for a more direct form of democracy, one which by-passed party politicians through extensive use of referenda – it being argued that voters were now mature enough to make policy decisions themselves, rather than passing this power to party-based MPs they anyhow distrusted.[55] This trend was again reflected in Labour's 1997 manifesto, which promised referenda on a range of constitutional reforms.

Rescuing party politics

The notion of direct, as opposed to traditional, representative democracy
has clear theoretical attractions for anyone who believes that power in
society should rest with the bulk of its citizens. However, the case for this
dynamic, Athenian form of government is weakened by one central reality:
there seems little public support for it. Voters may be unimpressed with
those elected to make decisions for them, but they still seem a long way
from wishing to take those decisions themselves.[56] Even on the crucial issue
of Europe, evidence of public enthusiasm for a referendum is sketchy, as
the most hardened of Euro-sceptic MPs are forced to acknowledge.[57] The
Referendum party – formed by Sir James Goldsmith to bring about such
a ballot – could only secure 2.6 per cent of votes in the 1997 general
election.

Apropos constitutional reform, this book does not propose to get embroiled
in such a complex issue. But if there is a movement towards a more
codified constitution, with more attendant powers for courts and judges,
we would make one very simple point: that government by elected party
politicians, no matter how imperfect, has the merit of accountability. Party
politicians may be obsessed with their prospects of re-election, but this is
not always a bad thing if it means being sensitive to public opinion. This
is a problem still to be solved by devotees of European integration, aware
that the present structure has an inherent 'democratic deficit'.[58] Both
Maastricht and the Amsterdam treaty of 1997 gave new powers of 'co-
decision' to the European parliament, whose elections British parties already
contest vigorously; yet its control over the EU executive in Brussels is at
present even less than that exercised by Westminster over Whitehall. If a
fully integrated European state is not to be dominated by unaccountable
officials, then the European parliament will have to be strengthened again –
in which case party activity within the EU will doubtless intensify. With
Britain's main parties respectively forging closer links recently with the
European Socialist party and European People's party, there are already
signs that they are poised to refocus their activities in a way that (they
hope) will give them more influence over the supra-national forces already
affecting Britain.

In this sense, some might argue that the Europeanisation of government
is in fact the saviour of party politics in Britain. As the *New Statesman
and Society* pointed out in 1990, it had already proved impossible for any
'progressive' governing party to ignore the internationalisation of markets
and the omnipresence of multi-national corporations – both of which had
the power to blow such governments off course at an early stage.[59] A
supra-national political system was needed precisely because parties in
national government were no longer the masters of their own fate, and
therefore needed to co-operate with like-minded parties elsewhere

(particularly Europe) in order to meet the radical expectations of their voters.

If the Euro-federalist dream is realised, the parties may have to refocus their energies not just at continental level, but also at a more local level. Federalists tend to argue that their scheme would involve national governments losing power not just to a federal government in Brussels, but to regional governments within their own national boundaries. According to this analysis, economic, environmental and foreign policy matters would be among those which passed 'upwards', while most other functions would pass 'downwards', to regional assemblies in Brittany, Tuscany, Bavaria, Humberside, East Anglia and so on – hence their vision of a 'Europe of the regions' so eagerly embraced by Plaid Cymru, the SNP and to a lesser extent parties in Northern Ireland (see chapter 8). As Gaffney's study points out, far from being redundant in a federal Europe, party activity could be realigned and rejuvenated.[60]

Cautionary tails

During the 1990s, such 'big' ideas have occupied many a seminar or tutorial in higher education. But, as is often the case with seminar discussion, it all has a rather surreal flavour. A 'Europe of the regions' or a 'United States of Europe' is a neat theory but one which tends to ignore huge practical difficulties. At the time of going to press, the timescale for a single currency, for example, still looks fraught with problems, with the task of convergence proving trickier than originally thought. By 1997, there was throughout the EU growing scepticism about the political and economic consequences of greater union, its enlargement only exposing the problem of central direction.[61]

In many ways, the credibility of federalism never fully recovered from the financial crisis of September 1992. In one respect, Britain's free-fall from the exchange rate mechanism was another blistering example of governing parties being powerless in the face of modern economic conditions; membership of the exchange rate mechanism had been crucial to the Tories' election manifesto just five months earlier.[62] Yet, in another sense, it showed that European integration was not after all the solution to the problem of governmental powerlessness and certainly no guarantee of economic security in government. This raises questions about 'throwing the baby out with the bathwater': is it wise to allow Europe to usurp further areas of non-economic policy if it cannot guarantee in return a more manageable and predictable economy for member states?

It is easy to forget that British governments still have immense discretionary powers which affect enormously the way we live. As a result, it is crazy to argue that it now matters not which party wins a British general election. Before 1997, there was nothing inevitable about (for example) changes in taxation, the centralisation of education or the corrosion of local government – policies which had a profound effect upon millions of people. Even in local elections, levels of party support can still make a huge difference to ordinary voters – witness the retention of state grammar schools in some areas but not others.[63]

One would also need a relentlessly jaundiced view of politicians to argue that those who seek office seek nothing more than personal glory. If politicians are unusually vain, their vanity often springs from a conviction that, through success at a British election, they can make a lasting impression upon the way we live. European union and a globalised economy have undeniably eroded the effect national politicians can have; but there is a huge difference between erosion and elimination.

Across the capitalist world, economic power has become more diffuse. This, in turn, has made people question the conventional sources of political authority. For this reason alone, the early twenty-first century is likely to see a continuing debate about which governmental structures are best suited to the vicissitudes of a modern economy. Yet it can be stated with a fair degree of confidence that, wherever representative government is seen to lie, party politics will closely follow. Parties may no longer be the sole or even main agency of political participation. But they remain exclusively capable of aggregating interests and ideas, while giving voters the chance to elect or dismiss governments – particularly important given that the bulk of voters still want only occasional involvement in the political system. At the close of the 1990s, the focal point of party activity may be shifting; yet its objectives remain unaltered and indispensable.

Notes

1   P. Seyd and P. Whiteley, *Labour's Grass Roots* (Oxford, Claremont, 1992); R. Morris, *Tories* (Edinburgh, Mainstream, 1991).
2   S. E. Finer, *Adversary Politics and Electoral Reform* (London, Wigram, 1975).
3   R. Jenkins, 'Home Thoughts From Abroad', in W. Kennett (ed.), *The Rebirth of Britain* (London, Weidenfeld and Nicolson, 1982), pp. 9–33.
4   P. Dunleavy, 'Send Her Victorious', *New Statesman and Society*, 16 September 1988.
5   P. Jenkins (London, Cape, 1987); J. Cole (London, BBC, 1987); D. Kavanagh (Oxford, Oxford University Press, 1987); H. Young and A. Sloman (London, BBC, 1987).
6   Kavanagh, *Thatcherism*, p. 283.
7   A. Gamble, *The Free Economy and the Strong State* (London, Macmillan, 1988), p. 315.
8   P. Riddell, *The Thatcher Decade* (Oxford, Blackwell, 1989), p. 208.
9   Riddell, *Thatcher Decade*, p. 216.
10 H. Young, *One of Us* (London, Macmillan, 1989), p. 544.
11 From P. Hennessy and A. Seldon (eds), *Ruling Performance* (Oxford, Blackwell, 1987), p. 285.

12   *The Campaign For Labour Party Democracy*, Labour party conference pamphlet, 1982.

13   S. Higgins, *The Benn Inheritance* (London, Weidenfeld and Nicolson, 1984), pp. 188–213.

14   B. Pimlott, 'The Audit of Thatcherism', *Contemporary Record*, autumn 1989.

15   J. Vincent, 'The Thatcher Governments 1979–1987', in P. Hennessy and A. Seldon (eds), *Ruling Performance* (Blackwell, Oxford, 1987), p. 285.

16   Riddell, *Thatcher Decade*, p. 207.

17   J. Kelly, *Trade Unions and Socialist Politics* (London, Verso, 1988).

18   Young, *One of Us*, p. 526.

19   V. Wright, *The Government and Politics of France* (London, Hutchinson, 1983), p. 167–97.

20   R. Rose (London, Macmillan, 1980).

21   D. McKie and C. Cook (eds), *The Decade of Disillusion* (London, Macmillan, 1972), p. 16.

22   A. Downs, *An Economic Theory of Democracy* (New York, Harper, 1957).

23   Rose, *Do Parties Make A Difference?*, p. 169.

24   R. T. McKenzie, *British Political Parties* (London, Heinemann, 1955), pp. 2–7.

25   Hennessy and Seldon, *Ruling Performance*, pp. 32–3.

26   B. Sarlvik and I. Crewe, *Decade of Dealignment* (Cambridge, Cambridge University Press, 1983), ch. 8.

27   I. Crewe, 'Values: A Crusade That Failed', in D. Kavanagh and A. Seldon (eds), *The Thatcher Effect* (Oxford, Oxford University Press, 1989).

28   J. Hayward, quoted in S. Ingle, *The British Party System* (Oxford, Blackwell, 1987), p. 191.

29   Rose, *Do Parties Make a Difference?*, p. 72.

30   D. Butler, *British General Elections Since 1945* (Oxford, Blackwell, 1995), p. 123.

31   D. Coates (London, Longman, 1980); T. Benn (London, Arrow, 1989); C. Ponting (London, Hamish Hamilton, 1989).

32   Harold Lever, *Listener*, 22 November 1984.

33   Hennessy and Seldon, *Ruling Performance*, p. 307.

34   J. Campbell, *Edward Heath* (London, Cape, 1993), chs 10–11.

35   Kavanagh, quoted in Hennessy and Seldon, *Ruling Performance*, p. 231.

36   Young, *One of Us*, p. 533.

37   *Whither Monetarism?* (London, Centre for Policy Studies, 1988).

38   D. Butler, A. Adonis and T. Travers, *Failure in British Government: The Politics of the Poll Tax* (Oxford, Oxford University Press, 1994).

39   Seyd and Whiteley, *Labour's Grass Roots*, p. 54; P. Whiteley, P. Seyd and J. Richardson, *True Blues* (Oxford, Oxford University Press, 1994), p. 65.

40   N. Acherson, 'Fuzzy Democracy', *New Statesman and Society*, 11 March 1994.

41   A. Marr, *Ruling Britannia* (London, Penguin, 1995); 'The Real Enemy is the Money Market', *Spectator*, 9 September 1995. See also P. Gummett (ed.), *Globalisation and Public Policy* (Cheltenham, Edward Elgar, 1996).

42   See C. Pilkington, *Britain in the European Union Today* (Manchester, Manchester University Press, 1995), ch. 5.

43   N. Nugent, 'The European Community and British Independence', *Talking Politics*, autumn 1989; see also A. Geddes, *Britain in the European Community* (Manchester, Baseline, 1993).

44   See J. McCormick, *The European Union* (Oxford, Westview Press, 1996).

45   R. Shepherd, *The Power Brokers* (London, Hutchinson, 1991), pp. 1–6.

46   M. J. Dedman, *The Origins and Development of the European Union 1945–1995* (London, Routledge, 1996), pp. 170–9.

47   T. Congdon, 'The Last of England', *Spectator*, 23 June 1990.
48   B. Gould, *Goodbye To All That* (London, Macmillan, 1995), pp. 265–8.
49   M. Newman, *Democracy, Sovereignty and the European Union* (London, Hurst and Company, 1996), pp. 85–94.
50   *New Statesman and Society*, 29 September 1995.
51   *Focus on Britain 1994* (Oxford, Philip Allan, 1994), p. 51.
52   *New Statesman and Society*, 3 December 1993.
53   *Daily Telegraph*, 29 September 1995; Whiteley *et al.*, *True Blues*, pp. 32 (Labour), 43 (Tory).
54   *New Statesman and Society*, 27 January 1995.
55   See C. Pilkington, *Representative Democracy in Britain Today* (Manchester, Manchester University Press, 1997), pp. 126–9.
56   See A. Batchelor, 'The Referendum We Never Had', *Talking Politics*, summer 1994.
57   See T. Gorman *The Bastards* (London, Pan, 1993).
58   Geddes, *Britain in the European Community*, ch. 7.
59   *New Statesman and Society*, 22 June 1990.
60   J. Gaffney (ed.), *Political Parties and the European Union* (London, Routledge, 1996).
61   See C. Booker and R. North, *The Castle of Lies* (London, Duckworth, 1996).
62   See N. Lamont, *Sovereign Britain* (London, Duckworth, 1995), pp. 12–19.
63   J. A. Chandler, *Local Government Today* (Manchester, Manchester University Press, 1996), ch. 9.

Index

Numbers in **bold** indicate main page references.